Debra,

Hope this is useful To you

Dale

ORGANIZATIONAL CAPABILITY

ORGANIZATIONAL CAPABILITY

Competing from the Inside Out

David Ulrich
Dale Lake

John Wiley & Sons
New York • Chichester • Brisbane • Toronto • Singapore

Recognizing the importance of preserving what has been written, it is a policy of John Wiley & Sons, Inc., to have books of enduring value published in the United States printed on acid-free paper, and we exert our best efforts to that end.

Library of Congress Cataloging in Publication Data

Ulrich, David, 1953–
    Organizational capability : competing from the inside out / by
    David Ulrich, Dale Lake.
        p. cm.
        Include biographical references.
        ISBN 0-471-61807-1
        1. Organizational effectiveness. I. Lake, Dale G. II. Title.
HD58.9.U47 1990
658.4—dc20   90-31355

Printed in the United States of America
        10 9 8 7 6 5

To our loving wives,
Wendy and Gerry,
and to our caring families,
who have been
patient and supportive.

To the portable computer that made it possible.

Preface

Books are written for many reasons—pride, fame, ego, temporary insanity. Our primary reason for this book is simple: We believe that for any organization (small or large, public or private, new or old) to compete successfully, attention must be focused on building *organizational capability*. Organizational capability focuses simultaneously on improving management processes and meeting customer requirements. It empowers employees because they see the results of their work. It permits organizations to compete from the inside out by building a set of competencies that meet customer requirements. It empowers executives to recognize that their success can come only from building internal support systems. It helps managers understand *why* their work is critical to organizational success. It allows each employee to sense a connection between daily work and long-term customer success.

As organizations face increasing change and turbulence, we believe that some companies have looked for elixirs—quick fixes that will meet the short-term requirements of investors. Our hope is that by focusing on organizational capability, we can not only meet short-term financial requirements but build a foundation for the future.

We recognize that paying attention to employees is not new. What is new is the magnitude and acuteness of the effort. In a world where parity in technology exists, where products can be copied in weeks, where capital exists to build new projects, and where global competition forces new management systems, those companies that build organizational capability will compete, succeed, and survive. A simple metaphor describes our hope for the book: the numbering system of U.S. freeways. Most of us drive on freeways all the time, but probably give little thought to why the freeways are numbered the way they are: even numbers for east and west, odd for north and south. The number represents the approximate land mass north, south, east, or west of the freeway. Three-digit numbers represent circles around major metropolitan areas.

Likewise, most managers have worked with and believe that people are "their most important asset." But, like the freeway numbering system, people are taken for granted; they are not treated in ways that build competitive organizations. By better understanding *why* people "are our most important asset," managers can move beyond platitudes and magical potions to long-term success.

Most managers consider themselves good people managers. Yet they often fail to recognize the significance of their managerial practices. In this book, we have tried to lay out a rationale for *why* managing people is so critical to competitiveness. In addition, we have provided a number of suggestions designed to help managers and employees find their way through the morass of people programs to build competitiveness.

As we look back to the decade of the 1980s, we see managers learning about competitiveness, customers, leadership, and excellence. We envision the decade of the 1990s as one during which the focus is on the synthesis of what goes on outside as well as inside a company. We see this as a major agenda for all managers seeking to find ways to continue to compete.

Dave Ulrich
Dale Lake

Ann Arbor, Michigan
May 1990

Acknowledgments

This book is an integration of diverse paths. Dale Lake's direction has been influenced by the study of processes for managing change and by the work of Ken Benne and Bob Chin. Dave Ulrich's direction has been influenced by the organizational philosophers J. B. Ritchie, Bill McKelvey, Bill Ouchi, and Steve Kerr. We appreciate and acknowledge their intellectual curiosity, which frames our arguments.

Our paths have merged to a great extent because of the stimulation and creativity of our colleague Noel Tichy. His work on change and leadership has helped us see means of integrating these diverse paths into a common direction. We are grateful to him for bringing us together and for being a constant source of stimulation.

In preparing this book, a number of colleagues were instrumental in refining and reshaping our ideas. We are grateful for cases, comments, and critiques by Dick Beatty, John Boroski, John Boudreau, Bill Bowen, Bill Brandt, Kim Cameron, Ram Charan, Frank Doyle, Ed Dunn, Lee Dyer, Cliff Ehrlich, Jane Henry, Todd Jick, Don Kane, Frank LaFasto, Gerry Lake, Phil Leyendecker, John O'Brien, Jim Peters, Tom Peters, C. K. Prahalad, Ray Reilly, Tony Rucci, Len Schlessinger, Ed Thompson, Wendy Ulrich, Jim Walker, Warren Wilhelm, Arthur Yeung, and Joe White.

We had outstanding administrative help from Ginger Bitter, Diane Haft, Margaret Oberle, and Esther Shear, who helped prepare various drafts of the manuscript. The editorial staff at Wiley was responsive and helpful. Above all, the editorial advice and work by Evelyn Toynton was nothing short of miraculous. She took a jargon-laden manuscript complete with mixed metaphors and images and molded it into the present book. Any errors that remain are ours.

Finally, we owe a special intellectual, personal, and emotional debt to Wayne Brockbank. His ability to conceive ideas and translate phenomena to principles has been of unequaled value. In addition, his personal friendship and emotional support have helped this project come to fruition.

Contents

1

Changing Vistas for Management Thought

If you give a man a fish, he will have a meal.
If you teach him to fish, he will have a living.
If you are thinking a year ahead, sow seed.
If you are thinking ten years ahead, plant a tree.
If you are thinking one hundred years ahead, educate the people.
By sowing a seed once, you will harvest once.
By planting a tree, you will harvest tenfold.
By educating the people, you will harvest one hundredfold.

Anonymous Chinese poet, c. 420 B.C.

For a piece of wood to catch fire, it must first be heated to a temperature at which it ignites; then it burns by itself. The initial heating requires energy from outside, but once the wood is ignited, the flame sustains itself and gives off light and heat.

A more intense fire than that of burning wood is produced from a mixture of aluminum powder and metal oxide. By itself, the mixture is cold and lifeless, but when heated to the ignition temperature it becomes a self-sustaining source of brilliant light and intense heat. Once it ignites it cannot be put out by ordinary means. The mixture will burn underwater or in any other environment that would extinguish an ordinary flame. When it burns, the fire is self-sustaining and does not depend on its surroundings for support.[1]

All managers want their organizations to succeed—or to continue to burn, as in the fire metaphor. In the last two decades, continued success has often been measured in terms of how well a company can meet customer needs. In both the private and public sectors, definitions of success have often focused on customer satisfaction.

In this book, however, we propose that in the 1990s a company's success will depend not only on ability to meet customer

1

needs but also on how well an organization's *internal* processes
work to meet external demands. By combining its processes with
its ability to meet customer expectations, the organization suc-
ceeds from the inside out—much like the ignited aluminum
powder and metal oxide mixture. The commitment and dedication of employees to fulfilling customer needs may become the
self-sustaining flame that perpetuates success. Competing from
the inside out means not merely managing employees to make
them comfortable within a company, but managing them in ways
that build the firm's ability to compete in the marketplace.

Traditional means of gaining competitive advantage—
building better products or services, pricing goods or services
lower than the competition, or incorporating technological innovation into research and manufacturing operations—must today be
supplemented by *organizational capability*,[2] or the ability of a firm to
manage people to gain a competitive advantage. Building organizational capability focuses internal organizational processes and
systems on meeting customer needs and ensures that the skills
and efforts of employees are directed toward achieving the goals
of the organization as a whole. In this way, employees become a
critical resource for competitiveness that will sustain itself over
time.

Developing organizational capability does not come by quick
fixes, simple programs, or management speeches, but involves
adopting certain principles and attitudes, which in turn determine and guide management behavior. It is a way of thinking as
well as of acting, and it begins with the realization that there is a
strong link between competitiveness and effective people management.

Some forward-thinking companies are becoming increasingly
aware of the connection between employees and competitiveness.
The three cases that follow illustrate how emphasis on building
organizational capability has helped these companies respond to
the challenges of the 1990s.

Marriott Corporation's new strategic agenda reflects innovative patterns of, and approaches to, competition within the service sector. The new organizational processes implemented by
Borg-Warner were designed to change the mindset of employees
after a capital restructuring. The merger between Baxter Travenol
and American Hospital Supply demonstrates that organizational
capability is a key factor in enabling diverse organization units to
develop a common focus.

MARRIOTT CORPORATION:
RETHINKING PEOPLE MANAGEMENT
TO IMPLEMENT STRATEGIC GOALS

Between 1964 and 1989, Marriott Corporation has been one of the most successful corporations in the world. The firm has maintained a 20 percent annual compounded top line growth—or increase in sales—along with a 20 percent annual compounded bottom line growth—or increase in profits.

Marriott began by focusing resources on food (airline food, Hot Shoppe restaurants) and single-product hotel chains. It expanded to become a major player in the service sector. In the food business, Marriott is a leader in both consumer food (Roy Rogers, Big Boy, and Travel Plaza restaurants) and institutional food (served in hospitals, airlines, airports, schools, and businesses). In the hotel industry, Marriott offers a product portfolio ranging from luxurious accommodations (Marriott Suites) to traditional rooms (Marriott) to lodging for family vacationers (Residence Inn), business travelers (Courtyard), and people seeking economy (Fairfield Inn). Painstakingly introduced, this product portfolio has ensured Marriott's success in a competitive market.

In the late 1980s, management identified two major factors as central to Marriott's continuing success. First, Marriott had to manage effectively its financial assets. Construction costs in the hotel division could be accurately predetermined and related to the type of facility to be built—for example, a conference center versus an economy hotel. The occupancy rates required to cover these costs could also be identified and established as goals. In the food business, Marriott knew the cost of each meal it produced and its net revenues on the food served. On an ongoing basis, these calculations enabled Marriott to monitor current expenses and anticipate future costs. Marriott also demonstrated commitment to effectively deploying financial assets by offering weekend rates to keep rooms filled on otherwise low-volume Friday and Saturday nights, by putting breakfast menus on beds at night to increase the use of kitchens, and by selling the hotels to syndications while maintaining management responsibility.

The second major factor in this company's success has been Marriott's efforts to meet its goal of becoming the provider of choice, or the preferred provider, in the hotel industry. In guest-satisfaction surveys, Marriott consistently ranks at the top. To meet guest demands, Marriott has initiated a number of programs aimed at maintaining its preferred-provider status: Concierge service, video checkout, frequent flier points, weekend rates, and customer-satisfaction cards all help ensure that guests' needs are anticipated and met. Likewise, in the food service sector, Marriott continually administers surveys to identify current and future customer needs to keep service well above par.

Managing financial resources and being the provider of choice are two key success factors that have enabled Marriott to maintain membership in the exclusive 20–20 club (20 percent annual compounded sales and 20 percent annual profit increase). But in the 1990s, will these two critical success factors be sufficient?

By the late 1980s, as Marriott management looked at changing economic, social, demographic, and technological shifts, it recognized that a third key success factor would be required (see Figure 1–1). With 225,000 employees in 1989 and the prospect of hiring more, Marriott executives saw the need to add a new dimension to their corporate strategy. To compete successfully, management realized that it also had to ignite within each employee a burning and self-sustaining commitment to outstanding customer service. To be consistent with Marriott's provider-of-choice philosophy, management set the goal of becoming the employer of choice. Being the employer of choice would be critical because (1) customers judge Marriott's service primarily on the basis of the impression created by Marriott employees, and (2) changing demographics, with fewer people in the 18- to 25-year-old age group—the traditional hiring pool—mean that the challenge of attracting high-quality employees will be greater than in the past.

Becoming the employer of choice would depend on two factors. First, employees must prefer working at Marriott, as measured by reduced turnover of high-quality employees. Second, high-quality job applicants must be attracted to Marriott, as measured by the acceptance rate among chosen job candidates.

To become the employer of choice, Marriott embarked on a number of activities. Rather than apply market research solely to customers, the firm conducted extensive surveys to learn what motivated, bothered, and challenged its employees. Based on these data, management could act to meet employee needs. For example, in one division of a food business, the general manager realized that in the 1990s Spanish would be the primary language of a majority of his employees. To help shape employee percep-

Figure 1–1
MARRIOTT CORPORATION'S THREE CRITICAL SUCCESS FACTORS

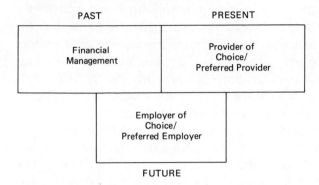

tions of Marriott, this manager recommended that all first-line supervisors become fluent in Spanish by 1993. His commitment was backed up with resources, such as Berlitz language courses for interested employees. He also realized that a key factor in becoming the employer of choice would be the relationship between employees and their immediate supervisors.

Other methods of attracting and keeping good employees included offering them training programs, career opportunities, and a variety of jobs; developing joint-venture internship programs with local high schools or colleges; and experimenting with alternative ways of designing work and giving employees feelings of ownership and of responsibility for their work areas. For example, a team approach to restaurant management or housecleaning was adopted, so that teams rather than individuals set standards and allocated work. In addition to hiring from the traditional labor pool of 18- to-25-year-olds, Marriott employed retirees and others who wanted to work part time. Division managers set standards for becoming the employer of choice, just as they had set standards for maintaining Marriott's position as the provider of choice. These standards translated into managerial rewards and incentives.

Thus, Marriott redefined the nature of competition in the service sector. Rather than compete merely on price, through its financial capability, or on product, through its commitment to being the preferred provider, Marriott realized that it had to compete by developing strong organizational capability. In competing exclusively on the basis of product, Marriott hotels took on firms such as Hilton, Hyatt, Sheraton, Four Seasons, and other hotels and chains. Focusing on becoming the employer of choice means that Marriott competitors now include firms like McDonald's, Burger King, Sears, and other companies that hire large numbers of employees from the traditional applicant pool. In addition to these private firms, Marriott views the U.S. military as a major competitor for employees in the 1990s. The military offers recruits job training, career advancement, opportunity for travel, and other amenities. To compete, Marriott has sought to become a more attractive employer than the military.

In brief, Marriott executives looked at the nature of competition in the 1990s and concluded that winning would require *organizational capability*, in addition to financial and product capabilities, and that would determine whether the corporation could reach its goals. By redefining the source of competition to include the military with its attractive employment practices, Marriott executives concentrated on achieving organizational capability. At Marriott, organizational capability has meant rethinking and redesigning the traditional processes to manage employees.

BORG-WARNER: RETHINKING ORGANIZATIONAL PROCESSES OF REWARDS, DEVELOPMENT, AND COMMUNICATION TO MANAGE CHANGE

In late 1986, Borg-Warner consisted of six major businesses: chemicals, producing plastics and other chemical products; automotive, producing products for the automobile drive chain; information services, through Chilton, a credit-reporting business; and financial services. Borg-Warner executives faced an unenviable situation. The stock was fluctuating between $30 and $35 a share.[3] And yet, if each of the four largest businesses were to be sold independently to a firm looking to expand in that particular industry, the break-up stock price would be about $60 a share. This situation made Borg-Warner a prime candidate for a takeover.

A number of investors, raiders, and greenmail artists began investing in Borg-Warner with the hope of realizing short-term profits through the acquisition and dismantling of the company. Believing that a takeover was inevitable and that they could manage the business more effectively than any other potential owner, Borg-Warner executives attempted a leveraged buyout (LBO)— that is, they borrowed money from a financial institution to buy the stock themselves. They then made the firm private rather than publicly traded. The result was a dramatic change in Borg-Warner's balance sheet, with the debt-to-equity ratio rising from about 30 percent (1:3) to a hefty 1,800 percent (19:1).

The principles of an LBO are similar to those of home ownership. Most people acquire a home by putting up a percentage of cash and borrowing the rest. When the home value increases because of inflation or some other reason, the leverage enables the homeowner to generate rapid wealth. This rationale argues for high leverage in buying a home (putting only a little down and maintaining a high debt-to-equity ratio). However, to keep the home the homeowner must pay monthly mortgage payments. The challenge for the mortgage issuer, of course, is to make sure that the prospective buyer can afford the monthly payments. If the debt-to-equity ratio is too high and the payments cannot be met, the borrower risks losing everything.

Before engaging in an LBO, a firm's executives and the investors who lend them the money must believe that the new company will be able to carry the high monthly debt service. If these payments are made and the company increases in value, both the executives and the investors earn enormous profits. At Borg-Warner, management believed that the LBO (1) met original shareholder expectations by adding value to their investment, since the managers acquired the stock at $48.50 a share; (2) avoided the possibility of a takeover and the ruthless dismantling of the firm; and (3) enabled managers and investors to earn high returns if they managed the business profitably.

Like the homeowner who makes a $50,000 down payment on a $1 million home and then must make high monthly mortgage payments, Borg-Warner executives faced the immediate challenge of meeting debt payments. By implementing several short-term tactics they were able to accomplish this. The chemicals business was sold to General Electric and the information services to TRW. These divestitures helped Borg-Warner reduce its debt load and make short-term payments. It should be noted that these divestitures, unlike those that would have occurred had a takeover "artist" acquired the firm, were carried out in a manner highly protective of employee interests. Some employees were given assurances of job security, and those whose jobs were duplicated received severance packages. Sensitivity to employee needs characterized the entire process.

Borg-Warner executives, however, did not consider these divestitures—while important—to be the key to meeting their financial obligations. They concluded that financial success under the LBO depended on changing the mindset of employees—from that of company agent to that of company owner. Before the LBO, managers saw themselves as agents of the owners. As agents, Borg-Warner managers acted on behalf of the shareholders. The board of directors and the executive committee set policies, which the managers implemented. For example, company policy allowed employees who traveled overseas on business to fly business class. As agents of the stockholders, managers availed themselves of this privilege.

After the LBO, however, Borg-Warner executives realized that managers had to begin to feel and act like owners of the firm rather than like agents. To this end, the top 267 managers were "strongly invited" to invest from $20,000 to $5 million in the firm, depending on their position and tenure. Once managers made this significant personal investment, their mindset shifted, and they began to view themselves as owners rather than as agents. Through the incentives offered them, employees had the fires of ownership and commitment lighted within them. They began to act with the owner mindset and make decisions that saved the company money. For example, they traveled overseas on reduced fares or even reassessed the need for the trip. Because of the changed incentive system, managers were motivated to make decisions that helped the firm reach its financial goals. Furthermore, the bonus program was dramatically changed to encompass more employees and to reflect the cash flow and operating income generated by specific units.

In addition to the changed reward system, new training and communications programs were instituted. The training programs helped employees at all levels develop the skills necessary to make the LBO successful. The communications program fostered employee understanding of the causes and impact of the LBO, as well as the management processes that were needed for continuing business success.

With the Borg-Warner LBO, the criterion of business success changed dramatically from earning profits to servicing debt. To meet its debt obligations, the company effected strategic changes and restructurings. However, the long-term ability to meet business requirements was enhanced by a focusing on *organizational capability*—in this case, a shift in the mindset of managers from agents to owners. In sum, the reward, training, and communications programs helped to develop organizational capability, enabled employees to shift mindsets, and strengthened the firm as it sought to reach its financial objectives.

BAXTER HEALTHCARE: RETHINKING ORGANIZATIONAL PHILOSOPHY, STRUCTURE, AND STAFFING TO ENHANCE STRATEGIC UNITY

The decade of the 1980s saw a rapid increase in the number and size of mergers, acquisitions, and consolidations (MACs). Whether these ventures were initiated for strategic or financial reasons, the ability to accomplish mergers or acquisitions often derived from the proficiency with which managers used organizational processes to manage people for competitive advantage—that is, organizational capability.[4]

The merger of Baxter Travenol and American Hospital Supply (AHS) is a classic illustration of the critical role of organizational capability in ensuring the business success of a MAC. Managers of the new company—Baxter Healthcare—focused on three initiatives to develop organizational capability: (1) defining a new operating philosophy, (2) designing an organizational structure consistent with that philosophy, and (3) facilitating the human aspects of the merger through communications, executive and staff selection, severance packages, and career counseling.

To increase organizational capability during the period of the merger, four major task forces were formed:

1. The *Merger Steering Committee* was composed of the chief executive officers (CEOs) and the chief operating officers (COOs) of Baxter and American Hospital. These four individuals conducted frequent reviews of the entire integration process.
2. The *Transition Team* was made up of eight senior executives, four from each company.
3. The *Top Management Organization* and the *Corporate Staff Integration* task forces were responsible for designing and staffing the senior management and staff functions within the organization.

These task forces were charged with building organizational capability through three initiatives, as follows.

Initiative 1: Achieving Greater Organizational Capability through Establishing a Shared Operating Philosophy

Before the merger, the two companies had substantially different operating philosophies. In each case, the operating philosophy represented organizational processes that affected the thinking and behavior of employees. AHS was characterized by a decentralized structure that included multiple units, each with its integrated and separate operating philosophy. By contrast, Baxter represented a much more centralized and functional operating style, with few autonomous units. Managers in such functions as human resources and finance reported directly to corporate headquarters.

After the merger, it became popular when discussing where the company was headed to formulate a dichotomy, an either-or choice between centralized and decentralized operating styles. Ultimately, however, the Top Management Organization task force determined that an either-or approach was inadequate for business needs and opted for a hybrid concept. This approach involved both decentralizing decision-making in areas such as marketing, which directly affect customers, and centralizing and consolidating decision-making in functions not seen as critical to customer interface. Areas such as research, manufacturing, and administrative support offered opportunities to realize economies of scale.

To arrive at an operating philosophy to build organizational capability, the firm had to identify the values and principles that would drive the new organization. From the outset, an explicit position was taken regarding *how* the merger would proceed. The following "process" issues found their way into the culture of the new company as the key philosophical objectives for Baxter Healthcare:

□ *Participative.* The design and integration of the merged organization would be undertaken with broad participation from executives of *both* companies.

□ *Strategic.* Any decisions made on activities that were essential to merge the two companies would be consistent with the strategic direction of the merger rather than being based on expediency.

□ *High standards*. An explicit decision was made to conduct the merger integration in an unprecedentedly humane way, both to avoid the traumatic impact on people and to select into the new organization the best individuals from each company.

□ *Dignity*. Executives would treat *all* employees from each company—both those who remained and those who were outplaced—in an open and honest fashion, with a sense of dignity and respect.

These philosophical objectives were a core element of building organizational capability for Baxter Healthcare, and provided the underpinning for the processes used to shape employee thought and action.

Initiative 2: Developing Organizational Capability through the Design of the New Organizational Structure

The operating philosophy reflected the principles on which Baxter Healthcare was established. After the hybrid philosophy was formulated, the Top Management Organization task force turned its attention to organizational restructuring, realizing that the structure itself would send a clear message to employees about management philosophy. To maintain the philosophical objectives, the task force identified "rational" groupings of operating units, based primarily on similarity of product lines and/or customer and market segments. This grouping process resulted in the formation of ten operating groups, seven focusing on similar product or customer types and three handling distribution, national accounts, and world trade. In addition, the task force identified the need for ten corporate staff functions. Consistent with all other aspects of the merger, within the staff groups, task forces with equal Baxter and AHS representation were formed in each functional area.

To examine each corporate staff area in depth, a formal organization design process was established (see Figure 1–2).

1. Each staff executive evaluated the strategic mission, or charter, of his or her function in the new organization.

Figure 1–2
FORMAL ORGANIZATION DESIGN PROCESS AT BAXTER HEALTHCARE

STEP 1: Define the strategic mission.
STEP 2: Identify programs, functions, and subfunctions.
STEP 3: Evaluate centralized and decentralized approaches.
STEP 4: Determine the resources necessary to accomplish the mission.
STEP 5: Create an organization structure.
STEP 6: Select the best people.
STEP 7: Implement the new organization structure.

2. Each executive identified all of the functions, programs, and systems that would be needed to meet the strategic charter.

3. Each executive evaluated whether a centralized or decentralized operation approach would be more appropriate.

4. Each executive estimated the resources, in terms of both dollars and staffing levels, that would be needed to accomplish the strategic mission.

5. Each executive recommended an organizational structure for his or her function that was consistent with its mission and the centralized or decentralized philosophy to be adopted.

In selecting the best people for the new organization (step 6), a series of processes were used to enhance organizational capability. First, the people-selection phase of the merger did not occur until the new organization and the new corporate staff structure were *completely* designed. This meant that executives on the task forces responsible for designing the structures and the staff organizations did not know whether they personally would be selected for a role in the new organization. The uncertainty created a climate of interdependence and cooperation. Second, organizational capability was increased because the selection process was geared to ensuring fairness and equity in staffing, thereby raising the level of employee competency.

Initiative Three: Building Organizational Capability through Successful Handling of the Human Aspects of the Merger

The people-selection process at the corporate staff level created unique challenges. First, the magnitude of the task was significant: Prior to the merger, the two companies had a total of nearly 3,000 people on their staffs. With a more decentralized operating philosophy, the goal was a staff of 2,000 (not all 1,000 reductions resulted in job loss, because many people were redeployed to operating units). Second, the decision to go to a more decentralized structure in some areas meant that at times one position existed for two qualified employees (one from each company). The CEO of the new Baxter Healthcare maintained that true integration would occur, with the best person for the job to be selected in each instance.

To meet the unique challenges of this merger and to enhance organizational capability, the people-selection process became formal and elaborate. It was characterized by the following principles and practices:

- □ Select the best person, regardless of company.
- □ Appoint a full-time staffing transition team.
- □ Establish terms to ensure analysis of staffing needs for each functional area.
- □ Set up formal placement centers.
- □ Offer career counseling.
- □ Freeze external hiring in all operating units.
- □ Appoint a review and appeals board.

These initiatives for establishing an operating philosophy, staff structure, and management practices were critical to the new company's overall organizational capability. Because resources and attention were dedicated to ensuring organizational capability as a critical element of the merger, Baxter's experience was higher than expected integration and the creation of a successfully operating firm.

MANAGING IN THE 1990S

The examples just given illustrate three major challenges to managers. A key factor in each case was the fundamental drive on the part of the managers to make their organizations more competitive. More competitive organizations meet customer needs, succeed in the marketplace, and survive and grow over time. To be competitive, Marriott worked on three management agendas (financial, preferred provider, and preferred employer). Borg-

Warner underwent an LBO to restructure its business and re-vamped financial incentives to change employee mindset. Baxter Healthcare merged to gain economies of scale and become stronger in the marketplace. In each case, managers recognized that building organizational capability was necessary to achieving competitiveness.

To illustrate the overall purposes of this book, we highlight the three major themes that managers at all levels must under-stand and deal with in order to succeed in the 1990s.

Theme 1: Using Organizational Capability to Achieve Key Goals

Organizational capability helps companies realize their strategic goals. Firms with high organizational capability are better able to implement their strategies. As discussed earlier, a key strategy of Marriott Corporation is to achieve excellence in customer service. This objective, which is critical to Marriott's success, is dependent in part on being the preferred employer, or the employer of choice. To become the preferred employer, Marriott dedicated resources to building organizational capability by upgrading its human resource practices, ensuring that employees believed that their needs were understood, and finding means of attracting and retaining high-quality employees. At Borg-Warner, the strategy was clear: obtain enough cash to cover debt. By modifying the financial reward system, managerial attention was redirected toward generating the cash needed to service the debt. At Baxter Healthcare, the goal was to become the most extensive and power-ful organization in the hospital supply industry. To achieve this objective, it was necessary to merge two diverse cultures, a feat that was accomplished, in part, through a commitment to initia-tives aimed at building organizational capability.

Many strategies are formulated without being implemented. Those that are formulated but not implemented do not add value to the organization. We believe that organizational capability makes it possible for strategies to be translated from elegant concepts into practical actions. By learning to manage people for competitive advantage, managers help their companies win in the marketplace.

By focusing on the importance of employees in sustaining competitive advantage, firms building organizational capability rebuild their commitment to and from employees. Traditional employee commitments to the firm have been based on job security and loyalty, which a firm promises its employees. Because of the turbulent business environment of the 1980s, with restructurings, mergers, acquisitions, and consolidations, most firms violated this traditional employee contract. Employees who worked under conditions and guarantees of loyalty and job security were faced with the stark realization that loyalty-based contracts were invalid. Firms that have not replaced loyalty contracts with innovative and defined employee guarantees face employees who have little long-term commitment to the firm. By building organizational capability, firms can re-establish their contracts with employees. At Baxter Healthcare, employee contracts of loyalty were violated with the merger. However, by involving employees in the merger process, this contract was replaced with a guarantee of involvement. Employees could be involved in decision-making processes that affected their jobs. Through building organizational capability, employee contracts may be re-established.

Organizational capability also reflects how effectively firms manage change. A capacity for change is central to managing people for competitive advantage. A popular assumption is that people always resist change and that the most common response to the question, "Is there always resistance to change?" is "yes." We disagree. If we won a $5 million lottery, we would probably accept the money. Our lives would probably change, but very likely we would not resist the change (at least in the short term). In their personal lives, people often resist change when they lack information about how the change will affect them, or when they perceive the change as having negative consequences. Within organizations, individuals often resist change for the same reasons: They lack information about how the change will affect them and/or are afraid the consequences of the change will be negative. Organizational processes designed to manage people can be modified to effect change positively. Communication, training, and staffing programs can be used to share information with employees about what the future may hold. In addition, incentive programs, rewards, and appraisal systems can be modified to ensure that the change will have positive rather than negative effects.

At Borg-Warner, managers who invested in the LBO and who received full information about and training for it actually welcomed the change. When individuals are able to accommodate change, firms increase their capacity for change and such firms can respond more quickly to market shifts. Such firms have competitive advantage in the marketplace. At Baxter Healthcare, information about the merger was shared through the task forces, employee meetings, and communication programs to help all employees understand not only what was happening, but why.

Finally, organizational capability shifts attention from strategic planning and intent to strategic unity.[5] Strategic planning, which was popular throughout the 1970s, encouraged businesses to set future directions through environmental scanning, market analyses, and portfolio management. Strategic intent, which became popular during the 1980s, focused more on setting a business's vision, mission, and longer-term orientation. Both strategic planning and strategic intent focus on how firms allocate resources. We believe that in the 1990s, strategic unity will become a more critical success factor. Strategic unity highlights the importance of building employee commitment to the plans and intents by dealing with employee attitudes and business culture. When Baxter Healthcare merged, two different cultures had to be brought into harmony. The operating philosophy, organizational structure, and people-management processes that were established helped employees from the two firms integrate their disparate values into a single style. The creation of strategic unity for the newly merged company enabled Baxter Healthcare to focus employee attention on common goals and values.

In firms with strategic unity, employees, customers, and suppliers have common, or shared, goals and values. Having a common focus enables employees to spend time and energy reaching rather than debating goals. Strategic unity also enables the firm to represent itself more clearly to customers, thereby giving customers a fuller understanding of the firm's values. With strategic unity comes competitive advantage, because firms are able to allocate their resources more effectively and efficiently.

In the past, arguments for allocating resources to managing people have been couched primarily in social terms. Managers worked to help employees feel good about working in the firm because feeling good was a value in and of itself. We do not refute that argument. We believe, however, that only those firms which manage their human resources effectively, and thereby create organizational capability, will enjoy sustained success in the marketplace in the 1990s. Once employees are recognized as a key competitive resource, effective management will finally come to be seen as an economic as well as a social value. When this fact is realized, firms will be much less willing to abandon human resource programs even during economic downturns.

Theme 2: Managing Paradox, Not Polarity, as a Way of Life

Throughout the 1970s and 1980s, a series of polarities was proposed for managers. Managers were urged to shift their focus from short-term to long-term results, from a domestic to a global market, from operational to strategic activities, from practical actions to strategic visions, from internal employees to external stakeholders (customers, suppliers, stockholders). They were ordered to stop thinking and start acting, to stop trusting their intuition and start basing their decisions on statistics. They were warned that the autocratic business leaders of the past had to evolve into or be replaced by democratic ones if companies were to survive.

All of these proposals call for moving from one practice or idea to its exact opposite. We suggest, however, that a crucial challenge for the 1990s will be managing paradox.[6] Managing the paradoxes inherent in any business transition means focusing not on conflicts and polarities (for example, ''Let's move the organization *from* one state *to* another state'') but on formulating responses that meet simultaneous, disparate demands and resolving the conflicts among them (for example, ''Let's make sure the organization accomplishes *simultaneously* its financial, strategic, and employee goals'').

A simple analogy illustrates the logic of operating within multiple goals. Imagine three glasses representing the financial, customer, and employee stakeholders of a firm and a pitcher of water representing managerial attention. Some managers pour all their energy (water) into one glass, concentrating on either financial, customer, or employee needs. We propose something else: Fill all the glasses, allocating energy to multiple goals. As a result, any one goal may not be met as completely as it would be in a firm that dedicated all its attention to achieving that goal alone, but the total success rate for the three goals will be higher. In effect, the total volume of water in the three glasses is greater than the volume in a single glass into which a firm has put all its energy.

Paradox management has a physiological analogy. The body survives only by integrating different functions. The heart pumps blood, which is central to all life-support systems. The brain provides electrical impulses to keep the body functioning. We would not call a person healthy who has only a strong heart or only a sound brain; both are critical to life, and we need both to function. Likewise, managers in the 1990s cannot rely on simple either-or solutions. They must learn to operate in the complex, ever-changing world of paradox as they seek to satisfy multiple and at times competing demands from multiple stakeholders.

At Marriott, managers were challenged by three competing and at times competing demands: to maintain financial standards, to remain the provider of choice, and to become the employer of choice. Winning *exclusively* at any one of the three would be likely to guarantee overall failure. For example, it would be easy to be the employer of choice simply by raising wages far above market rates. However, since each five-cent pay increase costs $30 million, giving away money to become the employer of choice is not a viable option. To be effective, Marriott management must maintain an ever-changing balance among money, product, and people.

Likewise, Baxter Healthcare and Borg-Warner were challenged to resolve seemingly conflicting demands for short- and long-term performance. Short-term performance for either company was a tempting choice. For example, cutting costs in research, engineering, overhead, and people would have helped Borg-Warner reach its financial goals quickly. And Baxter could have shown the investment community its immediate savings from the merger by laying off employees and closing facilities. Such short-term ploys, however, would have weakened both employee loyalty and the firm's ability to compete in the marketplace over the long term. If short-term tactics at Baxter Healthcare had imposed the value structure of either Baxter Travenol or American Hospital Supply on employees of the other company, the new firm would not have had the valuable synergy that resulted from a forward-thinking integration.

The continuing management of paradox is an integral part of organizational capability, since by its nature it involves developing management practices that meet multiple demands. While financial or technical demands may create seemingly contradictory goals, a firm's management processes must build the ability both to recognize and to integrate paradoxical demands. When executives develop organizational capability, they are able to manage paradox in ways that add value to all the stakeholders of a firm.

Theme 3: Developing Staff Leadership through Partnerships

Building partnerships inside and outside the firm helps managers use organizational processes to gain competitive advantage and to manage paradox effectively. Partnerships exist in many forms and at many levels. At Marriott, a partnership was formed among the financial, strategic planning, operations, marketing, and human resource functions to help the corporation become the employer of choice. Financial experts developed measurements and allocated resources. Strategic experts linked employee behavior to business strategy. Marketing experts applied market research tools to employee groups. Human resource professionals helped clarify employee values and goals and designed programs and activities to meet employee needs.

At Borg-Warner, the four managing partners possessed broad expertise: One was the former CEO, who had a strategic and customer focus; one was a financial expert; one a legal expert; and one a human resources expert. Their partnership enabled them to draw on each other's backgrounds to meet the needs of the firm. For example, the creation of the incentive package to change the mindset of employees from agents to owners had strategic, financial, and human resource implications. This senior management team operated as a partnership to meet its strategic objective of generating cash to service the debt.

At Baxter Healthcare, partnerships existed across functions as human resource professionals joined with managers to plan the integration of the two firms. Such partnerships enabled the new organization to combine the strengths of the original firms. It allowed for open discussion of key management positions and ensured fairness in the filling of those positions. Partnerships also existed at Baxter Healthcare among the temporary teams, which examined work functions, made recommendations, and spoke with one voice to move the organization toward its new structure.

Partnerships will be a management requirement in the 1990s. They will enhance organizational capability and enable people with different views to express their differences but come together when decisions must be made. An executive once expressed to her newly hired staff her commitment to participative management with the simple but elegant explanation: ''I am hiring you because you are different from me. If you and I thought alike one of us would not be necessary, and it would never be me. But once we make a decision, we go public as one." From this simple concept derive the three key elements of partnership.

First, partnerships exist when there is mutual respect. Because employees from different functions at Marriott respected one another, they were able to form and operate partnerships. Because the line managers perceived that the human resource professionls at Baxter added value, partnerships were formed.

Second, partnerships exist when each member of the partnership operates as a staff leader. Leadership was a major theme in the 1980s, and the need for it will increase in the 1990s. Organizational leadership cannot be exhibited exclusively at the top of the organization. Critical leadership will also come from staff professionals who offer expertise in their functional areas, thus adding value to other areas. The human resource managing partner at Borg-Warner, for example, initiated and framed the discussion of the new incentive program. He then acted as a staff leader, because he understood the need for a new incentive program, had the competencies to deliver it, and initiated the effort to design and implement it.

Third, partnerships exist through unity of voice. As the executive told her staff, "When we go public, we go as one." We believe that partners can draw individual strength from each other, then integrate their differences into one voice.

At a recent seminar where we introduced the concept of managing people for competitive advantage, a wise cynic pointed out that what we call organizational capability is nothing new. In part, we agree. The Chinese poem at the beginning of this chapter, written in approximately 420 B.C., espouses many of the principles discussed in this book. However, organizational capability is becoming a much more pivotal part of a manager's responsibility. It helps build competitiveness, resolves paradoxes, and builds partnerships—key success factors for the 1990s.

2

Forces for Change:
The Call for Competitive
Advantage

The more human beings proceed by plan, the more effectively they
may be hit by accident.

F. Durrenmatt

Don't expect anything original from an echo.

Michael Kami

A ll viable organizations react directly or indirectly to
the business environment in which they operate. In
viewing the interplay between the organization and its environment, two constructs may be helpful: niche and milieu. An organization's niche comprises the stakeholders who deal directly
with the organization and may include suppliers, customers, government agencies, trade associations, competitors, members of
the board of directors, strategic alliance partners, labor unions,
distributors, and investors. These stakeholders play an important
role in determining how management allocates the organization's
resources. Businesses succeed when they effectively and efficiently draw resources from input stakeholders (for example, investors, unions, suppliers), transform resources into goods or
services, and return resources to output stakeholders (for
example, customers), with value having been added in the transformation process. Adding value to customers is the essence of
competitive advantage and the key to gaining greater market
share within a niche. Within a niche, managers often deal directly
with stakeholders to make transactions more efficient in the short
term and more stable in the long term.

The second set of environmental factors—the external
milieu—affects not only the value chain but the processes by
which management makes decisions. The economic, technologi-

cal, and social conditions of the external milieu have an impact on business managers, but managers have little control over these factors. By understanding trends in its milieu, management can better predict how external forces will affect its niche and its business over time.

In the 1980s, the milieu in which managers operated underwent many dramatic changes:[1] Business became increasingly global, the composition of the labor force was radically altered, and new technologies created changes by themselves and caused the overall pace of change to accelerate. In the 1990s, change is expected to proceed at an even more rapid rate, and many of the changes that will take place are not readily predictable. Managements will therefore need to be flexible in order to respond quickly to events for which they cannot plan.

Concurrently, competition will not only increase but will itself become less predictable. Traditional competitors, whose behaviors are well known, will be replaced by nontraditional ones—for example, Sears, Roebuck & Company, a retailer, becoming a major player in the financial services industry. Also growing in importance will be foreign competitors, who often play by different rules—for example, Japanese companies whose business perspective has been long rather than short term, and who have therefore been willing to sacrifice short-term profits to gain market share.

Changes in the milieu often lead to increased competition, which in turn alters the milieu still further. Thus the 1990s are likely to place more demands on managers than ever before.

FORCES FOR CHANGE

The most significant changes in the business milieu in the next decade are likely to derive from five trends: globalization, technological change, growth of equity markets and corporate restructuring, changes in public policy, and demographic transitions. These trends will force managers to find new answers to such traditional questions as:

- □ What is our market share?
- □ Who are our primary competitors?
- □ What technological changes are available?

□ Who are our major customers?
□ What are the expectations of our employees?

Understanding these trends and their implications also creates a heightened need to focus on competitive advantage, as described in this chapter.

Globalization

Economic, technological, and social conditions over the past twenty years have culminated in what Marshall McLuhan has called a "global village." The shrinking globe is reflected in nearly every aspect of life: the growing number of North American university students from outside North America; increased leisure travel abroad; the growing number of firms buying supplies from other countries, obtaining capital from financial institutions overseas, and seeking access to markets around the world; and increased investment in the United States by non-U.S. investors.[2]

Globalization increases competitive pressures by bringing more entrants into a market. Many of these new players may have extensive financial resources in their native countries and may concentrate on long-term goals, such as gaining market share, rather than on short-term economic goals. With globalization, a niche is also expanded when the firm can include a larger number of potential suppliers from whom it can obtain materials and supplies, a larger source of investors, a more diverse labor pool, and more customers. Globalization increases geometrically the complexity of doing business, from learning to find and manage employees in different countries to establishing cross-national information systems to designing and delivering products and services uniquely suited for separate national markets. Honda, for example, a global competitor in the engine market, sells almost no snowblowers in Japan, but realizes that there is a market for snowblowers in the United States and Canada. Honda executives realized that to complete globally, they had to define the product needs of each country and work to serve that market.

Globalization also requires new ways of defining and accomplishing work. At a strategic level, organizations in a global market need to redefine their served market. In a recent seminar, we asked the executives of a manufacturing firm to write down their current market share. Within about a 5 percent variance, the executives claimed to have 20 percent of the market. Upon further analysis, each executive defined the served market as only North America. When the boundaries of this market were stretched to global dimensions, the firm's market share decreased to about 5 percent. The executives of this firm also defined primary competitors solely as other North American companies. Upon closer examination, it became evident that current and future competitors were outside North America. As the executives probed further, they learned that these competitors had already established a beachhead in the North American market through joint ventures and licensing agreements. They realized that their ability to compete globally would be a critical success factor in the 1990s.

At an operational level, globalization has an equally profound impact. Managers in manufacturing firms have learned that raw materials can be obtained from around the world more cheaply than from North American firms exclusively. Labor pools and a diverse work force have been recognized as primary global challenges. For years one U.S. firm obtained new employees through an established list of well-known American universities. Stretching to a global perspective required management to develop a global organizational capability by considering employees from diverse backgrounds, forming relationships with Asian and European universities, and creating a career-progression program for employees from other nations.

Readiness for globalization varies across firms. Nation-wide, only 9 percent of U.S. citizens hold passports; comparatively few speak a second language; and sensitivity to alternative cultures often remains at a neophyte level. While many companies have invested in strategic alliances, joint ventures, and other licensing arrangements, others still define their served market as within borders rather than across borders and lack the organizational capability to compete globally.

Technological Change

With today's computers and RAM storage chips, technology has become an "infohype," with more information available quicker than ever before in nearly every industry.[3] It has been suggested that the increased information flow results in a new competitive reality. The trend toward competing through the use of information pervades virtually all areas of business. Financial services compete through the use of automatic teller machines and point-of-sale terminals. Manufacturers use computer-aided design and computer-aided manufacturing technologies, frequently with the designers separated geographically from the manufacturing facilities. Retailers have the capacity to monitor inventory immediately and receive immediate point-of-sale payment for goods purchased. Airlines use computer-controlled reservation systems, allowing for hundreds of daily price and reservation changes. Throughout all industries, electronics and information systems have changed the nature of competition.

With technological changes, product life cycles have become shorter. In the automobile industry, the traditional development time for a car from conception to production was about seven years. The cycle has now been reduced to three years for North American firms and two years for Japanese firms. Technology has played a critical role in this shorter lead time through automated design, manufacturing, supply, and distribution systems.

Evidence of rapid technological change is everywhere. In the automotive industry, new technology will continue to result in improved products. Innovations abound in stereo systems, brake systems, transmission systems, and drive trains, to name just a few. Such technological innovations have had a marked impact on the quality of the products produced and the degree of customer satisfaction. Future technological innovations will continue to affect automobile systems. For example, automatic navigation systems have been designed and tested. In these systems, cars have an antenna in the roof and a map system on the dashboard. After the driver punches into the computer the starting and ending point of a trip, the computer plots on a dashboard map the most efficient route to the destination. Such systems have been tested in European cities to help traffic flow, with computers providing continual updates on least-congested travel routes. In addition, automobile companies have applied technology from the Air Force to project driving information (speedometer, odometer, and other information) in front of the windshield so that drivers do not have to avert their eyes from the road to check information. Additional innovations in plastics have enabled automobile manufacturers to reduce the weight of cars, make production easier, and increase gas mileage.

A variety of industries have arisen as a function of new technology—for example, genetic engineering, information systems, and telecommunications. In addition, many traditional ones, such as banking, have been restructured and redefined: Non-traditional banks such as Sears, K-Mart, General Motors, and American Express now provide many banking and financial services. Technology makes possible different kinds of transactions, such as point-of-sale debit, and allows for more cross-national transactions, such as those using internationally recognized credit cards. Technology redefines competitors, forces innovation, and encourages a commitment to constant change.

Maintaining technological currency is not an option for firms that seek sustained competitive advantage. Continuing technological change will necessitate continual education of employees to adapt to new technologies and alternative work systems, such as portable work stations that enable individuals to work at home.

Growth of Equity Markets and Corporate Restructuring

Since 1970, the concentration of stock ownership by institutional investors in Fortune 1000 companies has increased threefold (from 15 to 45 percent). Growth in pension funds and mutual funds accounts for some of this institutional investment. This concentration has contributed to the dramatic rise throughout the 1980s in the number of mergers, acquisitions, and consolidations (MACs). Mergers and acquisitions increased from $30 billion in 1980 to over $220 billion in 1988; and over 1,400 LBOs took place between 1982 and 1988.

These corporate restructurings have occurred in all industries and have changed the contract between firms and employees. Traditional psychological contracts based on loyalty between corporations and employees often falter in a MAC environment. With new ownership, there is a reassessment of the contribution of employees to firm performance, and the result may be the cancellation or renegotiation of traditional contracts. With MACs, there may be duplication of employee functions, and some employees may not fit into the new organization.

Changes in Public Policy

Public policy has also affected how organizations operate within their niches. Federal deficits have fueled the need to generate alternative sources of income. As the alternatives are assessed and implemented, they affect the cost, design, and distribution of products.

Deregulation in many markets has led to increased competitiveness. The trucking, telecommunications, financial services, hospital supply, airline, and oil industries have experienced significant shifts because of deregulation in the 1980s. As a result, new competitors have entered the markets, firms have experienced greater failure rates, and traditional avenues for competition have changed.

In some industries, regulation has increased. For example, in the hospital supply industry, federal stipulations of diagnostic regulated groups (DRGs) and reimbursement levels for each DRG have had a dramatic impact. Since payments for hospital services were fixed by legislation, competitors were forced to reduce the cost of producing and delivering the supplies. Such increased cost pressures led to many restructurings and mergers, among them that between Baxter Travenol and American Hospital Supply.

Throughout the 1980s, federal policies redefined the nature of competition. As businesses enter the 1990s, they will need to be aware of and responsive to changing federal policies. In a global market, understanding the policies of one's own government is not sufficient. To be successful in such an environment, managers must be sensitive to the regulations and practices of nations all over the globe.

Demographic Transitions

Demographic changes will dramatically affect business organizations of the 1990s. First, the population of Western nations is aging. The aging of the baby boomers will lead to new products, services, and market opportunities. Retailers will have growing markets for more conservative, traditional, and larger-sized apparel as they serve the needs of this growing population group. Home designs have already expanded the size of and products for master suites to provide adults with increased private and personal living space. Leisure-time activities for adults will continue to increase.

The aging of the population will reduce the overall labor force to levels below the number of jobs available. One European company estimates that the supply of college graduates in 1993 and 1994, based on the number of college entrants in 1989 and 1990, will be 10 percent below demand for employment. These statistics underlie Marriott's need to become the employer of choice, as described in Chapter 1. With a smaller labor pool from which to choose and an increase in the number of available jobs, the ability to attract employees may become an increasingly critical factor in the next decade, particularly for firms with large employee populations. The proliferation of help wanted signs, of temporary employment agencies, and of flexible jobs for retired, dual-career, and permanent part-time employees are signs of this change.

Change in family structure represents another major demographic trend. The traditional "Leave It to Beaver" family, with a working father, housewife mother, and two children, exists in only 19 percent of U.S. households. Single parents, single adults, and dual careers have become dominant forms of family structure. A future family transition may be care of the elderly as the financial and emotional costs of care for this age group dramatically increase. Couples who, after rearing children, seek the financial and social flexibility of the empty nest may face the challenge of caring for aging parents. These changing family patterns mean greater pressures on employees, leading to added stress in balancing work and family, changes in the mix of fringe benefits and reward packages required to meet the needs of diverse family structures, and restricted mobility.

Implications of the Forces for Change: An Economic Vicious Circle

As a result of global, technological, equity, public policy, and demographic transitions, business managers face two related challenges: change and competition.

Increasing Change

As a function of the kinds of changes just discussed, managers of the 1990s will face increasing rates of change. In the 1960s and 1970s, the pace of change could be likened to the progress of a ship in a placid and predictable ocean. The routine swell of the waves enabled managers to navigate their ships on a straight course with ease.

The 1980s brought storms to the ocean that will persist throughout the 1990s. Traditionally placid and predictable waves have become turbulent and unpredictable. In a storm, waves change in three ways. First, the *pace* of the waves increases, with the swells coming closer together. Second, the *intensity* of the waves increases, with the swells larger and the gulfs between waves greater. Third, the *direction* of the waves becomes less predictable. Rather than coming from the same direction, the waves come simultaneously from many directions. Navigating a ship in a straight direction in these stormy conditions requires great flexibility and navigational expertise. No formal training fully prepares a commander for navigating in a storm; no previous job experience can predict the unique challenges of stormy conditions. On the other hand, formal and on-the-job training are requirements for successfully navigating the ship. Navigating through storms requires traditional skill coupled with informed flexibility.

Managers of the 1990s will be like ship commanders in stormy seas. Just as storms turn placid waves into turbulence, the underlying forces for change create increased demands on executives. First, the pace of change facing executives will increase. New product cycles will be shortened, and the time period for competition to respond will be correspondingly reduced. Second, the intensity of the market changes will be greater. More upheavals may face executives as foreign competitors introduce and adapt new technologies. Industries may grow or shrink dramatically in short time periods. Third, the direction of change is less predictable. New challenges may come from traditional competitors, from competitors in nontraditional businesses, or from firms not previously considered competitors. In the early 1980s, banks would not have predicted that Sears, K-Mart, General Electric, and General Motors would be major competitors in the financial services industry as we moved into the 1990s. Each of these organizations made significant investments in financial services throughout the 1980s and now competes directly and indirectly with the large traditional banks such as Citicorp, Bank of America, Chase Manhattan, and others. In addition, the largest securities firm in the world, Nomura Securities, although headquartered in Tokyo, has established strong ties in New York City.

The dramatic political and social changes in Western Europe and South Africa which concluded the decade of the 1980s may be a glimmer of the rapidity and extent of globalization. Decades of political history become transformed in months; individuals who have been reared and taught within one political view recognize and accept change. Businesses who considered themselves global by first expanding to neighboring countries (one U.S. firm declared itself a global competitor by offering products to Canada), have moved to Asia and Western Europe. With the pace of globalization, Eastern Europe, Latin America, Africa, and other continents may become central sites for global competition.

The forces of competition have increased the pace, intensity and unpredictability of the direction of change. Consider the example of Coca-Cola and Pepsico. In the early 1980s, these two companies dominated the cola market, each with one main product, Coke and Pepsi. Throughout the 1980s, new cola products were introduced at an astonishing rate: diet, caffeine-free, flavored (cherry) coke, and any combination of these. Now there are sixteen combinations to meet specific consumer needs. While only a small percentage of consumers may want diet, caffeine-free, or cherry coke, there is a target segment for this market niche, so specialized cola products are offered for these customers. The Coke and Pepsi competition has increased the pace of new product introductions and the intensity of the competitors toward each other. In addition to experiencing the increased pace and intensity of change, the cola market has taken some unforeseen directions. Jolt, a cola drink with double sugar and caffeine, has entered the market and—against all predictions—gained wide customer acceptance.

Increasing Competitiveness

Global, technological, equity, public policy, and demographic transitions have also caused an increase in competitiveness. As business becomes more global, any given market includes more competitors. Traditional competitors who played by traditional rules have been supplanted by competitors who play by different rules. Japanese firms entering the electronics and automotive industries in the 1980s did so with a longer-term perspective than most North American firms. Rather than seek immediate financial return for investors, the immediate goal of many of these firms was to gain market share through reduced price, even at a possible loss of short-term profits. North American firms understood the short-term profit motive more than they did the Japanese goal of gaining market share.

In addition, restructuring has increased the intensity of competition. In the soft drink business, Pepsi and Coke have acquired many firms (Sprite, Minute Maid, 7-Up) to consolidate the industry, but consolidation has made the competition between the two major players more intense. Similar consolidations have increased competition between the major players in the electronics, oil service, and telecommunications industries. Larger firms have more slack and are more able to allocate resources to compete with each other. When the major firms in an industry become increasingly competitive with each other, the minor firms face an even greater challenge to their position.

Finally, competition has increased because business growth has changed in nature. While globalization has opened new markets, it has also become evident that business growth will come equally from entering new global markets and from taking market share from competitors in existing markets. For example, Coke and Pepsi work to enter new markets around the world through aggressive growth marketing, but each firm realizes that ultimately its growth will have to come at the expense of the other.

Vicious Circles

As change increases, it fuels competition, which leads to more change, resulting in a vicious circle. The change–competition vicious circle (see Figure 2–1) exists in many industries because of the global, technological, equity, public policy, and demographic forces we have discussed.

Vicious circles exist in many relationships. They may, for example, exist between parents and adolescents. The parent tells the teenager to turn down the music, the teenager immediately turns up the music; the parent tells the teenager, with greater

Figure 2–1
CHANGE–COMPETITION CYCLE: A VICIOUS CIRCLE

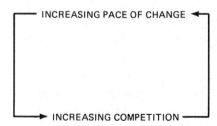

INCREASING PACE OF CHANGE

INCREASING COMPETITION

intensity, to turn down the music, but the volume rises. A vicious circle has been established. A parent tells a child to clean her room, but the child resists; as the room gets messier, the parent issues further directives to clean the room. Here too a vicious circle has been created. Vicious circles also exist between spouses. When one spouse believes that too much money is being spent and tries to control the other, the other is angered by the attempt at control and spends even more; the first spouse becomes even more frustrated by the spending patterns, and a vicious circle is created.

The economic vicious circle exists when change fuels competition, causing competitors to change and in turn increasing competition. Soon after Coke introduced diet and caffeine-free Coke, Pepsi followed with its diet and caffeine-free product, but added to it a lemon flavor. Coke responded with Cherry Coke, continuing to fuel the vicious circle. Soon after Ford introduced a European-look car (the Taurus), General Motors and Chrysler introduced cars with smoother, curved lines. Soon after Saks Fifth Avenue introduces a new line of fashion apparel, competitors like Macy's and Lord and Taylor follow suit.

The downside of a vicious circle is that it focuses energy on the wrong thing. After a teenager and parent form the vicious circle over cleaning a room, more energy is spent trying to control each other and demonstrate independence than cleaning the room in the first place. More effort may be spent trying to control a spouse's habits than building relationships. In the office-automation industry in the 1980s, two firms entered into a vicious circle. The first firm announced a new desktop product with some unique features (A and B). Rather than be outdone by the first firm, the second firm announced a new product with additional features (A, B, C, and D). Immediately the first firm, not to be outdone, announced its new product with features A through F. After awhile, these two firms were more focused on announcing additional features than on producing products that met customer needs. Both firms were promising far more than they could deliver, and as a result lost customer confidence by missing deadlines and promised delivery dates.

To break a vicious circle, one of the two parties to it must change. In the case of the loud music, either the parent or the teenager must change behavior to stop perpetuating the vicious circle. Parents may focus on rewarding good behavior rather than on scolding bad. Adolescents may surprise parents by cleaning their rooms, doing chores, getting good grades, or moderating the volume of music to break a vicious circle.

In the economic arena, either the pace of change or the nature of competition must be managed to alter a vicious circle. Managers may wish for a return to a peaceful environment in which change was predictable and controllable. Unfortunately, such wishes are more fantasy than fact, and wishful thinking will not stop the forces for change we are witnessing today. The only way out of the economic vicious circle is to redefine the nature of competition. Our proposal is straightforward: As change accelerates, vicious circles are created; since no one can halt the onslaught of change, we must focus on redefining competitive advantage to break vicious circles.

COMPETITIVE ADVANTAGE: TWO KEY PRINCIPLES

Gaining competitive advantage has been defined as the process by which a firm assesses its position in its niche, compares itself to competitors, and enhances its position by adding more value to suppliers and customers than do its competitors.[4] Finding new and sustainable ways to gain competitive advantage enables companies to confront both change and increased competition. Competitive advantage may be dissected into two critical elements: perceived customer value and sources of uniqueness. The extent to which executives understand and manage these two elements determines a firm's competitive advantage.

Perceived Customer Value

Competitive advantage is achieved if and only if customers perceive that they receive value from their transactions with a business. A product or service may be the best in the world, but if customers do not gain a perceived value from it, the business will have no competitive advantage. For example, if someone wanted to open a unique restaurant, she could go to Scotland and hire the world's best haggis chef. Haggis is a Scottish speciality composed of sheep stomach stuffed with minced heart, liver, and lungs and a blood–oatmeal concoction. In all probability, she might have the best haggis around—but if no one came to her restaurant, she would not have a competitive advantage. The restaurant would fail despite its excellence because haggis has not gained widespread popularity outside Scotland—nor even inside it, for that matter.

Often the responsibility for meeting customer needs rests with marketing or public relations people. But such a focus ignores a vital factor in competitive advantage—the employees throughout an organization who understand and work to provide customer satisfaction.

It is vital that all employees be dedicated to meeting customer needs. To ensure that they are, a customer-orientation philosophy must be established throughout the organization. There must be a commitment between customers and employees, as is demonstrated when employees involve customers in firm activities. Executives play a critical role in this area.

First, management must continually assess customer values. It can find out what customers want from the firm over the short and long term. Managers can invite customers to the company facilities to meet with employee groups. And managers can constantly reinforce, by word and by example, the importance of good customer relations.

Second, management can analyze the competition to broaden its understanding of the marketplace. Managers can learn why customers choose to do business with their firm over their competitors' by understanding how their product or service offerings differ from their competitors'.

Third, management can communicate to all employees the extent to which perceived customer values are being attained. Market research information can also be shared wisely among employees. Employees may be involved in focus groups to learn customer needs or may participate in customer interviews and surveys to learn what customers expect and how customers believe they have benefited from doing business with the firm.

Perceived customer value is critical for both private and public sector organizations. Private sector organizations must add customer value or customers will not continue to purchase the firm's goods or services, and economic viability will be sacrificed. Public sector agencies must also add customer value.[5] These agencies have two critical customers. First, the legislative bodies that allocate resources and fix budgets must perceive value added from the resources of the agency. Second, the public served by the agency must perceive value added from the services of the agency or it will resist the agency's efforts along with its support of the agency.

Maintaining Uniqueness

The second element of competitive advantage derives from creating *sources of uniqueness*—products or services that competitors cannot easily imitate or copy. If a competitor can easily copy a product or service, a business will not have a long-term competitive advantage. If someone opens a hamburger restaurant and a competitor moves in next door and serves hamburgers that taste and cost the same, the first proprietor is likely to lose a large part of his business to the competition. In order to continue to attract customers, the original restaurant needs to offer something unique—such as better-tasting hamburgers, a greater of variety hamburgers, lower-priced hamburgers, or a wider variety of foods. Only in this way will the first restaurant build a competitive advantage.

ORGANIZATIONAL ACTIONS THAT MAINTAIN UNIQUENESS

In strategic planning and competitive advantage literature, three traditional means of offering customers perceived uniqueness have been identified: financial or economic capability, strategic or marketing capability, and technological capability (see Figure 2–2).

Financial or Economic Capability

A business may create uniqueness through its *financial or economic capability*. Financial uniqueness comes when a business has a

Figure 2–2
TRADITIONAL SOURCES OF COMPETITIVE ADVANTAGE

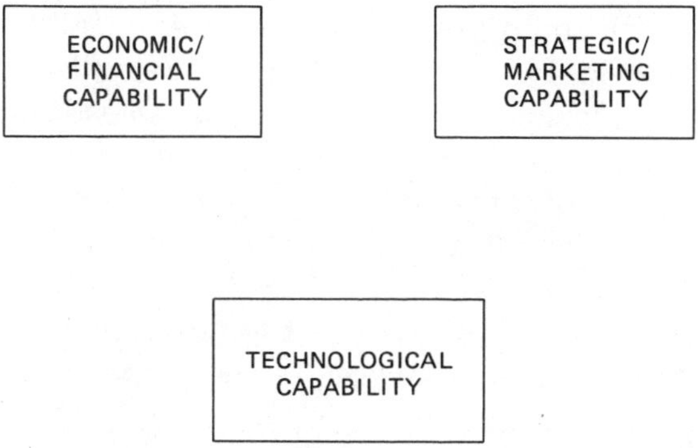

product or service that a customer perceives as having economic value. Generally, financial capability means that the business is able to produce the good or service at a lower cost than its competitors. Many avenues exist for gaining financial or economic capability.

A business may have unique access to capital that translates into lower costs to customers. For example, the owner of the hamburger restaurant may have received money to build the restaurant from family or friends who do not expect immediate repayment. Thus, the owner may be able to charge less for the hamburgers than a competitor who had to borrow money from a financial institution and has to repay the loan at high interest rates. The lower-priced hamburger becomes a source of uniqueness that customers value, so they continue to eat in the restaurant.

If a business manages its financial systems and costs more effectively than its competitors—for example, through inventory turnovers, lower supplier costs, more efficient distribution, economies of scale, lower overhead costs, and shortened receivables—then it may translate these activities into lower product or service costs, which lead in turn to lower prices for customers. Businesses may base their competitive strategies on their financial capabilities.

Strategic or Marketing Capability

A business may create uniqueness through its strategic or marketing capability. This uniqueness comes when a business offers customers products or services that differentiate it from its competitors. From strategic and marketing capability, customers receive product features that they perceive as adding value.

In the hamburger wars among McDonald's, Burger King, Wendy's, and Hardee's, each chain has attempted to offer unique products, features, and services to attract customers. Salad bars, potato bars, taco bars, breakfasts, kids' meals, special sales, and games or prizes are all examples of attempts on the part of these chains to make their products unique and appealing to customers.

Strategic or marketing capability may involve product portfolio mix as well as product features. Marriott developed strategic capability and offered customers a full range of lodging options: Marriott Suites at the highest end, Marriott at the upper end,

Courtyard and Residence Inn at the middle level, and Fairfield Inns at the lower end. Customers desiring any form of lodging may turn to Marriott to receive perceived value added.

Technological Capability

A business may create uniqueness through its technological or operational capability. This means it has a unique way of building or delivering its product or service, so that customers obtain innovation and high-quality, state-of-the-art products. To continue the hamburger example, the cooking techniques used to prepare the hamburgers may distinguish one hamburger restaurant from another (broiled versus flame-grilled, for example). Customers may prefer one method over another and thus patronize one restaurant more than another. In more complex businesses, technological capability may derive from research and development, engineering, computer systems, and manufacturing operations.[6] Eastman Kodak's manufacturing facility gives the firm a unique ability to produce its products. Kodak Park, with over 17,000 employees, operates efficiently through focused factories committed to each line of business.

For many businesses, allocating resources to improve manufacturing, engineering, and inventory-control processes has translated into customers receiving greater perceived value.

3

Competitive Advantage from the Inside Out through Organizational Capability

The three traditional sources of uniqueness (financial, strategic, and technological capabilities), which have been well explored in strategic planning and competitive advantage literature, undoubtedly build competitive advantage and must be taken into account in management decision-making. We contend, however, that these sources describe only a portion of what managers will need to do to build sustained competitive advantage in the business milieu of the 1990s.

Any approach to competition that takes into account only the traditional sources of uniqueness cited above has four deficiencies. First, in any traditional approach, the implicit assumption is that businesses operate exclusively through rational processes and that by analyzing these processes management can always make decisions that will help a business prosper. As many organizational analysts have suggested, however, businesses do not operate on rational premises alone. A firm's culture, history, management style, and organizational structure are also important factors. Purely rational analyses may not take into account the kind of nonrational decision-making that often occurs within businesses.

Second, the traditional sources of uniqueness may rely on a static view of competitive advantage. Often factors that enable a business to compete successfully today will not serve the same function tomorrow. The capacity to manage strategic change often determines how firms will create and *sustain* competitive advantage. Without the capacity to manage changing strategies, firms may lock themselves into historical success patterns rather than adapting to new situations. Relying on past strategies and their fit with industry forces encourages firms to emphasize the use of existing competencies rather than develop new approaches to new situations.

A third problem with defining competition in terms of the traditional sources of uniqueness is that such an approach evades the question of how strategies are *executed*. Strategic planning often serves two purposes. On the one hand, it helps a firm allocate its resources—for example, for capital investments or for mergers and acquisitions. Most strategic-planning assumptions focus on this purpose. However, strategic planning should also lead to action through creating a strategic unity—or shared understanding among employees and customers of how to go about accomplishing a strategy. Focusing on strategic unity requires an emphasis on strategy execution, not formulation.

Organizations do not think, make decisions, or allocate resources; people do. New organizational strategies or programs emphasizing strategic, technological, or financial goals must be implemented through people. Any analysis of how a firm's internal systems adapt to changing strategies for gaining competitive advantage must include the role of people. Yet the people component of competitive advantage is often included only as an afterthought. After financial, strategic, or technological plans have been specified, concern finally shifts to generating commitment from the people in the organization.

Finally, the three traditionally acknowledged sources of uniqueness are not necessarily integrated with each other. At times, financial strategies may be disconnected from and even in conflict with marketing and technological strategies. For example, one danger of LBOs is that financial capability is often emphasized at the expense of technological capability; to maximize profit, resources are shifted away from research, development, and engineering. Technological capability may also conflict with marketing capability when outstanding research produces elegant technical products not valued in the marketplace. A major challenge of creating sources of uniqueness is to ensure that these sources do not operate in isolation, that they are integrated, and that a process is established to ensure that they are in balance and trade-offs are made.

ORGANIZATIONAL CAPABILITY AS A SOURCE OF UNIQUENESS

To complete and integrate the traditional view of what builds uniqueness, we propose a fourth critical source of uniqueness: organizational capability (see Figure 3–1). As defined in Chapter

1, at its most fundamental level organizational capability is the ability to manage people for competitive advantage. A more complex and encompassing definition of organizational capability is *a business's ability to establish internal structures and processes that influence its members to create organization-specific competencies and thus enable the business to adapt to changing customer and strategic needs.*

Organizational capability includes, besides the management of people, the means through which the organization implements policies and procedures to develop and sustain employee commitment. Organizational capability, much like success in sports, depends on teamwork. Having the five best athletes in the sport will not guarantee that a basketball team will win. In many cases, the best athletes do not win critical games: The Soviet Union beat the United States in basketball in the 1988 Olympic games; Kansas beat Oklahoma for the 1988 NCAA championship; and Indiana beat Syracuse for the 1987 NCAA championship. In each case, both teams had good players, but the winning team had organizational capability—a synergy that made the team play better than the individual skills of its members might have indicated.

We can illustrate organizational capability by continuing the restaurant example presented in Chapter 2. A hamburger chain's organizational capability is determined by the employees who are hired, how they are trained, how they feel about working with the company, how they are rewarded for meeting customer needs, and how they communicate with customers. While a customer may enter the restaurant because of the price (financial capability)

Figure 3–1
ORGANIZATIONAL CAPABILITY AS A CRITICAL
SOURCE OF COMPETITIVE ADVANTAGE

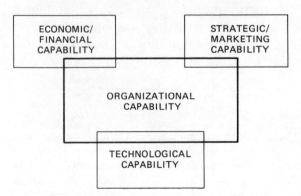

or uniqueness of the hamburger (strategic capability) or because of how the hamburger is prepared (technological capability), the customer's lasting impression of the restaurant will depend in large part on the ambiance and feelings experienced there. Employees' attitudes and behaviors create this ambiance.

John Teets, Chairman of Greyhound Corporation, has acknowledged the importance to Greyhound's success of the firm's financial, strategic, and operational (technological) capabilities. However, when referring to organizational capability, he became more adamant when he wrote a letter to all employees in 1989:

> None of these capabilities (financial, strategic, or operational) can be attained without the last—organizational capability. Each of you, the individuals behind the name of Greyhound, makes things happen and "People + Sales + Control = Profit." In every Greyhound company, your pay and benefits depend on business results, and each of us is responsible for contributing to the competitive advantages that will make Greyhound successful.

From a simple hamburger business to a complex conglomerate like Greyhound, organizational capability is critical to competitive advantage.

We have seen that merely hiring the best people will not guarantee organizational capability. Hiring competent employees, and then developing those competencies through effective human resource policies and practices, is more likely to create organizational capability.

Generating Organizational Capability versus Creating Quick Fixes

Throughout the 1980s many firms adopted slogans and quick fixes that reflected a superficial understanding of organizational capability.[1] These slogans often espoused some version of "People are our most important asset," led to extensive discussions within organizations, and raised employee expectations. However, they usually did not lead to long-term, sustained change. A quick-fix people program can be likened to a situation in which a basketball coach hires a consultant to give advice on winning more games. After extensive data collection—through surveys, interviews, and videotapes—the consultant returns to the coach and claims, "I have figured out exactly what you have to do to win more games." The enthusiastic coach asks what the secret is, and the consultant responds, "You have to score more points than your opponents."

Although people slogans sound like easy solutions, they ignore the challenging question of *how*. Organizational capability not only helps executives understand *what* needs to be done but focuses on *how* it needs to be done. By serving as an integrative function, this approach avoids quick fixes; helps management execute strategies based on the assessment of financial, strategic, and technological capabilities; and links sources of uniqueness.

Organizational Capability and Financial Capability

People costs are often one of the major costs of an organization. These costs translate directly into overall cost, and the price of a product may determine the extent to which customers derive value from an organization. When attempting to gain financial capability through cost management, a major cost category becomes people. Organizational capability may be combined with financial capability to lead to perceived customer value, or competitive advantage. Since people costs are unique to each business and depend on the business's access to employees, its hiring practices, the number and required skill levels of its employees, the extent of required employee training and development, span of control, and employee compensation, people costs in one business may be difficult to replicate in another.

Many organizations recognize that organizational and financial capability are intertwined. At United Parcel Service (UPS), each year's annual report reveals that people costs (including direct costs such as salary and benefits and indirect costs such as employee travel, training, and relocation) represent approximately 60 percent of the overall operating budget. In addition to tracking material, inventory, and distribution costs, UPS executives issue, receive, and monitor information on people costs on a monthly and quarterly basis. By recognizing that people costs are a predictor of financial capability, UPS executives focus attention on organizational capability.

For public sector agencies, the percentage of operating budget allocated to people may go as high as 80 percent. Even in the midst of an enormous build-up of technology and computer systems in the 1980s, the Federal Aviation Administration (FAA) found that 75 percent of its operating budget represented people costs. As a result, FAA management realized that how it worked with and developed its employees would be critical factors in accomplishing its goals of aircraft safety and efficient airport and airway management within budget.[2] In public agencies committed to adding value to their constituents, financial and organizational capability are intertwined, since a large portion of any agency's resources is dedicated to people.

In the airline industry, the major costs that determine the price of air travel include equipment, fuel, maintenance, and people. After deregulation in 1978, when competition increased throughout the industry, airline executives examined these four cost categories and realized that the only one in which they could gain a competitive advantage was people. While competitors could purchase essentially the same aircraft, fuel, and maintenance, the ability to manage people costs became a primary variant in creating distinctive competence and building a financial capability that would lead to competitive advantage. Almost all the major air carriers—Northwest, TWA, United, American, and Delta—began to review their employee management systems. The result was that they adjusted direct salary costs with two-tier pay systems, reduced base pay and increased incentive pay, and created organization designs with fewer layers of management and overhead. The reasons for these human resource changes were straightforward—they represented a way to increase organizational capability and thereby increase financial capability. By combining financial and organizational capability, airlines could better meet customer demands.

Across all U.S. industries, people costs represent approximately 55 percent of operating budgets.[3] While this cost varies widely from one industry to another, with capital-intensive industries like utilities having much lower people costs than employee-intensive industries like food-service firms, the simple fact remains: financial capability is linked with organizational capability. A business seeking competitive advantage through financial capability must do so by managing its employees in such a way that customers receive good value for their money.

Organizational Capability
and Strategic Capability

When a group within a Fortune 50 corporation decided to increase
its commitment to strategic planning, a senior officer who had
worked in the finance function for several years was assigned to
manage the strategic planning process. This officer, whom we'll
call Jim Crystal, spent a year researching the strengths, weaknesses, opportunities, and competitive threats significant to each
of the five businesses with the group. He hired expert consultants
to perform market research, examine present and future market
opportunities, and recommend the optimum product portfolio. In
the process, he issued quarterly summaries of his work to the
management team.

At the end of a year, Jim Crystal was asked to present his
conclusions to management. At a business retreat, he asked for
and was granted one hour at the end of the day to make his
report. He began by reviewing the market data, environmental
opportunities, and product mix for each business within the
group. He then recommended that one business be divested, one
be extensively expanded, one be joint ventured, one be further
examined, and one be the "cash cow" to finance expansion in the
growth business. At the end of the session he asked for questions
but received none from the silent executives. When he returned to
work the next day, he felt that he had made enormous progress
during the year, had made an effective presentation, and could
now move ahead quickly to finalize his plans. Two weeks later,
much to his surprise and chagrin, he was reassigned to his old
finance position, and the strategic-planning effort was disbanded.

Jim Crystal learned by experience a common fate of strategic
plans: SPOTS, or Strategic Plans On Top Shelf.[4] While many
companies have allocated resources to formulating strategic
plans, they do not necessarily follow through and implement
such plans. In fact, elegant and empirically correct plans often
end up in leather binders on bookshelves, never to be translated
into managerial action.

SPOTS is experienced also in the public sector. One federal
agency spent two years designing a new strategic direction for the
next two decades. The plan arrived at was complex and required
the integration of computer systems, technology, and client relationships. Ultimately, the plan was presented in a 300-page book
that contained extensive technical information, analyses of client
trends, and recommendations for new computer systems. Not a

single page, however, considered the changes involving people that would be required to implement the strategy. Five years into the plan, the agency was way behind schedule.

Without carefully assessing how changes involving people need to be managed and adapted to organizational changes, strategies remain merely blueprints. Jim Crystal missed two opportunities to prepare his strategic plan for execution. First, he did not manage the process of creating the strategic plan. His quarterly reports *to* managers in the group were one way; he did not elicit feedback or dialogue with managers in the five businesses. As a result, his reports, for the most part, were quickly scanned and then ignored. When the executives heard his recommendations, they were surprised and annoyed. They believed that as a group staff member Jim Crystal had no right to tell them how to operate their businesses. While they admired his research, they felt it was their responsibility and role as management to make strategic decisions, not Jim Crystal's. He had focused more on the *content* of the strategy than on the *process* of creating the strategy.

Nor did he assess and integrate organizational capability into his strategic plan. Jim Crystal did strategic planning from the *outside in*: that is, he recognized the broad implications of his market research, but was unable to identify the systems available to prepare and motivate people to implement the plan. He did not tie strategies to staffing decisions, compensation systems, organization restructurings, or performance appraisal systems. Had he linked his strategic plans to these human resource practices, the management team could have better understood how his proposals could be put into practice within the current business context.

Likewise, managers at the federal agency who focused their strategic-planning activities on a large technical document failed to integrate organizational capability into their process and proposals. They failed because the formulation of agency strategy was carried out by senior officers and selected technical experts, who understood technical issues while important human resource issues were not addressed. As a result, the agency's strategy statement did not include a reference to the management practices that would be necessary to accomplish the plan. For example, the introduction of new computer systems and technologies required new staffing criteria, training programs for employees, alternative reward systems, and agency-wide communication programs. None of these issues was addressed in the plan.

The internal processes that create business-specific personal competencies can be linked to strategic capabilities to help accomplish strategies. Organizational capability as a means of achieving competitive advantage calls for developing processes that create personal distinctive competencies which are unique to the business and nontransferable. One practice that has translated into competitive advantage has been the Japanese system of career management. Within the automotive industry, for example, managers in the United States are given experience in far fewer functional areas than are Japanese managers. The traditional U.S. career track encourages specialization, allowing employees to move from one firm to another as functional specialists. The Japanese system, on the other hand, prepares managers to move from one area of a firm to another, giving them an integrated sense of how the firm operates.[5]

Organizational capability includes creating the processes for accomplishing strategic capability. The higher the level of organizational capability, the greater the strategic capability. Ethicon Corporation, a subsidiary of Johnson & Johnson, dominates the U.S. market for hospital sutures (needle and thread or staples used to close surgical incisions). The suture business is characterized by extremely high margins, because the cost of producing sutures is minimal. In terms of financial capability, any number of competitors—domestic or foreign—could maintain adequate margins in this industry. In terms of strategic capability, the products can be easily copied. How then does Ethicon maintain its large market share? One reason might be neglect on the part of potential competitors. If this were all Ethicon had to count on, however, its luck would run out as soon as a potential competitor recognized the opportunity and entered the market.

Ethicon's real insurance for continuing success lies in its organizational capability, as evidenced by the project Ethicon embarked on to determine what customers valued in their suture supplier. From interviews and research, the firm learned that hospital purchasing agents and physicians who influence purchasing decisions desired responsiveness and service quality. They wanted assurance that the required sutures would always be in stock and available for any emergency. They wanted a long-term relationship with their supplier so that they could contact the supplier's representative at any time and be personally assured that the sutures would be delivered. Developing this relationship was perceived as the most important way Ethicon could add value to its customers.

In light of what it had learned about customer values, Ethicon examined its policies vis-à-vis sales representatives. Like many companies, Ethicon always recruited sales representatives from a selected list of twenty to thirty universities. As sales representatives succeeded in their territories, they were given greater responsibility and were moved up in the firm. But with the customer data in hand, Ethicon executives began to reassess these policies.

Building long-term stability in sales representatives became a major goal. Rather than hiring from selected universities and transfering employees to locations where they might not want to stay for an extended period of time, Ethicon began to hire sales representatives from universities within the territory in which they would be working. The company also wanted to ensure that sales representatives would have good relationships with hospital decision-makers. To facilitate this process, Ethicon began to help underwrite representatives' home mortgages, country club memberships, and school fees in areas where physicians lived. Ethicon's commitment to organizational capability increased the stability of its sales force and enhanced relationships between sales representatives and hospital purchasing agents.

Organizational capability built stable relationships, which in turn allowed Ethicon to maintain its strategic position. A competitor attempting to penetrate the Ethicon market would need to undo old relationships and establish new ones, an undertaking that would require enormous resources. Thus, Ethicon not only built a competitive advantage through organizational capability but built in safeguards to maintain its advantage as well.

Organizational Capability and Technological Capability

Technological capability without people is like computer hardware with no software. All the hardware in the world is useless unless software is available to make it functional. Likewise, all the technology in the world will not give a business competitive advantage if it is not accompanied by effective management of people.

Throughout the 1980s, General Motors invested heavily in the Saturn project. This was a "greenfield" endeavor—that is, designing and producing a car from scratch, or "in a green field." Much of the excitement surrounding the project stemmed from the chance to apply state-of-the-art technologies in engineering and manufacturing. Computer-assisted design and manufacturing as well as extensive use of robots were central features of the venture. Concerning the new technology, however, William Hoglund, Vice President of Saturn, stated that technology would be important, but not the most critical element in the Saturn project. He noted that within the automobile industry, Ford, Chrysler, Toyota, Honda, and other foreign competitors could easily acquire the same technology, so technology alone would not be a long-term source of competitiveness. In addition, he acknowledged that even with the latest technology, the operation of the technology would require the dedication and commitment of Saturn employees—that is, organizational capability. To gain this commitment, General Motors formed a cooperative venture with the unions, hired employees who demonstrated the personal competencies necessary to build the innovative car through teamwork, established incentives for team performance, and shared extensive information with new employees. As a result, the success of the Saturn venture depended less on technology than on management practices.

The research and development (R and D) element of technological capability derives from organizational capability. 3M, known for innovation, research and development, and the ability to introduce new products to the marketplace, attributes some of its R and D success to its incentive system. The company ties manager and executive incentive pay to the number of products sold in their divisions over three-year periods. The incentive system is central to 3M's organizational capability and its ability to maintain technological capability through R and D. 3M also encourages engineers to devote a portion of their time to initiating and championing new, innovative projects: The incentive system offers engineers the opportunity to run any new business that is generated by their ideas.

ORGANIZATIONAL CAPABILITY AND COMPETITIVE ADVANTAGE

Chapter 2 examined two criteria for competitive advantage: (1) adding perceived value to the customer and (2) offering uniqueness that cannot be easily replicated by a competitor. Organizational capability is a means of achieving both.

Organizational Capability and Perceived Customer Value

From financial capability, customers receive lower prices; from strategic capability, customers receive product features; and from technological capability, customers receive innovation. From organizational capability, customers receive responsiveness, relationships, and service quality.

Responsiveness

For a business to succeed, customers must perceive its suppliers' employees as responsive.[6] Responsiveness implies that the business understands and meets customer needs more quickly than its competitors. Responsiveness can also lead to shortened product introduction cycles. When Ford introduced the Taurus in 1985, the normal product introduction cycle in the U.S. automotive industry was about six years from concept to production. With the Taurus Ford reduced the time significantly, to 42 months. This shortened cycle was made possible largely because of the way Ford organized the Taurus project. Rather than relying on traditional sequential product-development techniques, Ford implemented parallel development through the formation of a Taurus team made up of representatives from each of the major components of the production chain: researchers, design engineers, manufacturing engineers, suppliers, quality engineers, production representatives, distributors, and customers. The Taurus team had overall responsibility for taking the car from concept to production; no hand-offs were attempted between research and design, engineering and manufacturing, or production and distribution. Because the Taurus project cycle was shortened by 40 percent, Ford's perceived responsiveness to consumer needs was enhanced, thereby creating competitive advantage.

In the service sector, responsiveness derives directly from organizational capability. Car rental, food services, and financial services have found that the single biggest factor in customer loyalty is perceived customer responsiveness of employees.[7] Training employees to be sensitive, supportive, and responsive has become a major element in creating and maintaining a positive business image. As consumers, when we receive bad service from bank tellers, car rental personnel, or waiters and waitresses, we become angry at the individual and infer that the entire business lacks customer responsiveness.

One expert argues that time is a source of competitive advantage,[8] because customers perceive added value in shorter time frames. We argue that shorter product cycles derive primarily from organizational capability, since the time necessary to get work done is reduced when incentives are offered to individuals and teams and when there is good communication so that employees understand what is expected of them.

Relationships

Organizational capability enables employees and customers of businesses to form endearing and enduring relationships. When such relationships exist, customers may feel the same loyalty to employees that employees feel to their firm. Relationships may be formed somewhat indirectly—between customers and the organization represented by employees—or directly—between customers and specific employees.

Research that focused on customer and employee attitudes toward a bank demonstrated clearly that when employees had positive attitudes about the bank, customers also had strong positive attitudes.[9] The reason for this finding is straightforward. Customer-contact employees—tellers, loan officers, and so on—are the medium through which customers interact with the bank. Employees with good feelings about the bank will reflect these positive attitudes in the way they interact with customers, who in turn will sense these feelings and themselves form positive images about the bank. Organizational capability, which helps employees develop good feelings about a company, thus works to build both positive images and customer loyalty.

While customers generally have only indirect, anonymous relationships with bank employees, in some businesses employees form direct relationships with customers. Consumer businesses have often formed exclusive clubs, including airline, car rental, hotel, and retail clubs (Saks Fifth Avenue has created a Fifth Avenue Club for frequent shoppers) to interact more directly with key accounts. These special-recognition clubs enable employees to recognize regular customers and work to solidify these relationships. In businesses in the industrial sector, employees and customers may also form direct relationships. The Ethicon example in the hospital supply business illustrates how organizational capability leads to long-term relationships with buyers, thereby helping the firm to achieve strategic and financial capability.

For small businesses, too, the forging of long-term relationships with various types of stakeholders is a critical factor in maintaining competitive advantage. In the building industry, for example, where small contractors must increasingly compete with large firms in the trade-up, high-quality home market, long-term relationships with qualified subcontractors are crucial to success. Small builders have devised various strategies to ensure that their subcontractors are not wooed away by the larger firms. Many have installed computerized estimating and purchasing departments to relieve the subcontractors of some of the paperwork burden. One builder allows favored subs to review other bids and then rebid the job; another makes sure he pays his subs more promptly than the large firms.[10]

Relationships also matter between contractors and future homeowners, as anyone who has faced the ordeal of building a house has learned. In contracting to build a house, thousands of decisions are required, many of which cannot be defined in explicit contract terms prior to the building of the home. As changes in the design occur, the relationship between the builder and the homeowner becomes critical. Relationships of trust must overcome differences in opinions about who is responsible for what work.

Service Quality

Service quality is particularly important in industries in which output is intangible—and approximately 60 percent of all the people employed in the United States work in such industries. These businesses include transportation, utilities, telecommunications, wholesale, retail, finance, and pure services. Service also refers to how manufacturing businesses interact with customers, for example, how Ford works with dealers and how dealers work with customers.

Two experts in the field of industrial policy have underscored the need to focus on service throughout all sectors of the economy and the importance of organizational capability in building service quality:

> Organizations concerned with honing a competitive edge for the 1980s, 90s, and beyond must develop two new capacities. The first is the ability to think strategically about service and to build a strong service orientation around and into the vision of their strategic future. The second capacity, which is perhaps more difficult to develop, is the ability to effectively and efficiently manage the

design, development, and delivery of service. In our view, the ability to manage the production and delivery of a service differs from the ability to manage the production and delivery of a commodity.[11]

We agree with this argument. Service is critical to all businesses because customers perceive added value in service. Achieving a high quality of service requires organizational capability, because people, not technologies, make service happen.

We envision the 1990s as a decade in which service quality becomes so critical that service guarantees will have to match traditional product guarantees. For example, if customers are not satisfied with the service they receive, they could be given discounts on future transactions with the firm. The Promus Companies—which includes Embassy Suites, Hampton Inn, and Homewood Suites—has made a service guarantee promise. They guarantee that guests will have a positive experience in their accomodations or the stay is free. This service guarantee indicates an enormous commitment to service quality. Such service guarantees require that all employees be charged with and committed to service quality in every customer interaction. Only through organizational capability can a firm ensure that its hiring, training, and reward policies are designed to promote service quality and that employees are provided with the information necessary to sustain it.

Organizational Capability and Uniqueness

The second criterion for achieving competitive advantage is offering goods or services that cannot be easily replicated by competitors. Of the four sources of uniqueness, we believe that organizational capability is the most difficult to copy.[12] Financial capability may be duplicated if competitors are equally capable of reducing costs, gaining access to capital, or managing the balance sheet. Strategic capability is often copied, because new product features are routinely analyzed and replicated soon after a product is introduced. Technological capability, while not as easy to copy, may also lose its uniqueness over time because competitors may acquire the same equipment.

Copying organizational capability, however, is much more difficult and complex. It requires not only changing one's method of managing costs and capital, modifying products, or purchasing technologies but also implementing pervasive new ways of thinking among all employees. To change individuals' perceptions and job performance is a complex and all-encompassing task; it is not a one-step action.

Along with being more difficult to copy, organizational capability is also the most difficult source of uniqueness to change. From our experience, we believe that changing organizational capability requires two to three times as much time as changing strategic capability. If product development (a technological and strategic capability) requires two years, then a change in organizational capability would probably require four to six years to accomplish.

THE CHALLENGE OF BUILDING ORGANIZATIONAL CAPABILITY

When we discuss the need for building organizational capability with managers, most of them agree with the concept and its rationale. Yet many find it difficult to understand *how* to translate organizational capability into executive actions. Managers need to identify the specific areas in which greater organizational capability is needed, define choices in each area, and suggest actions that will build organizational capability.

In essence, organizational capability consists of four critical elements:[13]

1. *Shared mindset*. The people within an organization and the stakeholders outside it have common ways of thinking about goals and the means used to reach the goals. Creating a shared way of thinking about these goals may be a core element of organizational capability. Shared mindset is the focus of Chapter 4.

2. *Management and human resource practices*. Managers have tools with which to create organizational capability, and thus competitive advantage. These tools, or levers, influence how people inside and outside the organization think and behave (Chapter 5). We believe that management and human resource tools accomplish three goals for organizational capability. First, they generate competencies within the organization through selection or

development (Chapter 6). Second, they reinforce competencies within the organization through appraisal and rewards (Chapter 7). Third, they sustain competencies within the organization through organization design and communication (Chapter 8).

3. *Capacity for change.* Organizations with a capacity for change have increased organizational capability. Organizational capacity for change derives from individuals being empowered and able to influence others (Chapter 9). The capacity for change requires that a firm's management diagnose and manage change (Chapter 10) and develop the competencies to build flexible organizational arrangements (Chapter 11).

4. *Leadership (Chapter 12).* Organizational capability is driven by leadership, from individuals with vision at all levels of an organization. The visionary capacity of leaders has received much attention in recent years. Generating commitment to vision and to institutionalizing it have received much less attention. We focus on these aspects of leaders by calling attention to what must happen *inside* an organization once vision and strategy are clear. While most literature having to do with leadership focuses on senior executives, we propose that leadership must exist at all levels in the organization and that specific individual competencies must be developed to build leadership.

The book concludes (Chapter 13) with seven critical questions that managers who wish to build organizational capability must ask. We also identify some basic principles that may help in responding to these questions. We have added an Epilogue, which focuses on the importance of managing the environment to reduce the threat of misusing resources. We believe this material is critical to seeing how the principles discussed throughout this book will apply in the decade of the 1990s.

As we proceed, we will examine *how* executives can use each of these elements to enhance organizational capability and build competitive advantage. Our analysis will not make organizational capability easy to accomplish, but it will show the path whereby competitive advantage can be achieved from the inside out and will identify specific actions that may be taken to begin the process.

4

Creating Shared Mindset: Unity of Culture[1]

> Therefore, appraise it [war] in terms of the five fundamental factors.
> . . . So you may assess its essentials. The first of these factors is
> moral influence. . . . By moral influence I mean that which causes
> the people to be in harmony with their leaders, so that they will ac-
> company them in life and unto death without fear of mortal peril.
> When one treats people with benevolence, justice, and righteous-
> ness, and reposes confidence in them, the army will be united in
> mind and all will be happy to serve their leaders.
>
> Sun Tzu, *The Art of War*

At the heart of the ability to manage people for competitive advantage is the creation of shared mindsets. Shared mindsets stem from organizational culture;[2] they
exist within the overall corporation, or within businesses, departments, functions, or groups. They represent a uniform way of
thinking, perceiving, and valuing both the goals of an organization and the processes used to reach those goals. They can be
characterized as attitudes, values, or basic assumptions. If shared
mindsets exist, the employees within an organization and the
stakeholders outside it experience strategic unity—a common understanding of the organization's goals as well as the process used
to reach those goals.

In discussing the importance of shared mindsets, John Sculley, chief executive officer at Apple Computer, described his successes at Pepsico and his goals at Apple in his book *Odyssey: Pepsi
to Apple:*

> Today, we are moving from a mass-production orientation to mass
> customization. As we gain the ability to customize products for
> people, localities, regions, and markets are splitting. There are
> many varieties of autos—you can order one built to your own specs
> in terms of add-ons. There is no one car market any more. Con-
> sumers are not middle class or upper class; they're hybrids.

These days someone might buy a cheap digital watch, yet drive a BMW. Or drive to a fast-food restaurant in a Mercedes. To reach these hybrid consumers, we try to attract a *"share of mind"* rather than traditional "share of market." To do that, we have to position not just the product, which has an ever-shrinking shelf life, but the company—who we are, and why we are important to consumers beyond the life of the product, today and tomorrow. That's what we were able to do at Pepsi with the Pepsi Generation, and that's what we try to do at Apple.

Most marketing strategies hype the product. Event marketing goes well beyond the product. Apple had to sell personal computing more than the personal computer. . . .

Every new, highly innovative product creates a new problem for society which only it can solve: The airplane made transportation by any other mode seem disadvantageously longer than in the era of the train and horse and buggy. The telephone made anything less than instantaneous communication a fearsome obstacle. So the Macintosh—the computer for everyone—was designed to make standard communication forms a severe limitation to personal productivity. Computers make us recognize our handicaps; without them we would realize how clumsy we are at drawing, how we often fail to express ourselves well, how there is, inside of us, someone who strives for much more than we can achieve. With the Mac, who would want to go back to using ditto machines and typewriters?

If Mac introduced a problem, we would have to sell the solution only it could provide. And we had to do this at the very moment the home computer market went bust. That was first. Then, we had to sell what almost can't be sold because it didn't really exist: We had to sell the future, our vision for a world enhanced by personal computing. To see our product, we had to alter the culture, reshape the public consciousness. We had, in other words, to lay claim to *"share of mind."* . . .

Unlike "share of market," "share of mind" is much more lasting.*

The introduction of Macintosh through the "1984" ad at the 1984 Super Bowl—showing a woman throwing a hammer through a big screen to indicate a break from tradition—was an attempt to create a new and different mindset among potential customers. If shared mindsets, were established, Sculley believed that Apple could gain long-term market share.

*Excerpt from *Odyssey: Pepsi to Apple* by John Sculley and J. A. Byrne. Copyright © 1987 by John Sculley. Reprint by permission of Harper & Row Publishers, Inc.

But it was not merely the customer who needed to think differently about computers in general and Macintosh in particular: Apple employees also needed to develp the new mindset if the organization was to succeed.

THE CONCEPT OF SHARED MINDSET

In the quote at the beginning of this chapter, Sun Tzu used the word "harmony" to describe the processes by which individuals are *united in mind*. Of the five fundamental factors for being successful at war, the creation of harmony is the most critical. Shared mindsets represent the harmony, or unity of mind, that may also lead organizations to gain more competitive positions.

A basic premise of the shared mindset is to explain why people do what they do as a function of how the human brain processes, stores, and retrieves information.[3] The images or patterns of our activities in our memories which reflect how we think about activities affect what we do in relation to a particular activity. As a simple example, we asked participants in a recent workshop who liked to fish to report what images they had when they thought about fishing. Individuals who liked fishing offered a number of verbal descriptions of these images: the outdoors, friendship, drinking, fresh air, relaxation, peacefulness, excitement. We then asked persons who do not like fishing to report their images of the sport, and these included up early, worms, smelly, seasickness, boring, waste of time. We asked each group a simple question: What is the probability in the next year that you will go fishing? The first group responded almost uniformly 100 percent; the second group responded uniformly almost 0 percent.

A shared mindset explanation of this story is straightforward: Members of each group have a mindset regarding fishing which predicts whether the individual is likely to go fishing. We have done similar exercises with ballet, baseball, yachting, golf, eating at McDonald's, and dozens of other activities. In each case, we can identify how individuals store information and predict how people will act based on mindsets.

Two factors important in the construction of mindsets are information and behavior. The more individuals are exposed to consistent patterns of information, the more they establish a mindset.[4] In the fishing example, the mental image of the sport may be influenced, in part, by the amount of information a person possesses about fishing. Individuals who are familiar with spinners, rods, lures, and varieties of fish will be more likely to have favorable mental images of fishing than those who know less. In our seminars, we ask those who like and those who dislike fishing to describe a spinner. Those who like to fish know the language of fishing and can describe in great detail the nuances of spinners. Those who do not have favorable images of fishing generally do not know much about spinners.

In addition to information, behavior also influences mindset.[5] First, as individuals engage in activities, they receive an immediate and relatively credible source of clear information. Those who spend time fishing learn more about the language of fishing. This information then sustains a fishing mindset. Second, persons tend to view their behavior in regular patterns, which shape mindsets.[6] After spending time fishing, we reconstruct the value of fishing because we don't want to admit having wasted time. Third, given that individuals prefer to exhibit consistency between the private and public self, when individuals undertake public action, they tend to restructure their mindsets to be consistent with their public behaviors. When we talk to others about fishing, we become known publicly as persons who like to fish. This reinforces our mindset about fishing.

Just as individuals have mindsets, or images, about activities, which affect how they act with respect to those activities, organizations can also have shared mindsets. A shared mindset represents a way of thinking that is shared by members of an organization.[7] When a shared mindset exists, unity of purpose and activity follows, and individuals work together toward a common goal.[8] The basis for organizational capability is a shared mindset when employees inside an organization and customers and suppliers outside share the purposes and means to reach the organization's objectives.

Two factors are significant with respect to shared mindsets in organizations: (1) *what* is shared and (2) *who* shares the mindset.

What Is Shared

Shared mindsets may be created about the means or ends within an organization, department, function, or group. Shared mindsets about the means implies a common understanding and way of thinking about *how work is done* within the organization. Everyone understands, accepts, and participates in the processes used for accomplishing work. In a university, for example, the processes for generating and disseminating knowledge through attending seminars, writing papers, and doing homework assignments are understood, accepted, and shared by students, faculty, administrators, support staff, and donors. The notion that universities require faculty engaged in both research and teaching and students who attend classes is accepted to a greater or lesser extent. When these activities are understood and accepted as normal ways of behaving in a university, shared mindsets exist about how work in the university is done.

In describing the cultures of two companies, one researcher emphasized the extent to which shared mindsets about means exit in each company.[9] At Action Corporation, employees are accustomed to dialogue, debate, and open confrontation. It is considered normal for employees to cross organizational boundaries, to form committees composed of representatives from different areas, and to move up and down the hierarchy to lobby for positions. At Multi Company, however, the means of getting work done are quite different, relying more on formal organizational systems and procedures and on deference to superiors in the hierarchy.

The means of getting work done in these two companies— both in the same industry—differs dramatically, because in each case the employees have different mindsets concerning how work is to be done. As the industry has grown more competitive and change has accelerated, the Action mindset has enabled the firm to adapt more effectively than Multi Company.

At Apple, John Sculley's challenge as chairman was compounded because he felt there was a need to modify the mindset of employees about how work was to be done. Under Steven Jobs, Apple's founder, employees had been free to make independent decisions. They were encouraged to explore alternatives and engage in research and other activities, with little worry about management control. The pirate emblem on the Macintosh building symbolized the ''rebellious'' mindset among Apple employees. Sculley's challenge was to maintain the benefits of the piratelike, creative mindset but at the same time instill discipline in procedures and processes.

At Nordstrom, there is an enormous commitment to customer service, which influences activities of all Nordstrom employees. Individuals are hired who demonstrate sensitivity to customers; policies are set that encourage customer commitment—for example, a no-question return policy. These practices have established a shared mindset about how work is to be done within Nordstrom.

Shared mindset may also be established around organizational outcomes, thus ensuring that individuals feel similarly about *what the organization is trying to accomplish* and understand and participate in goals or outcomes. In a university, multiple goals exist. Faculty may define success as the extent to which the university produces high-quality research or teaching. Students may view learning as a goal, while administrators focus on stability and reputation. Donors may measure success in terms of athletic victories, theatrical productions, or student graduation rates. Legislators of state universities may define success by the rate of acceptance of in-state students, cost-effectiveness, enhancement of jobs in the state, or enrollment of students with diverse backgrounds. The extent to which stakeholders pursue their individual goals while recognizing and accepting the shared goals of the university defines the degree of shared mindset that exists.

At Apple, Sculley had to change the mindset not only about how work was done, but why it was done. He had to modify the mindset that employees shared about the outcomes of the company. Creating computer products that would change the world for the benefit of humankind was an important outcome mindset that Jobs had established at Apple. Sculley's challenge was to complement this altruistic and visionary mindset with one that acknowledged the importance of market performance. He needed to persuade employees that gaining high market penetration was an important ingredient in Apple's long-term success.

Who Shares the Mindset

Shared mindsets may exist for stakeholders *inside* or *outside* the organization. Within the organization, shared mindsets mean that employees share common views of how the organization operates. At Action Corporation, all employees who have remained with the company have come to understand the "Action way" of doing business, and allegiance to this mindset has helped the firm perpetuate itself over time.

Shared mindsets outside the organization signify that stakeholders—financiers, investors, suppliers, customers, competitors, trade associations, legislators—share perceptions with those inside the organization. At Action, customers, suppliers, and other external stakeholders have come to understand and appreciate the "Action way" of accomplishing work, which has enabled them to build strong long-term relationships.

Nordstrom too has worked to establish shared mindsets between persons inside and outside the organization. Nordstrom management oversimplifies its commitment to service by saying, "All we do is hire nice people."[10] Employees, as we have seen, are chosen based on their commitment to customer service. Then, once hired, the company's formal and informal lines of communication reinforce salespeople who have made extraordinary commitments to customer service. When employees demonstrate outstanding service, they are given "Customer Service All-Star" awards. At Nordstrom, employees set goals and are rewarded for meeting their customer objectives. Policies and practices have created a unity of mindset among persons within the organization.

The mindset is also shared by those outside the organization. Customers become addicted to Nordstrom, developing a personal loyalty to the store, becoming an extended sales force. Suppliers too feel a commitment to Nordstrom. Leonard Lauder, the chief executive officer of the cosmetics maker Estée Lauder, said, "All retailers in America have awakened to the Nordstrom threat and are struggling to catch up. Nordstrom is the future of retailing."[11]

TYPES OF SHARED MINDSETS

We can identify four types of organizational shared mindsets, based on what is shared and who shares it. As the four types expand, a unity evolves that builds organizational capability and competitive advantage (Figure 4–1).

Type I: Internal Ends

Shared mindsets exist to the extent that employees throughout an organization understand and accept the mission of the firm. An organization with a shared mindset about internal ends may be characterized by employees at all levels who understand the financial, strategic, and technological goals of the business and

Figure 4–1
SHARED ORGANIZATION MINDSETS

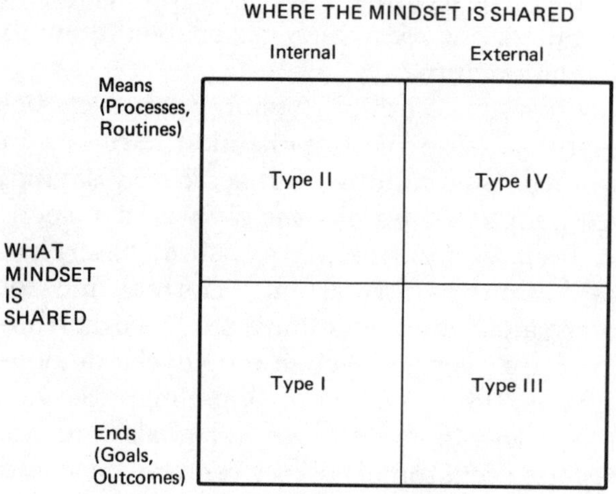

WHERE THE MINDSET IS SHARED

	Internal	External
Means (Processes, Routines)	Type II	Type IV
WHAT MINDSET IS SHARED		
Ends (Goals, Outcomes)	Type I	Type III

how the business stacks up against competitors. We believe the internal leader of an organization is responsible for creating this mindset (see Chapter 12).

In a a study of over 1,200 businesses, researchers found that some firms are characterized by a unity of vision among employees.[12] In businesses where employees share a vision of the organization's goals and perceive the firm's objectives as credible, they also reflect a unity of understanding about the context in which the business operates. When unity of vision and shared perceptions of the business context prevail, the same research found, employees tend to be high-performing.

Unfortunately, in many businesses, strategic plans are viewed as confidential and are not shared with employees, and workers are discouraged from trying to become informed about the organization's strategic, technological, or financial goals. With plans locked away, employees inevitably feel locked out of the organizational mindset.

At Apple, John Sculley remarked that a primary challenge was to create an identity for employees: "We talk endlessly—about what we do: 'We build people, not computers'; or 'The best way to predict the future is to invent it.' I know most cultural gurus would have companies memorize their corporate vision. We define our identity as the company that 'builds great personal computers.'" (*Odyssey*, p. 186) Inducing employees to share Apple's identity required that Sculley openly and candidly discuss his views on Apple's vision, mission, and strategy.

In addition to understanding a business's goals, employees may share an understanding of its competitive position. A consultant visiting a Komatsu facility in Japan asked an employee what he was trying to accomplish at work that day. To his surprise, the immediate response was, "I am trying to beat Caterpillar." When he randomly asked four other Komatsu employees the same question, he received the same response. Komatsu managers had drilled into their employees not only Komatsu's identity and goals but its position relative to competitors. In contrast, U.S. assemblyline workers might be more likely to respond, "I am working to get my pay check" or "I am working to meet my quota" or "I am working to help increase productivity." While these responses may indicate varying degrees of commitment, they do not reflect a shared mindset about the strategic and competitive goals of the company.

Employees who share a mindset about company goals and how the company ranks against competitors are more committed to the organization and therefore perform better. A simple test for this shared mindset is to ask employees what they perceive is the strategy or competitive position of their organization. The shared mindset about internal ends exists to the extent that employees respond in similar ways.

A consumer manufacturing company, recognizing the need for a strong employee shared mindset about internal ends, set out to develop one. First, the five core values of the company were extrapolated from its mission and strategy statement. After these values were identified, a survey was administered to a sampling of employees at all levels of the organization asking them the extent to which they perceived these values as critical to the company's success. The results of the survey were discouraging: the further the employees were from the top of the organization, the less they perceived the importance of the five core values.

Management then set about building a unity around these values. It talked about them with employees, created a communications program using videotapes and recorded dialogues, reoriented the incentive systems to reflect them, and made sure company decisions were consistent with its values. Two years later, another survey showed that employees at all levels of the company had a much greater understanding of the importance of the five core values. Management believed that the employee unity which had been created helped to focus attention on key organization activities. This unity helped the company compete in changing markets.

Type II: Internal Means

Shared mindsets also exist when employees share an understanding of *how work is done* in the organization. *Means* of accomplishing the work include such factors as work ethic, decision-making processes, what information is shared, and how employees allocate their work time.

Several work processes may be identified and examined: the processes for inventory control; for accounts receivable and payable; for product design; for marketing analysis; for hiring, transfering, or promoting people; and for sharing information. In work on continuous improvement through quality, one researcher has suggested that major improvements in quality programs derive from a focus on reducing variances in work processes. When employees identify specific work processes with extreme variance and try to reduce variance in these areas, processes become stabilized and customer requirements are better satisfied.[13]

A number of businesses have worked to develop shared mindset about internal means. Disneyworld management has sought to build within each employee a commitment to guest service. Employees receive extensive orientation not only in their jobs but also regarding the vision of Disneyworld as a place where guests can escape from their daily routines. Disney management sets standards and offers incentives based on the extent to which employees meet company standards, and Disneyworld employees are trained and encouraged to share the company goals of ensuring that guests have a good time when they visit.

Employees are trained to share the means by which the Disney goals are to be realized. They are taught how to conduct themselves with guests, how to respond to guests' questions and how to dress. Special Disney "language" reinforces their commitment to the organization. This language includes calling visitors guests rather than customers, being "on stage" when with guests and "off stage" when away from guests, wearing "costumes" rather than "uniforms," and being hosts and hostesses rather than employees. By creating a common mindset among employees about how work is done, Disney helps ensure that guests will achieve the goals for which they came to Disneyworld.

The shared mindset about customer service among Nordstrom employees helps everyone not only to understand and accept Nordstrom's goals, but to agree to the customer-commitment processes that accomplish the goals. Knowing customer names, calling other Nordstrom stores to locate out-of-stock items, helping customers select clothes, and making personal calls to customers builds over time a mindset among employees about how to treat customers. As this mindset becomes shared company-wide, a unity of agreement is created concerning how work is to be done at Nordstrom. Employees become "Nordies" and come to live the culture they represent.

At Apple, Sculley implemented a series of work processes and approaches around which employees could rally to achieve a shared mindset about how work is done. These included creating an informal atmosphere, fostered by the absence of suits or uniforms, and an open office structure; offering employees untraditional work alternatives—for example, working at home or in others' offices; and allowing employees to name their own conference rooms and buildings and to create logos and symbols unique to their work settings. By giving employees "ownership" of their work processes, management helped to build a shared mindset about how work was to be done.

Some people have argued that building shared mindset is merely brainwashing, which fosters homogeneity at the expense of creativity. We disagree. In fact, a shared mindset can reflect a common acceptance of diversity. At Digital Equipment Corporation, for example, a shared mindset exists about "valuing differences." Employees are encouraged to acknowledge and reward diversities of opinion. Debate, dialogue, and the offering of ideas and proposals by employees are the norm. Digital management believes that valuing differences enables employees to respond more effectively to the diverse global cultures in which they operate and to a wide variety of customer requirements.

At Disney, Nordstrom, Apple, and Digital, employees share a mindset not only about the organization's goals but about how the goals are to be accomplished. Through sharing this mindset, employees achieve the harmony Sun Tzu described in the quotation that opens this chapter. While this kind of harmony may not lead people to die for their businesses, it may help create employee unity around what work needs to be done (ends) and how work is to be done (means). Such internal unity ultimately helps businesses reach their goals.

Type III: External Ends

Most discussions of shared values, culture, or mindset focus exclusively on how *employees* come to acquire a common set of shared values.[14] We believe that shared mindset may also be defined as the extent to which stakeholders outside an organization understand and accept the firm's goals. Suppliers, customers, and other stakeholders may come to accept and agree with what the business is attempting to accomplish. When an external shared mindset exists, stakeholders experience a unity of values and beliefs with those inside the organization. They therefore believe that their needs will be met through working with the business.[15]

When people are asked what comes to mind when they think of Disneyworld, they may name a series of favorable images: fun, warmth, escape, Mickey Mouse, vacation. If these are the images Disney management wants customers to have, a shared mindset exists about external ends. Stakeholders that share a mindset with the firm are more likely to engage in activities favorable to the business.

Similar shared mindsets about external ends exist in many industries for many stakeholders. Throughout the 1980s, Ford Motor Company concentrated on building a shared mindset among suppliers and distributors. Suppliers, who were required to pass rigorous quality-certification tests, were trained in quality procedures and were requested to furnish statements and demonstrations of their commitment to quality. Ford's purpose was to build a shared mindset about external ends, focusing on quality among suppliers, dealers, and other stakeholders.

John Sculley's statements early in this chapter indicate the extent to which shared mindsets were critical to success at Pepsico and Apple. Both companies were attempting to create a new way of thinking about soft drinks and computers. Pepsico sought to be identified with the "Pepsi Generation," a generation dedicated to excitement, which was to be achieved in part through consumption of Pepsi. Management at both Pepsico and Apple was intent on ensuring that employees *inside* and customers *outside* shared a mindset about what the organization was trying to do. Apple, with the Macintosh, wished to create a new understanding of how usable and friendly computers could be and how great an asset a friendly computer could represent. When customers believe in the goals and outcomes of a business, a shared external mindset exists that often leads to customer commitment.

Nordstrom set out to build a mindset about customer service among employees as well as customers. The approach was based on the premise that if customers think of Nordstrom and service simultaneously, Nordstrom will have a competitive advantage. In our seminars, we ask which participants have heard of Nordstrom. We then list the first word that comes to mind. Almost uniformly, the word "service" comes out on top. We then request, and almost always receive, stories from participants who have experienced exceptional Nordstrom service. In one case, a woman visiting Salt Lake City wanted a new outfit to wear to a family dinner. She purchased an outfit on sale at Nordstrom and wore the outfit that evening; the next morning she noticed that the outfit had a tear in the back. She did not know whether the outfit was torn when she purchased it or whether it was torn during the evening. Thinking Nordstrom might offer a partial refund, she returned to the store and described the situation. The salesclerk immediately took the outfit, saying, "You cannot have this outfit if it is torn." She asked if the woman still wanted the outfit; then, when not finding a replacement in the store, called other Nordstrom stores. On being unable to locate the outfit, she demanded that the customer take a refund, but asked if the customer would still like the outfit. The salesclerk took the customer's name, and three weeks later the outfit arrived in the mail. The salesclerk had called throughout the entire system and found the outfit in another store in another state. Versions of this story are repeated many times over by customers who have come to understand and accept the Nordstrom culture.

An external shared mindset goes beyond advertising alone to merge internal and external images of the company. In the mid-1980s, Hewlett Packard embarked on a "What if . . . " advertising campaign, which was designed to encourage both customers and employees to redefine their expectations of the company. Customers could expect that the firm would pay attention to innovation and creative product design, while employees could expect to produce creative products through attention to customer requests. The point was to unify customers' and employees' beliefs about the company.

To create an external shared mindset, businesses may open a direct channel to customers, explicitly identifying to the customers the business's desired outcomes. When the president of Vidal Sassoon Hair Products declared to television viewers that ''If you don't look good, we don't look good,'' the message was that unity existed between the customers' goals and the company's.

Type IV: External Means

A fourth type of shared mindset may exist when stakeholders share the *process* the business uses to accomplish work. Sharing processes with stakeholders means that supplies, customers, financiers, and other groups understand and agree not on on *what* the organization is attempting to accomplish but on *how*. We may identify three approaches to sharing how work is done.

The most common, and the most superficial, approach to sharing processes is to invite suppliers and customers to visit plants to learn firsthand how work is done. When suppliers and customers visit facilities, information is shared, and behavior is created that brings at least minimal unity between the employees inside and the stakeholders outside a business. Apple regularly invites customers to visit its facilities to see how its products are developed as a means of building ongoing communication between customers and employees.

Similarly, with internal divisions, shared mindsets can be created through visits. Johnson Wax in Racine, Wisconsin, discovered there was a lack of unity between its employees in England and those in Racine. To remedy the situation, the chairman of the company chartered a Boeing 747 and flew employees from England to Racine for a week. During that time, employees from the two continents shared information, talked, and became more sensitive and responsive to each other. Merely spending time together helped people from different backgrounds build community.

But on-site visits may not engender long-term commitment. A second approach to building shared external mindset about processes is to involve stakeholders in product design and delivery. Hewlett-Packard engineers, for example, spend enormous amounts of time in customer labs and offices working with customers to define product requirements. In the aircraft engine business, a manufacturer's representative is assigned to work full time in the aircraft assembler's facility. This practice helps to establish an ongoing relationship between the engine manufacturer and the aircraft assembler and fosters the sharing of new product information that affects them both: The engine manufacturer shares information about specifications for new engines, while the aircraft designers share information about design and dynamics.

As advocated by Tom Peters, providing service excellence requires that businesses spend large amounts of time with customers talking about product design, business strategy, and product delivery.[16] Making the customer part of the product-design process builds a greater level of customer commitment than merely inviting customers to tour facilities.

A third, more complex level of customer and supplier commitment may be derived by involving customers not only in product decisions but also in management processes.[17] A number of firms have begun to dissolve the traditional boundaries between a firm and its suppliers and customers and to integrate customers and suppliers into management processes. A food-supply firm with a reputation for high-quality employee training began to invite customers to its internal training programs. In one case, the firm sponsored a training event exclusively for customers. In addition, the firm sponsored a training session primarily for customers that was presented by managers of the firm. The goal was to help customers learn what they could do to be more competitive in the next five years. The food-supply firm found that account turnover was cut 70 percent among customers who attended the program. Why? Customers appreciated being treated with dignity, and a shared mindset evolved about how work was to be done.

One firm in the retail paint business now involves customers in hiring decisions. When an account representative job is open, the firm invites its major distributors to interview potential job candidates to find out which ones they believe would best meet their needs. Involving customers in staffing decisions may generate increased customer commitment to the individual hired. It also generates a shared mindset with the customer about how work is done within the business.

Several firms have begun to involve customers in the performance-appraisal process. At the design stage, the firms invite a focus group of key customers to review performance-appraisal forms and procedures and respond to several relatively straight-forward questions: To what extent will employees who meet these standards and criteria be of value to you? What other standards and criteria would you like to see more or less of? Involving customers in the design of appraisals helps ensure that appraisals reflect customer needs. Firms have also begun to involve customers in the delivery of performance appraisals, and employee performance reviews are based in part on customer perceptions as well as on supervisor and peer reviews.

As customers, suppliers, and other stakeholders become more involved in how a business does its work, a shared external mindset about means emerges, leading to unity of purpose and commitment.

ENHANCING ORGANIZATIONAL CAPABILITY THROUGH ESTABLISHING SHARED MINDSETS

Shared Mindsets and Customer Values

We have identified many of the customer values that affect competitiveness: price, product features, technological innovation, reduced product cycle times, long-term relationships, and service quality. Shared mindsets ensure that these values are not only desired but are designed into organizational procedures. Nordstrom built internal and external shared mindsets involving both goals and how work is done.

When a firm's stakeholders share values with its employees, long-term relationships are established which ensure that customers will receive value. For example, Disneyworld customers travel thousands of miles to visit the theme park. As their needs for fun and excitement are satisfied through activities they participate in, and as Disney employees come to share these values with customers, a unity is created. Customers receive value from their transactions with Disney employees, while employees receive work satisfaction from knowing that they have lived up to customer expectations.

Shared Mindsets and Uniqueness

The second criterion of competitive advantage is uniqueness: doing something that cannot be easily replicated by a competitor.

We propose that shared mindset is unique and nearly impossible to replicate—or change, for that matter.

Once a company has established a shared mindset, it endures over time. The commitment to service by Disney employees becomes self-perpetuating. New employees learn from seasoned ones the importance of offering outstanding customer service and come to perceive such service as the norm rather than the exception.

A simple example from sports illustrates this point. When a high school basketball player decides to attend the University of Indiana to play for coach Bobby Knight, he quickly adopts the mindset of the Indiana team. As a coach Knight drills his players and requires excellence in the fundamentals of basketball: making the right pass, staying between your man and the basket, blocking out on rebounds, and so on. This way of playing basketball at Indiana is entrenched; it is part of the mindset.

Similarly, a new player attending Loyola Marymount with Paul Westhead as basketball coach would be required to adopt a particular mindset. Westhead's philosophy is "run and gun." Players are expected to play an up-tempo game—to shoot within seven seconds, to make long passes, and so on. These mindsets have become a known and ongoing part of basketball at Indiana and Loyola Marymount. They become self-perpetuating as players choose the schools consistent with their own philosophies and playing styles. These unified mindsets result in a unique and distinctive approach to basketball at each school, which translates into competitive advantage.

Shared mindsets are not only durable but difficult to replicate. Developing Apple's mindset about innovation and creativity or copying Disney's about fun and excitement is easier said than done. Shared mindsets are created over time. Competitors who attempt to copy shared mindsets generally fail, because the supporting foundations of shared mindsets are complex and have evolved over time.

Shared mindsets are also difficult to change. Because they represent thought patterns about what we do and how we do it, they cannot easily be modified. When Jaguar experienced several problems in the area of service in the early 1980s, its customers developed a mindset that the firm offered poor service, poor quality, and poor reliability—a factor that severely handicapped the company in its entry into the North American market particularly. To change this mindset required three years of dedicated efforts by the management team, which had to reprogram how employees thought about working at Jaguar, how customers felt about buying Jaguars, and how suppliers, financiers, and other stakeholders thought about doing business with Jaguar. Changing a product feature was easier than changing internal and external shared mindsets.

THE ROLE OF MANAGEMENT IN CREATING, MODIFYING, OR SUSTAINING SHARED MINDSETS

Shared mindset is the first element of organizational capability. To establish a shared mindset, we suggest that management ask five questions:[18]

Question 1:   What is the current shared mindset?

This question has two parts. First, management needs to identify the current shared mindset *of employees*. It can examine how employees do their work, perceive the goals of the organization, make decisions, allocate resources and handle disagreements, and allocate their time. Management may also assess the extent to which a shared mindset exists within the organization; that is, to what extent do employees share similar views about the organization's means and ends?

Second, management can identify the current shared mindset *of stakeholders*. Management may wish to interview, survey, or visit key stakeholders to learn how they perceive the means and ends of the organization.

In our experience, there is often a great disparity between the mindset of employees and that of stakeholders. In one research effort, we collected from the top managers of a firm data about their perceptions of the firm's goals and the means used to achieve these objectives. We then interviewed a sample of key accounts— customers who had worked with the firm for many years. The two lists had almost no overlap. Management and customer perceptions differed so dramatically that it almost appeared as if we were talking about two separate firms. Communicating these results to managers not only got their attention but made it clear how urgent it was for them to understand the mindsets of the stakeholders.

From question 1, management may be able to define current shared mindsets inside and outside the business.

Question 2:   **What informational and behavioral practices create and institutionalize a shared mindset?**

For the group as well as the individual, the two major factors affecting perception are information and behavior. Our mental images are influenced by the information we receive and the behaviors we engage in.

Managers wishing to examine shared mindset may focus on the informational and behavioral patterns that institutionalize the mindset. Informational patterns include both the information itself and how it is disseminated. Since shared mindsets derive to a great extent from information, management can trace information flows to discover the antecedents of shared mindsets. In addition, managers may be able to identify specific employee behaviors that reinforce or sustain the existing mindset.

In one organization, management learned that a series of weekly reports flowed from each individual to the department manager. The practice of submitting weekly information reports had been initiated at a time when the organization had relatively few employees and when one manager supervised only five or six employees. In the current organization, with over 30,000 employees, the span of control was much broader (up to 30 employees to a manager), and managers who received weekly reports found the practice to be more burdensome than helpful. The information flow helped reinforce the bureaucratic mindsets established among the firm's employees. Before changing this mindset, managers had to examine the information flow in the organization and the processes that reinforced the mindset.

Question 3:   **Who is committed to the current mindset?**

Change is often difficult (see Chapter 10). It requires letting go of something and replacing it with something else—and often we gain more from not letting go than from letting go. In assessing ways of modifying shared mindsets, it is important to assess the value of the current mindset and to recognize that some people derive benefit from it. A manager in the company cited above did not want to give up the practice of weekly reports because he believed they helped him establish and maintain authority over his employees. Accepting that the reports served a purpose for him and that letting go of them would require finding new ways to accomplish the same purpose was an important step in modifying a shared mindset.

Since relationships in most organizations must be managed within a political context, it is important for management to determine who perceives what value from a shared mindset.

> *Question 4:*   **Given the strategic, financial, and technological goals of our business, what future mindsets will be required?**

Predicting the future is difficult and never infallible. It requires the ability to look ahead without having one's vision impaired by knowledge of the past. To define a mindset required for the future, management may consider questions that posit both an external and internal view of the future. Questions that may help with this dialogue include:

- □ What do we want customers to say about us in three years?
- □ How do we want to be known by our suppliers, financiers, and community leaders?
- □ If a prominent business periodical were doing a special issue on our business in three years, what would we like it to highlight? What will we have done over the next three years to merit such attention and acclaim?
- □ Three years from now what would we like employees to tell their friends who ask them what it is like to work here?

As these questions are raised and discussed, a new identity may begin to emerge that defines a shared mindset about both the ends (what we are trying to accomplish) and the means (how we are trying to accomplish it).

> *Question 5:*   **What will be the informational and behavioral implications of the new mindset?**

Just as information and behavior can be important diagnostic tools, they can also be levers with which management may establish new mindsets. If a new mindset can be specified, or at least partially described, management may then pursue the information processes for communicating the shared mindset. What messages need to be sent? What tools are available for sending the messages?

In addition to information, management may begin to specify behaviors consistent with the new mindset. The manager who had a difficult time letting go of the weekly reports found that when he stopped asking for the reports he could maintain his credibility in other ways. He could spend more time one on one with engineers who reported to him; he could focus on significant managerial challenges rather than on mundane reports; and he could spend time with customers and other external stakeholders. In effect, he had to learn that he could replace his old habits with new ones and that the new behaviors would be valuable. Over time, by changing behaviors, he changed his mindset.

As Apple was developing a shared mindset of a "small computer systems company," John Sculley had to convince the entrepreneurial engineers that the new mindset did not represent a total break with the old one but rather was an evolution of the old mindset consistent with market conditions. This required that he share information with employees who rebelled against the idea of letting go of their sense of the company as a stand-alone competitor of IBM. Management had to help these employees understand the behavioral requirements of the new mindset: working to integrate and extend current systems rather than continually inventing new ones.

5

Management Practices: Tools for Action

Nothing is as useful as a good theory.

Kurt Lewin

To Tom Watson, IBM is nothing more than the total of the individual contributions of the people within it. He would tell them that when things were tought. His message was, ''Look, you can take away almost anything from IBM. You can take away our technology. You can take away our plants. You can take away our labs. You can take away any facility. You can take away our headquarters, but leave our people and this business will recreate itself overnight.'' He believed it. His people believed it. Out of that came a tremendous unleashing of human effort.

Harry Levinson and Stuart Rosenthal,
CEO: Corporate Leadership in Action

If a shared mindset constitutes the heart of organizational capability, a business's management practices represent its mind. While shared mindset resides in values and beliefs, management practices comprise the formal processes for governing how employees think and behave. Management practices are embedded in an organization's policies, standard operating procedures, traditions, and work practices. They determine what information individuals receive, how they receive it, and when it is disseminated to them. Management practices also affect how individuals behave—where, how, and with whom they spend their time. They are tools management uses to shape and direct employee attention, time, behavior, and energy.[1]

We suggested earlier that organizational capability consists not just of employing people as a competitive advantage but includes using *processes* to gain competitive advantage through people. Management practices account for many of the processes that affect individual behavior within an organization. Our belief is that managers who are able to use management practices creatively and strategically to influence employees will build sustainable competitive advantage.

The criteria for judging the effectiveness of management practices must be modified to reflect the importance of these practices in building competitive advantage. The following questions need to be asked about each management practice within an organization:

1. To what extent does it add value to customers outside the business?
2. How dies it help in the implementation of economic, strategic, and technological strategies?
3. To what extent does it serve to create and preserve a shared mindset within the business?
4. Does it help the business to respond to change, become more competitive in the marketplace, or better meet customer needs?

A FRAMEWORK FOR DISCUSSING MANAGEMENT PRACTICES

Management Practices and Human Resource Departments and Professionals

In some organizations, when reference is made to management practices, the assumption is that these are merely processes carried out exclusively by professionals within human resource and personnel departments. We believe that this kind of thinking ultimately endangers an organization's capacity to compete. Management *practices* are the processes and approaches any manager uses that affect how people think, behave, and do their work. Narrowly categorizing management practices within one department or function is like saying that only the finance department of a business worries about money. All managers worry about money; all managers also worry about management practices. A simple test to assess an orientation to management practices within an organization is the following question:

Who has the primary responsibility for managing human resources in the organization?

a. **Line managers**
b. **Human resource professionals**
c. **Both**

Most people answer "c"—both. We disagree. We believe that the *primary* responsibility rests with line managers—"a." Each manager needs to be accountable for understanding, defining, and implementing management practices that build competitiveness. Human resource professionals may play partnership roles in designing and implementing management practices, but theirs is not the primary role.[2]

Categories of Management Practices

Within an organization, dozens of formal policies and procedures exist for managing how people think and behave. These policies represent the processes for combining personal competencies to form an organizational capability that is greater than the sum of the individuals within the business. They provide individuals in the organization with consistency and stability, thereby enabling the organization to establish and meet individual expectations. Many people take for their adage, "Organizations don't think, people do." While we agree, we go further and suggest that *management practices institutionalize the way people think and behave.* Organizations assume a life beyond and in addition to the sum of personal competencies. An important step toward developing organizational capability is to define a framework that managers may use for categorizing management practices.

Having a framework in which to discuss management practices helps avoid the problem of randomly discussing policies and procedures.[3] With it managers are able to assess practices on an ongoing basis. Having a framework also ensures that when organizational strategies are implemented or changes are attempted, the entire set of management practices may be examined, not merely one practice in isolation.

A number of managerial analysts have defined the domain of management practices empirically,[4] and the framework presented here builds on their work. We start with the assumption that individuals bring unique personal competencies to an organization. Organizations compete when they have more competencies than other organizations. To translate personal competencies into organizational capability, managers need to generate, reinforce, and sustain competencies. To meet competency requirements, six management practices may be defined. Selection and development primarily help generate competencies; appraisal and rewards primarily help reinforce competencies; and organization design and communication primarily help sustain competencies.

Generating Competencies

The first challenge of any business is to generate the competencies necessary to provide output that will be valued by customers. This is an ongoing need, because no organization can survive without individuals who have the personal competencies necessary to accomplish the work that is valued in the marketplace.

A colleague of ours, Thom Nielsen, who had a secure job as a college professor/administrator was approached by an associate with an idea for producing a new device that would balance grinding machines with greater precision than was possible with any technique then in use. The invention surpassed all state-of-the-art balancing technologies. While the market was not huge, Thom quickly learned that there was a strong demand for the new type of balancer. The product idea represented a niche in which Thom chose to join with partners to start a small business, called Balance Dynamics. Thom's first challenge was to ensure that the fledgling company had the competencies to meet market needs. Initially, these competencies were relatively easy to define: competence in designing and producing the balancer, in acquiring funds to launch the business, in marketing the balancer to customers, and in managing the business effectively. To generate these competencies, Thom worked with the inventor and with a third partner who had marketing and sales experience. Together they formed a partnership, with each of the three partners bringing a unique set of competencies to the business.

Generating competencies is the first challenge managers of people must meet. In the relatively simple world of a start-up venture, employees must have competencies to design, produce, and deliver a product that customers value. In larger, more mature, and more complex organizations, generating competencies involves the same issues but in addition the history, politics, size, and traditions of the organization must be taken into account. Yet the basic tools for generating competencies are similar in both young, small businesses and large, more mature ones. Two management approaches may be employed—selection and development.

A selection approach to generating competencies *buys* competencies from outside the organization. At the outset, Balance Dynamics had little choice but to acquire the competencies required to develop and distribute its product. Attracting partners who had complementary skills enabled the firm to succeed. By buying competencies an organization can obtain the exact set of skills it requires. Buying competencies is expensive, however, and at times politically unfeasible. Organizations committed to promoting from within cannot constantly go outside to buy competencies.

Selection processes deal with the flow of talent into, through, and out of the organization. Selection helps a firm respond to three critical management questions:

1. Who is hired into the organization?
2. Who is promoted within the organization?
3. Who is outplaced from the organization?

(Chapter 6 reviews choices, options, and success indicators relevant to each of these questions.)

If selection processes were perfect and organizations were able to hire only employees who had the competencies required to meet both present and future needs, all other management practices would be irrelevant. In practice, however, making accurate long-term selection decisions is difficult. Organizations must often compromise in their hiring and promotion decisions—for example, take the "best available" candidate rather than the "ideal" candidate. Furthermore, business conditions change, so that the competencies generated today may not be appropriate in the future.

A senior executive in the automobile industry in the late 1970s, when faced with the need to produce more cars to meet increased market demand, lamented that he knew the technology in the 1980s would require a new breed of employees—individuals who could work in flatter, more technologically driven, more flexible organizations. Yet because people were needed to produce cars to meet current production and market demands, the company knowingly hired employees who would probably not have the necessary skills and abilities to adapt to the more technology-driven and flexible organization that would evolve in the late 1980s and 1990s. When the technological and organizational changes of the 1980s arrived, the company committed itself to retraining employees. Unfortunately, because employees had been hired for expediency rather than with strategic goals in mind, many were unable to make the transition, regardless of the resources dedicated to retraining. Retraining is not the answer when employees lack the ability to adapt. We believe that the company's hiring philosophy in the 1970s was faulty: More attention should have been paid then to identifying long-term company needs. To find and hire the employees that could have adapted to the changing organization, however, would have been a time-consuming process, because long-term staffing processes were not already in place. And, in the face of market and product demands, hiring employees to fill immediate needs offered a superficial treatment for a serious, long-term disease.

Of all management functions, staffing is the most critical, because the quality of the people who enter the organization is the single greatest determinant of the organization's effectiveness. Peter Drucker argues that if an organization cannot staff itself effectively, it will have little chance of success.[5] If a company commits to the wrong talent, it will never be able to meet customer demands. Hiring decisions are among the most strategic decisions any manager makes, because they have such a significant impact on the long-term viability of the business. At the same time, the staffing process has a profound effect on people's personal lives and careers.

While employee selection has always been and will always be a critical issue for organizations, much of the attention to and research on selection began during and after World War II. Competency tests were designed to profile the kinds of persons needed for key jobs. The U.S. Army sought to identify the qualities of the ideal officer and then selected officer candidates based on those profiles. The Navy wanted to identify the psychological profile of individuals best suited to serve on submarines. For example, individuals were needed who could work in close proximity to others for long periods of time.

In a recent study of management practices in U.S. industry, researchers found that the criteria for attracting and promoting appropriate employees remain[6] the management practices given most attention by executives in the late 1980s. Again it was evident that executive attention paid to staffing is directly linked to business success.

A development approach to generating competencies is predicated on *building* new competencies within existing employees. Through training and retraining programs, job rotation, new job assignments, career moves, coaching, or counseling, organizations may be able to adapt the skills of an existing work force to meet changing business needs. In small businesses, where buying all of the competencies necessary for success is prohibitively expensive, all employees must make a personal investment to widen their competencies. At Balance Dynamics, for example, each partner had to develop new skills for the company to succeed. One had to learn more about marketing, sales, business plans, and production schedules. Another had to become proficient in finance, accounting, invoicing, and the technologies necessary to run the business. Because each partner was willing to dedicate time to gain additional competencies, Balance Dynamics was able to compete successfully.

The concept of development is based on the assumption that individuals can acquire new skills through training and other developmental experiences. This approach is at the core of our society. Throughout the primary school years, children are taught basic literacy and math skills on the assumption that they can build on these competencies. In many therapeutic situations, individuals are encouraged to develop new patterns of feeling and behaving that will be less-destructive than their previous ones. Government-sponsored programs attempt to help disadvantaged youth acquire job skills to break out of the dependency trap.

While selection *buys* competencies and manages the flow of people, development *builds* competencies and manages the flow of talent. The developmental practices of organizations should be based on well-thought-out answers to the following questions:

1. How can training generate personal competencies among employees?
2. How can alternative activities generate personal competencies?

Although these questions sound simple, the processes for generating competencies through development may be complex and difficult. (See Chapter 6 for an in-depth discussion of this issue.)

The literature on how individuals learn new concepts through developmental experiences is extensive.[7] We know that training and practice enable an individual to acquire technical, concrete skills. For example, we can teach someone to type, to speak a foreign language, or to analyze and interpret financial data. Research has demonstrated, however, that using development as a means of changing attitudes and ways of thinking is extremely difficult. Even in the most extreme cases, when individuals are completely removed from their environment—such as going away to a federal jobs program, going to prison, or joining a cult and being isolated from the world—long-term attitudes are difficult to change. Within organizations, employee attitudes cannot be changed simply by allocating more resources to training and development programs. In Chapter 6, we define the choices that businesses must make concerning who must be developed, what should be taught, and how the processes aimed at generating competencies should be designed and implemented.

Generating competencies through selection and development is a primary challenge of management. We believe that if selection and development are successful, so that organizations generate appropriate competencies, reinforcing and sustaining those competencies becomes much easier. While neither selection nor development can be made easy or fail-safe, a high degree of attention to these matters is required on the part of management.

Reinforcing Competencies

After an organization has generated the competencies necessary for its business success, it needs to put into place mechanisms for reinforcing those competencies. Reinforcing competencies ensures that individuals will continually focus their attention on, and behave in a manner consistent with the competencies required. Reinforcement can focus either on maintaining existing competencies or on adopting new ones. Two management practices are primarily responsible for achieving this objective: appraisal and rewards (see Figure 5–1).

Appraisal processes deal with setting performance standards, ensuring that people work according to standards, and providing feedback on performance. Appraisal processes address such questions as:

1. What are the performance standards of individuals, groups, and departments within the organization?
2. What mechanisms exist for giving feedback to employees about how well their performance meets established standards?

Figure 5–1
FRAMEWORK FOR MANAGEMENT PRACTICES

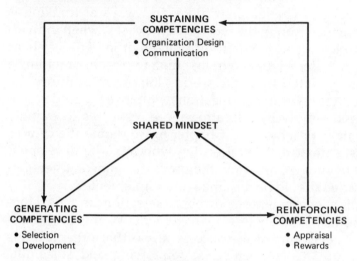

3. What *processes* are used to ensure accurate, meaningful, and effective appraisals?

(Chapter 7 identifies the attitudes and actions that must be adopted to ensure that appraisals reinforce personal competencies and build organizational capability.)

Balance Dynamics, although it had few employees, established performance standards for each employee and for the company as a whole. Employees received ongoing feedback on their performance from peers and supervisors. If performance was not up to standard, the partners worked with the employee to redefine the job or replace the individual. If an employee's performance was consistently above standard, the partners needed to find ways to reinforce success.

Appraisal processes define expectations, set standards, and offer individuals feedback on their performance. They help to reinforce competencies, create shared mindsets, and build organizational capability.

While appraisals are the first step in reinforcing standards, they work only if they are coupled with rewards. Rewards reinforce both behavior and thinking patterns and motivate employees to devote greater attention and energy to some activities than to others. Rewards may come in a variety of forms, ranging from financial incentives to informal group acceptance. Reward processes deal with such questions as:

1. What are the criteria for selecting alternative reward systems?
2. What alternative types of financial rewards can be used to reinforce behavior?
3. What alternative types of nonfinancial rewards can be used to reinforce behavior?

These questions lead to a series of choices about how rewards are allocated to reinforce employee competencies within the organization (see Chapter 7).

In Balance Dynamics, rewards played an important role in attracting and motivating employees. The partners chose to dedicate their professional careers to the company in the hope of receiving economic, social, and personal rewards. As owners, they had equity positions, which, if the company succeeded, could be very profitable. Social rewards stemmed from working with associates who were trusted, respected, and pleasant to work with. Personally, at Balance Dynamics the partners and employees were able to be part of a team that could build a quality product with a legacy of its own. These rewards were important motivators for both the original partners and the additional employees hired into the company. While the original partners retained most of the equity in the firm, the employees valued the rewards of a socially constructive work setting and opportunities for growth and advancement.

Offering rewards reinforces behavior for a simple, fundamental reason: most individuals are hedonistic and would rather do things they like to do than things they do not like to do.[8] When people are rewarded in ways that are pleasing, tasks that might otherwise be unpleasant become not only palatable but exciting.

Sustaining Competencies

Once the systems are in place to generate and reinforce the competencies necessary for an organization's success, the challenge remains to make sure the competencies persist over time. Sustaining competencies involves perpetuating the required competencies, offering individuals institutional support for demonstrating those competencies, and ensuring that the competencies are regenerated, so that they endure beyond the tenure of any single individual. Organization design and communication are the primary management practices for sustaining competencies.

Organization design includes processes used for allocating responsibility, defining roles, establishing control and accountability, and designating decision-making authority.[9] This aspect of a business sustains competencies through creating an organization identity that goes beyond the sum of the individual parts. This identity is often reflected in a shared mindset, but is sustained through the ways in which employees formally interact with each other. Patterns of individual interaction derive to a large extent from the structure, shape, and control processes within the firm. Organization design addresses such questions as:

1. What should be the shape of the organization, for example, how many levels, what roles, what reporting relationships, what division of labor?
2. What type of governance system should be established in the organization to allocate responsibility and ensure accountability?
3. What processes can be managed to reassess organization design on an ongoing basis?

These questions lead to a series of choices that will help sustain personal competencies (see Chapter 8).

Balance Dynamics, like many small companies, maintained a fluid organization design in its early stages. With three partners, roles and responsibilities overlapped extensively. While one partner focused on invention, another on marketing, and another on administration, the three collaborated to a great extent and shared the responsibility for design, assembly, and distribution of the new product. Rather than control the behavior of employees through formal rules and policies, informal processes prevailed. Accountability was shared and assigned to all members of the group. As Balance Dynamics grew to need additional sales and manufacturing personnel, the organization structure took on a more formal look. Roles were more clearly delineated, responsibility and accountability were specified, and control systems became more formal. The ongoing processes established by the partners to reassess their business structure enabled them to modify their organization design as needed. Regularly scheduled, periodic reviews forced them to analyze the changes that were necessary and ensured that they implemented these modifications on a timely basis.

Issues of accountability, role definition, control, and decision-making go beyond the workplace. Families also continually struggle with these matters. Within today's flexible, dynamic family structures, processes need to be established to decide who has what responsibilities, how decisions will be made, and the roles individual members will play. In a constantly changing setting, these decision-making processes become as important as the decisions themselves. Responsibility for food preparation, child care, car pooling, and verification of homework may vary according to individual obligations.

Organization design is an important means of sustaining employee competencies. The specific nature of reporting relationships, roles, and control systems within the organization, and the ways in which responsibilities are allocated, send cues to individuals about how they should spend their time. In organizations with narrow spans of control—for example, where fewer than five people report to each superior—a clear and tightly adhered-to hierarchy, control through rules and policies, and clear distinctions among roles, individuals know their roles, understand the consequences of inappropriate behavior and learn to look for guidance before making decisions. In organizations with wide spans of control—for example, where more than ten people report to each supervisor—diffuse power, control through shared values, and greater shared decision-making authority, individuals sense different behavioral cues. They learn to think about their work and spend their time in more flexible ways. Thus, the personal competencies that an individual brings to a job will be sustained or impeded, depending on the organization's structure.

Communication processes, which include all aspects of information flow within the organization, also sustain individual competencies. Communication sustains competencies by providing employees with information about the activities that are valued by the organization, involving selected individuals in the communication process, and using a variety of methods to share information. Communication deals with such questions as:

1. What information should be shared in the organization?
2. Who should be involved in sharing and receiving the information?
3. How can information be shared most effectively?

(The specific managerial choices for dealing with these questions are outlined in Chapter 8.)

At Balance Dynamics, with relatively few employees, communications were open and fluid. Information about customers, design, production, and distribution was shared among all employees. Most of the information was shared directly through face-to-face interactions, since all employees worked in the same location and saw each other daily. To formalize and ensure information flow, weekly and monthly meetings were held to share updates on business progress, and reports were distributed to keep employees abreast of new findings and insights.

Decisions on what information should be shared, who should share it, and how it should be disseminated should always be made with an eye to how choices in this area affect the organization's efforts to sustain employee competencies. When the right choices are made, individuals learn that their knowledge, skills, and abilities are valued and critical to business success. Through good communication processes, individuals acquire a shared mindset that sustains the competencies they bring to the organization.

MANAGEMENT PRACTICES AND COMPETITIVENESS

The ways in which executives apply management practices affect a firm's competitiveness for four reasons.

Gaining Customer Commitment

First, management practices help build customer commitment.[10] As discussed in Chapter 4, commitment increases when individuals receive information about and participate in an activity.[11] When customers take part in an organization's management practices, they also receive information about the business. Customer participation in a business's management or human resource practices ranges from involvement in designing management practices to active participation in implementation. For example, in staffing an organization, customers may play a role in designing a hiring process by helping to define the abilities required of new employees. An electronics firm invited key customers to participate in defining the job requirements of sales personnel. The customers worked with members of the firm in focus groups and extensive interviews to identify the abilities needed by successful sales personnel. These recommendations were then translated into competency profiles that were used in screening job applicants.

More direct and extensive customer involvement in staffing involves having customers actually interview individuals prior to their being hired or transferred. A paint manufacturer that distributes through a national retail chain had to replace the account representative for the chain. Rather than make the hiring decision exclusively on the basis of data collected within the firm, the company invited representatives of the chain to interview a slate of three to five qualified candidates. The customer interviews helped the organization in selecting the best candidate to serve the customer. As a result, both company managers and decision-makers in the distribution chain felt a greater commitment to the account representative eventually chosen.

Involving customers in both the design of the selection process and in actual staffing decisions may result in greater customer commitment to the organization. Such a commitment creates in the customer a perception of receiving increased value from its transactions. Here too the organization builds a competitive advantage through management practices.

Developing a Capacity for Change

Second, effective management practices foster the building of competitiveness by increasing the capacity of an organization to change. As discussed in Chapter 2, organizations of the 1990s will face increasing environmental pressures for change. Organizations that change quickly—that reduce response times and that adapt to changing customer and supplier expectations—will be better equipped to meet customer needs and remain competitive. (See Chapters 10–11 for a complete discussion of this issue.)

Capacity for change in an organization is based on individual capacity for change. Individuals resist change when they lack information about the desirable outcomes of the change, or when they perceive that the change may have a negative rather than a positive effect on themselves. Management can turn resistance to change into increased capacity for change by using all six of the management practices depicted in Figure 5–1. Hiring new employees, offering development experiences, redesigning appraisal systems, tying rewards to flexibility, creating more flexible organization structures, and sharing information are tools executives may use to help individuals recognize, accept, understand, and enact change. As individuals create the capacity for change, organizations also create the capacity for change.

Implementing Business Strategies

Management practices also build competitiveness by helping managers implement business strategies. Strategies to enhance a business's financial, technological, or market capabilities are shaped to a great extent by how individuals focus attention (see Chapter 2). Individual attention may be focused by ensuring that all six management practices are consistent with the desired strategy.

One manufacturer in the late 1980s created a strategy designed to transform itself into becoming a player in the global marketplace. To help implement this plan, it had to modify a number of management practices. Rather than interview and hire from a set of twenty North American universities, as it had traditionally done, the firm began to employ experienced managers from overseas firms and to establish a campus presence in leading European and Asian universities. Its employee development programs began to emphasize competing in a world market, and a senior management development program was held in Europe, with program participants calling on key accounts. Career paths to senior management positions were structured to include a foreign assignment. Appraisals began to include input from both immediate supervisors and peers and subordinates and were designed to establish *when*, not *if*, high-potential employees would be assigned overseas. Incentives for gaining global experience were added to the employee reward system. Organization design began to focus on strategic alliances and trading partnerships with overseas subsidiaries. In communications, senior managers emphasized the importance of being a global rather than a domestic player. Definitions of market share that were reported to employees began to include the entire globe as the served market. The organization began to view its competition as European and Japanese rather than exclusively North American firms.

These six management tools became means by which management in this company sought to implement its global strategy. No one practice dominated; all six management practices complemented each other and affected how employees viewed their own work as well as their firm's competitive position.

Competitiveness increases when businesses have the ability not only to formulate but to implement a business strategy. Ultimately, it is the people within an organization who make a strategy happen. Management practices may be used as processes to encourage the people inside an organization to work toward implementing strategy.

Creating Strategic Unity

Finally, management practices build competitiveness by creating strategic unity. As discussed in Chapter 4, shared mindset is a critical source of uniqueness that offers customers added value. We have seen that shared mindset is created through management practices that affect how people think and behave. These practices are primary means of shaping individual thought and action, and they send out signals about the mindset that needs to prevail within an organization.[12]

At Apple Computer, management practices played a critical role in creating a new mindset. The hiring of John Sculley as chairman, rewarding employees for generating systems solutions to problems, building a group identity among product design units, and communicating with employees directly and through the media helped create the desired mindset that enabled the organization to achieve a competitive advantage.

MISUSES OF MANAGEMENT PRACTICES

While executives should use management practices as tools to create sustained competitive advantage, they often fail to do so. Management practices have not served as competitive weapons because executives have historically tended to regard them as ways to build organizational stability rather than competitiveness. In the past, management has also relied too heavily on human resource professionals to serve as guardians of management practices. Traditionally, however, human resource people have drawn boundaries around their work, not letting others see the details of what they do. In particular, we have experienced four major misuses of management practices, which may keep them from being used as competitive weapons.

Human Resource Jeopardy

First, management practices are often applied as all-purpose solutions rather than as responses to specific questions and situations.

We call this phenomenon "Human Resource (HR) Jeopardy." It is played when human resource professionals or managers have predetermined, even before asking questions, what management practice they intend to recommend. Since, in HR Jeopardy, the answers precede the questions, solutions may be offered to problems that have never been defined in the first place.

For example, in some companies the management practice that is seen as a solution to all problems is employee training. Regardless of their overall strategies, such firms always decide that a new training program needs to be put into place. While the program may be elegant, thoughtful, and cleverly taught, if it is developed before a specific need is identified, it will have only a pot-luck chance of adding value to the business. Other companies play HR Jeopardy with performance appraisal. If the market is shrinking and a reduction in the work force is necessary, the firm knows in advance that it will revise the employee performance-appraisal system. If, on the other hand, the market calls for the organization to grow the next year, the firm will again revise the appraisal system to do so. If the market demands higher quality, again, we know how the firm will respond—it will revise the appraisal system.

It may happen, of course, that the new training program or appraisal system does indeed fit the needs of the business. But it is equally probable that it will not. HR Jeopardy also reinforces an insular view of management practices—the idea that these practices do not need to relate to business conditions because the firm can change them at any time.

HR Jeopardy is a game with many players. Player number 1 could be the human resource professional who is an expert in a particular area who fervently believes that his expertise alone can solve company problems. Player number 2 could be the manager who has read about the latest management fad or attended a workshop where she learned about a new appraisal program. Her well-intentioned request to learn more about how the new program could work in her company may result in other managers assuming that she is committed to the program and therefore focusing resources exclusively on it. Player number 3 could be the consultant who has survived by helping companies succeed through the services he provides. He believes that if the company will act on his counsel, it will succeed. Unfortunately, his solutions are "canned," or take one form for all situations.

Each of these players misuses management practices. Each comes to business meetings with solutions rather than questions.

That is one reason we have framed this book around key questions rather than answers. We believe that the greatest value of the book *In Search of Excellence*, by Peters and Waterman, lies in the introduction of the concept of "search"—of continually seeking new ideas by asking important questions—rather than in its discussion of "excellence." Unfortunately, it is easy to lock into the principles of excellence and stop searching. Likewise, the greatest value of the framework given in Figure 5-1 is when it is used to ask questions, not find solutions.

Narrowness of Focus

Management practices are also misused when any one of the six tools is emphasized to the exclusion of the others. In Figure 5-1 we identify six management tools that can be used as competitive weapons. A major challenge of using management practices is to integrate all six practices into a coherent system that will become a competitive weapon. For example, in the face of global competition and changing market conditions, one corporation drew up a new structure that transformed the firm from a functional organization into business units. Alone this response would not have helped the organization gain a competitive edge, but when coupled with modifications in the other five management practices, organizational capability was enhanced:

- ☐ Staffing criteria and processes changed, and the company began to hire entry-level employees who had the potential for moving into business generalist positions. To acquire the competencies necessary to operate independent businesses, some senior managers were hired from outside the organization.
- ☐ Development experiences were designed for both the classroom and the field, to help middle and senior managers gain a broad business pespective.
- ☐ Appraisal standards shifted to encourage and provide feedback on the extent to which managers had the ability to run independent divisions.
- ☐ Rewards were based on the performance of the manager's business rather than on that of the corporation as a whole.
- ☐ Dozens of communication vehicles—meetings, videos, newsletters, interviews—were used to help employees understand why the organization was restructured.

In this case all six management practices were integrated and modified to help the company respond to increased global competition.

Another destructive form of narrowness occurs when human resource professionals alone define and implement management practices. If representatives from the entire organization do not share responsibility for designing programs and processes and have no part in carrying them out, the strategic goals of the business will not be served. Creating limited "kitchen cabinets" to identify how management practices should be used as tools to build competitiveness is also a form of narrowness.

Means versus Ends

Further misuse of management practices occurs when such practices are defined as *ends* rather than as *means* of building competitiveness.[13] In a number of our seminars, we ask participants to describe what comes to mind when they hear the term "human resources." A consistent list emerges: people, training, performance management, pay, hiring, motivation, succession planning, career paths, workshops. While these responses accurately describe programs, they imply that management practices are ends in and of themselves—that the goal of a management practice is to establish a program and that a successful practice is an ongoing program. This misunderstanding often prevails among human resource professionals. When we ask human resource people what they have done for their organization in the last year, their comments often focus on the programs they designed and delivered. When we ask how they know they have been successful in the last year, a common response is that their programs were well received, that they seemed to find favor among managers, and that they continued to receive funding.

We believe this type of misunderstanding also leads to misuse of management practices. Development and other programs must be viewed as means for building competitiveness, not as ends in themselves. Forward-thinking human resource professionals respond to the question asking them what they have done for their business by discussing business conditions and how their firm operates to meet customer needs. Then they explain how the programs and processes they developed have improved business responsiveness.

Failure to Link Practices
to Business Needs

Finally, a management practice is misused when it is initiated not to meet a specific organization need but for reasons having to do with tradition, stability, security, political safety, and managerial requests. When we explore why a particular management practice exists and persists in an organization, we often find that the practice began as a response to an undefined need and has continued as an accepted, unquestioned part of the organization. In the early 1980s, for example, dozens of companies initiated quality circles, where groups of employees met to discuss ways to improve quality. When we looked for reasons for these efforts, many managers said that they had heard about quality circles at seminars, from books, or from colleagues in other companies who liked the concept. The motives given for investing in these programs varied: to be politically safe (''other companies are doing it; we don't want to be behind''), to respond to the request of a manager, who read a book or attended a seminar, or to help employees ''learn more about quality.'' While these are sometimes noble, and at times legitimate, reasons for initiating quality circles, they do not build competitive advantage, nor do they lead directly to improved customer value. As a result, many such programs that are based on noncompetitive criteria are simply quick-fixes that fail to endure.

CRITERIA FOR MANAGEMENT PRACTICES
AND HUMAN RESOURCE PROFESSIONALS[14]

To ensure that management practices become means for gaining a sustained competitive advantage, human resource professionals need to become strategic business partners and gear their activities to improving business performance. To do this they require a good working knowledge of the organization and its strategies. In assessing the role of human resources in an organization, management needs to determine the extent to which these professionals meet the following criteria:

1. Spend time with customers and clients—diagnosing, discussing, and responding to needs.

2. Actively participate in business planning meetings and offer informed insights on strategic, technological, and financial capabilities.
3. Act as both the guardians of and agents for changing shared mindset.
4. Understand business conditions.
5. Demonstrate competence in:
   a. Business knowledge, particularly customer relations.
   b. Delivery of world-class management practices.
   c. Management of change.

With these criteria, management and human resource professionals can collaborate and can better focus the human resource role in a competitive organization.

The ultimate responsibility, however, for using management practices to build organizational capability and competitiveness rests with all managers. As managers spend time on activities that affect employees and external stakeholders, they need to ensure that the practices they use add value for customers, implement business strategies, create and preserve a shared mindset, and help the business gain a stronger position in the marketplace.

6

Generating Competencies: Selection and Development

By and large, executives make poor promotion and staffing decisions. By all accounts, their batting average is no better than .333. At most one-third of such decisions turn out right; one-third are minimally effective; and one-third are outright failures. In no other area of management would we put up with such miserable performance. Indeed, we need not and should not. Managers making people decisions will never be perfect, of course, but they should come pretty close to batting 1.000.

Peter Drucker[1]

Regardless of an organization's product, access to capital, or leadership, if it lacks the ability to attract the right talent it will not be competitive and will eventually fail. A first step, then, is to generate employee competencies that provide the organization with the right mix of talent to meet existing and future needs.

Two organization processes are specifically aimed at meeting this objective. *Selection* generates competencies by the acquisition of new talent into an organization or the targeted promotion of employees who have demonstrated unique talents. Recruiting plays a primary role in generating competencies. Strong college athletic teams stay successful, to a great extent, because of their ability to attract outstanding athletes. Every year, the quality of each college team's new recruits is rated as a group, and these ratings prove to be surprisingly accurate predictors of the team's national ranking two or three years later. When Lou Holtz arrived at Notre Dame as football coach in 1985, he began aggressive recruiting efforts. In his first three years, his classes of recruits were ranked among the top five in the country each year—and a few years later the Notre Dame teams composed of these recruits won the national championship.

Development generates competencies through enhancing the talents of individuals already in an organization. Holtz would not have won national football championships without enhancing the talent of the players who were already on the Notre Dame team. Other coaches may have equally outstanding recruiting years but fail to develop talent as effectively. Recruiting good talent offers the foundation for success, but development translates good raw recruits into outstanding athletes. Recruiting is a necessary but not sufficient condition of success.

Both selection and development processes, if designed and implemented effectively, can help to build organizational capability. This chapter examines the key issues, managerial choices, and success indicators for using selection and development as tools for competitive advantage.

SELECTION

No single set of decisions affects a business's long-term viability more than who is hired. To build organizational capability, managers need to assume themselves—not delegate—hiring responsibility. This means they must learn and apply the skills necessary for effective hiring and aggressively monitor the hiring process.

Staffing and promotion decisions are critical to an organization for a number of reasons.[2] They determine whether an organization will have the talent necessary to meet customer expectations and implement strategy, respond to changing business conditions, and establish a shared mindset. Staffing decisions are also among the most costly for any organization. At IBM, a manager calculated the cost of hiring and retaining an employee for 35 years. Costs included direct costs of salary and benefits and indirect costs of office space, supplies, moving, training, and so forth. The total was $9 million over 35 years. Farm Credit Corporation put the figure at $4.5 million for 35 years. An expert in this field estimates that the cost to an organization in terms of lost productivity and training of an employee who fails and leaves after a few months ranges from $5,000 for an hourly employee to $75,000 for a manager. The cost may be even greater, he claims, if the misfit employee stays on.

To demonstrate the importance of staffing, we have done exercises in managerial seminars aimed at identifying the single most lethal weapon managers could employ against a competitor. After the managers have examined such areas as improving product quality and service, taking away customers, and reducing the competitor's access to capital, they nearly always conclude that the single most critical weapon would be to control hiring for six months at the competitor firm. If they could control who was hired, they could ensure that the competitor would be at a disadvantage not only for six months but over the long term.

Selection consists of three elements: hiring, promotion, and outplacement. The right choices in each of these areas will enhance an organization's competitive position.

Who Is Hired: Managerial Choices

The process of hiring involves five steps (see Figure 6-1). The ways in which each of these steps can be used to contribute directly to organizational capability are outlined as follows.

Setting Standards

Needs Analysis   A needs analysis analyzes the position to be filled and specifies the competencies (knowledge, skills, and abilities) that are required to perform the job. In too many firms, needs analysis is skipped completely or is done only in passing. Even when this is not the case, however, the emphasis is generally on past rather than future job requirements. To identify current and future business needs relevant to the position, questions need to be asked about the kinds of individuals who have filled the position in the past—that is, the competencies that persons who were successful in the job demonstrated—and about how anticipated

Figure 6-1
STEPS IN THE HIRING PROCESS

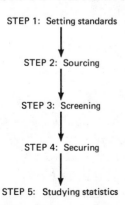

STEP 1: Setting standards

STEP 2: Sourcing

STEP 3: Screening

STEP 4: Securing

STEP 5: Studying statistics

changes in technology or customer requirements over the next five years will affect the competencies needed. The likely career path for this position, and the development that may be necessary to pursue it, should also be clarified. From the answers to these questions a profile will emerge of the type of person who could most effectively fill the job, which becomes a tool for assessing candidates.

Involving the individuals who will interact with the person to be hired will increase their awareness of the importance of the position and of management's commitment to filling it with a qualified candidate. Including them in the process helps the new employee gain acceptance and commitment even before a specific individual is selected to fill the job.

Technical and Cultural Fit   Often a needs analysis results in only a *technical* assessment of the knowledge, skills, and abilities that are required for the job. Hiring employees who will help build competitiveness means also allocating resources to ensuring the *cultural* fit of the future employee. At a U.S. Honda plant, job applicants must supply not only the traditional background information (degrees, previous experience, and so on) but they are asked to write an essay entitled, "How My Working at Honda Will Be Consistent with My Life Values." The essay enables managers to assess the extent to which the applicant's psychological background fits with the culture of company. In addition to the usual "technical" questions, interview questions include:

- ☐ Do you maintain your own car or motorcycle?
- ☐ What are your short- and long-term goals in life?
- ☐ What are you looking for in an employer?
- ☐ Why do you want to work for Honda?
- ☐ What is the best thing and the worst thing you've ever heard about Honda?
- ☐ If you were offered two jobs at the same pay and with the same benefits, what else would you consider to determine which company to work for?
- ☐ If you were working on the assembly line and couldn't keep up with it, what would you do?
- ☐ If somebody who had worked on the assembly line for five years kept passing you bad parts, what would you do?
- ☐ What would be your reaction if you were hired by Honda, but not assigned to work in your specialized area?

- □ In what areas are you most creative?
- □ Do you share your ideas with others?
- □ What is your definition of teamwork?
- □ What do you believe are some of the advantages and disadvantages of teamwork in the workplace?
- □ What is your average work week?

Cultural screens also have been used in hiring in the public sector. The Federal Aviation Administration (FAA), assesses candidates for positions as air traffic controllers first on the basis of their technical competencies—verbal ability, the ability to see in three-dimensional space, and so forth. In addition, cultural fit is an important predictor of a successul air traffic controller. FAA managers learned, for example, that creativity was not a cultural fit for an air traffic controller—the agency does not want to know if the controller can land an airplane looking in a mirror between his legs. Consistency, precision, commitment to the chain of command, and ability to make quick decisions were identified as some of the personality traits required for successful air traffic controllers. Knowing the importance of these qualifications in conjunction with technical competencies enabled the FAA to recruit from settings in which individuals with these characteristics are likely to be found—for example, the military and police and fire departments.

Hiring on the basis of technical fit alone may create problems. Data General, in the mid-1980s, wanted to compete more effectively with IBM. To do so, it hired a cadre of former IBM executives, believing that these individuals possess the competencies required to help Data General. The effort failed. In hindsight, Data General management determined that the mindset at IBM was that of a market leader rather than a market follower, with efforts aimed at acquiring large, national accounts rather than gaining market share piece by piece. In addition, their IBM training had inculcated in these individuals the habit of following rules and procedures, which was not compatible with Data General's more flexible and dynamic culture.

Data General's experience is not unique. Hiring employees who have technical skills but not the right personality characteristics may be a reason for Drucker's estimate that batting averages for hiring remain at .333. Drucker (1988) notes:

Some of the worst staffing failures I have seen involved brilliant Europeans hired by U.S. companies—one based in Pittsburgh, the other in Chicago—to head up new European ventures. Dr. Hans Schmidt and M. Jean Perrin (only the names are fictitious) were hailed as geniuses when they came in. A year later they were both out, totally defeated.

No one in Pittsburgh had understood that Schmidt's training and temperament would make him sit on a new assignment for the first six or nine months, thinking, studying, planning, getting ready for decisive action. Schmidt, in turn, had never even imagined that Pittsburgh expected action and immediate results. No one in Chicago had known that Perrin, while a solid and doggedly purposeful man, was excitable and mercurial, flailing his arms, making speeches about trivia, and sending up one trial balloon after another. Although both men subsequently became highly successful CEOs of major European corporations, both executives were failures in companies that did not know and understand them.

Sourcing Job Candidates

Internal versus External   Job candidates can be found both within and outside the company. Relying exclusively on either source can create problems: Hiring solely from outside reduces opportunities for current employees and thus weakens their commitment to the organization; exclusive hiring from within may limit the number of fresh ideas brought to the organization. Based on a study of 114 organizations, we have found that businesses tend to have optimum innovation, performance, and flexibility with an 80/20 ratio: 80 percent hired from within and 20 percent from outside the immediate business unit.[3]

Degree of Professional Experience   Candidates with varying degrees of professional experience can be recruited. Persons just out of school are likely to be more malleable in terms of ideas and approaches to work, more flexible and adaptive in terms of work assignments, and less expensive than experienced candidates from other companies. The latter, of course, come with more expertise, a greater ability to work on specific projects, and an ability to add value more quickly—and at a higher cost.

Whether to hire recent college graduates or professionals should be a decision based on the needs and philosophies of an organization. In businesses that compete through lower cost, standardized products, and long-term relationships with customers and have a philosophy of long-term employment, promotion from within, and stability of the work force, college graduates are generally more appropriate hires. Many businesses—among them utilities, telecommunications, consumer products, and pharmaceutical industries—that fit this description primarily hire college graduates. In businesses that compete through developing customized products, responding to changing technological conditions faster than competitors and entering new markets quickly, a balance between recent college graduates and experienced professionals may increase competitiveness.

Expanding the Pool   One way to meet the challenge of finding employees at all levels is to expand the pool of candidates. When the talent pool from which to draw employees is large, the probability of identifying better candidates increases.

Expanding the pool of employees who are paid by the hour is a major challenge in a shrinking labor market (see Chapter 2). Firms that hire large numbers of employees, for example, McDonald's, Marriott, and Sears, have used a variety of tactics to expand the labor pool. Encouraging referrals from existing employees, offering career progression and training, providing incentives to current employees (for example, $100 per candidate hired) for attracting new employees, providing transportation to and from work, and providing more flexible work hours and locations are among the tactics that have been used to expand the candidate pool. The ability to create a larger pool of candidates through marketing the company by building on existing relationships generally works better than advertising through signs, newspapers, and announcements.

Expanding the pool of college graduates is a relatively straightforward proposition. Identifying universities that have expertise in developing the competencies required by the business may lead to a targeted list of universities from which to recruit. Remember, however, in considering the competencies developed by the university, that cultural "fit" is also a component. One firm focused its hiring on only the "top ten" schools, mostly large universities with outstanding academic reputations. On studying the candidates that came out of these prestigious schools, however, management discovered that when these people were assigned to nonurban locations, their turnover rate increased dramatically. The firm began to expand its list of targeted schools to include universities in rural locations. While candidates with degrees from these schools did not have as much prestige as those from the top universities, their commitment to and performance in the firm were outstanding.

Companies are beginning to recognize that in global markets, selecting universities from which to recruit may require going beyond national boundaries. Businesses that have been most successful in entering the global market have sought employees from overseas. IBM, for example, with its strong presence on the campus of the University of Tokyo, has been able to hire graduates who can help IBM compete in Asia.

Identifying the universities or schools from which to recruit candidates is only the first step in expanding the external candidate pool. Working to expand relationships within the university to develop a favorable reputation further expands the candidate pool. Companies have used many techniques to become better known to students on campus: ongoing internship programs, monetary donations to the university, visits to classes and student groups, and meetings with faculty. By helping the company to gain a presence within the student community, these efforts expand the candidate pool of college hires.

To expand the pool of professional candidates, long-term relationships with head-hunters that parallel relationships with universities can be developed. Hiring from search firms is more problematic. Some firms have tried to expand the individual contributor candidate pool by staying in touch with individuals who did not accept job offers right out of school, forming joint ventures with other firms to share employees, and soliciting references from employees.

Although enlarging candidate pools takes time and money, the investment pays off if companies are able to choose from among a greater variety of candidates and thereby increase their chances of hiring people who meet their needs and help build their competitive position.

Screening

Candidate Interviews   The most common screening tool is the job interview. Unfortunately, many interviews are conducted ad hoc, and the resulting candidate selection may be equally random. If interviewers are not well trained to focus on the candidate's competencies and job fit, they may fall into the trap of recommending candidates who resemble themselves rather than ones who meet specific job requirements. The results of an interview may say more about the interviewer than the interviewee.

To use interviews more effectively, preparation should include a thorough analysis of the needs for the job and a plan for the interview itself, with a set of questions designed to probe the candidate's competencies. At least an hour of quiet, uninterrupted time should be set aside for the interview. Interview questions should encourage the candidate to cite examples from his or her experience, on the job or otherwise, that can be used to evaluate his or her competence. Open-ended questions beginning with "what," "how," "tell me about" encourage a candidate to talk. Once the interviewer has obtained a clear impression of the candidate's qualifications, it is important to communicate a realistic and accurate view of current and future job opportunities. For the candidate, it is as important to determine whether the position matches his or her interests and expectations. Finally, at the end of the interview, the candidate's questions about the company should be answered.

Multiple Interviews   Since the investment in people is so extensive in many companies and the costs of making poor hiring decisions are enormous, most firms conduct multiple interviews. At IBM, potential managers spend up to a week being interviewed by many individuals throughout the company. At the end of the week, all of the interviewers share notes, and each ranks the candidates. Generally, the top and bottom quartiles of the rankings are consistent. At Trammell Crow, candidates for managerial jobs are interviewed not only by multiple partners but also by a secretary or one of the company's younger leasing agents. This practice eliminates job seekers who impressed the partners but snubbed those lower in the hierarchy.

Other companies, as we have already seen, have begun to have customers or suppliers interview candidates for key positions. Particularly in cases where the employee will have direct customer contact, customers may be involved in screening final candidates. This practice ensures that customer needs are taken into account and at the same time makes a customer feel more committed to both the firm and the new person to be hired.

Multiple Candidates   A senior manager in a General Electric division interviewed over twenty candidates for an important position before he found someone who filled the requirements. While he was at times frustrated, and the hiring process stretched out over three months, he was confident that by the time he had finished the applicant selected would be the right person for the job. The traditional process whereby the hiring manager interviews two or three candidates prescreened by a personnel or human resource department has changed; the line manager may now actively interview dozens of potential hirees.

Realistic Job Previews   At present, what are known as job previews often consist simply of having the interviewer describe what a day on the job might be like. To be more realistic, however, job previews need to go further and actually simulate work conditions. At McKinsey & Company, four or five candidates meet with two or three McKinsey managers. These candidates are given a brief description of a current consulting assignment and are then asked to work as a team for a set period of time (two to three hours) to formulate a recommendation to the McKinsey interviewers as if they were the client. During this process, McKinsey managers observe each candidate's ability to apply technical expertise to the problem, deal with complex issues, function as part of a team, determine how to approach a client, and make recommendations consistent with McKinsey's philosophy.

At Toyota's assembly plant in Kentucky, teams of four or five candidates spend a half day in a simulated business. Each team is given a circuit board, a description of the company that makes the boards, and play money. Teams must make decisions about the most effective and profitable ways to find suppliers, assemble the boards, and maintain quality control. There are also mock production lines, where applicants assemble tubes or circuit boards. The candidates then spend six hours in a room assembling and disassembling a set of plastic pipes and equipment. The idea is to identify candidates who can keep a fast pace, endure repetitive work, and stay alert.

At Mazda and Diamond-Star, a joint venture between Chrysler and Mitsubishi, applicants are told they must learn several jobs, change shifts, work overtime, make and take constructive criticism, and submit a steady stream of recommendations for improvement. The screening process excludes about 24 percent of applicants based on written, drug, and medical tests; another 40 percent fall out based on the simulation experience. Mazda, Toyota, and Diamond-Star spend approximately $13,000 per employee to staff their U.S. plants.

The extensive screening efforts of Japanese firms starting plants in the United States has begun to be replicated by firms such as General Electric, General Motors, Ford, and Marriott. Realistic job previews ensure that future employees will have the capacity to build competitiveness, adapt to change, accomplish business strategies, and contribute to unity within the company.

Securing

Company Commitment   The screening undertaken by Toyota, Mazda, and other companies is simultaneously a commitment-building process. As employees spend more time in simulations and continue to pass the ''hurdles'' of entering the company, they become increasingly committed to being a part of the successful venture. The Marine recruitment slogan, ''We are looking for a few good men'' builds the commitment of the ''few'' who are selected to join the ranks. As the enlisted Marines feel special and part of a unique group, they come to feel the commitment of the Marine Corps to them.

Company commitment is also demonstrated by outlining for the applicant the career opportunities that might exist in the organization. At Marriott, employees who begin in strictly operational jobs (doorman, waitress, bellman) are told that the organization is committed to helping them move into managerial jobs to the extent that they demonstrate interest in the career opportunities available. McDonald's has gone so far as to initiate a ''university'' to train future managers and help employees with career progression.

Some service firms have followed the lead of major league sports, offering sign-up bonuses to secure large numbers of employees. The bonus may take the form not of money but of incentives such as a free television set, VCR, or tickets to an event if the applicant performs well on the job for a period of time (often three or six months). By being sensitive to individual needs, the company demonstrates its commitment to all its employees.

In the ranks of managers and technicians, company commitment to employees is critical, particularly for persons in specialized jobs. To demonstrate commitment to promising job applicants, companies may stay in close touch by phone—with senior managers almost daily—and issue invitations to company functions. In addition, many companies focus on securing candidates by being sensitive to their overall life situations. In the case of candidates with families, companies may invite the spouse to visit the firm's facilities, arrange visits with schools and community leaders, or aggressively seek employment for the spouse in neighboring companies. For single employees, companies may highlight the social setting outside work.

The changing demographics of the work force will make securing candidates with the desired competencies increasingly difficult. Offering attractive work environments, career paths, and outside opportunities will be critical success factors for companies hoping to attract the most qualified employees.

Studying Statistics

To ensure that the hiring process operates effectively, a number of statistics need to be monitored. First, the total number of employees required must be calculated. This number may be a function of business strategy, technological change, competitive pressures, and/or market conditions.[4] To determine the number of employees needed in different job categories, managers need to identify how current and future business trends will influence the number and types of employees needed.

Second, statistics can be kept about the mix and diversity of employees within a business. Demographic data on employees— sex, race, age, and nationality—may help a business focus its hiring decisions. For example, one organization routinely declared hiring freezes and offered early retirements during downturns. However, after collecting data on the age of the remaining work force, management found that 95 percent of employees were between the ages of 30 and 50. They realized that such a narrow age span would lead to long-term problems and possible gaps in managerial talent as the organization recovered and again began to grow. As a result, management initiated policies and procedures to widen the age range of employees.

Organizations have traditionally maintained a diversity of race, sex, and nationality among employees primarily and exclusively to meet government Equal Employment Opportunity (EEO) requirements. Such thinking is now obsolete. Today, maintaining diversity of race, sex, and nationality enhances a company's competitive advantage. When a firm can attract from a large talent pool, it is more likely to find better-qualified job candidates. We asked the vice president of the research lab of a New York-based software company why he was committed to maintaining a diversity of talent in his business. He told us that while he agreed with the social agenda, he was also driven to do so by an economic agenda. In his research domain, 25 percent of the college graduates were women and minorities (broadly defined as non-Caucasian). He explained that if his business was attractive to these diverse groups, he had a larger talent pool from which to seek candidates.

Third, statistics can be kept about the status of employees within the organization. At Eastman Kodak's Kodak Park, which employs about 20,000 people, 10 percent of the work force is composed of "supplementals," or part-time workers who serve as "buffers" for Eastman Kodak. In times of slow growth, these workers are more likely to be laid off. They buffer the permanent work force from employment swings and make possible greater employment stability. Some New York law firms currently contract services from free-lance attorneys. Using contract employees allows the firms to meet customer expectations and at the same time retain flexibility.

Who Is Promoted: Managerial Choices

Managers must make three types of choices when considering promoting an individual within the organization (see Figure 6–2). First, a series of content issues must be examined to ensure that *what action is taken* is appropriate. Second, choices must be made with respect to the promotion process, to ensure that *how the action taken* is appropriate. Third, the level at which the promotion occurs also must be considered.[5]

Content

Tie to Business Needs Any promotion that is intended to build competitiveness must be tied to future business needs. When Reginald Jones selected Jack Welch as his successor at General Electric, he said that he looked into the future—the 1980s and

Figure 6–2
WHO IS PROMOTED: MANAGERIAL CHOICES

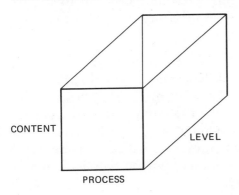

CONTENT   LEVEL

PROCESS

1990s—and saw a need for a leader with skills very different from his own. Jones believed that the head of General Electric needed to be technically knowledgeable and be able to make difficult decisions and respond rapidly to changing business conditions. Welch, with a Ph.D. in chemical engineering, possessed these characteristics—as he has clearly demonstrated during his tenure as CEO of General Electric.

Identifying future business needs requires assessing changes that may occur among the firm's stakeholders—customers, suppliers, financiers, unions, competitors, and government agencies. It also requires examining industry trends in developing world markets, in technology, and in economic growth. These business needs then translate into a specific set of competencies consistent with changing conditions.

Tie to Performance Promotion within a company may be tied more to internal politics and relationships than to demonstrated performance. Effective promotion systems demand performance rather than politics as the fundamental criterion. At IBM, General Electric, Rockwell, AT&T, and other companies,[6] checks and balances have been established around succession planning to ensure that relationships do not outweigh performance as a factor in promotion. One tool for maintaining these checks and balances is the slate system. In this system, a manager with a job opening prepares a slate of candidates who she or he thinks are qualified to fill the position. Then, rather than merely select her choice from the slate of candidates, this slate is then considered by a corporate review committee, which can add to, subtract from, or return the slate to the manager with no changes. The manager is then asked to interview all the candidates on the slate. Under the slate system, potential candidates who might not have been on an original slate are given consideration and opportunity for promotion.

Track High-Potential Candidates Successful succession-planning systems track high-potential candidates and ensure that they have the competencies necessary to take on future work. These succession-planning systems also ensure that individuals receive the development opportunities they need to stretch their skills. In one company, for example, decisions are systematically made about when individuals should be given the opportunity to gain experience outside their native country.

Balance Internal and External Promotion   Hiring exclusively from inside the business may limit creativity and flexibility, while finding employees only from outside may reduce morale and limit career opportunities of employees. The optimum ratio of internal to external hiring depends on business needs. Research indicates that companies which undergo strategic redirection, or shift their business strategies, often do so about two or three years after hiring a senior executive from outside the company.[7] Businesses needing to redirect their strategies may be well served by promoting from outside the company, although, as we have seen, extensive hiring from outside creates blockages and morale problems among employees.

Use Dual Ladders[8]   In traditional promotion patterns, employees rise through one function or specialty and then move laterally into a managerial career track (one can move up the technical career ladder only so far and then must shift to the managerial track). Increasingly, businesses are finding that dual career paths are more appropriate. In companies that use dual career paths, employees in a functional specialty remain in that specialty yet receive remuneration consistent with that of persons on the managerial track. For specialists, the rewards on the technical track may be high. They may include, in addition to salary, resources (money, staff, and equipment) for research, time off for further education and for professional exposure and development, and greater flexibility in and control over one's work.

Process

Allocate Responsibility   Primary responsibility for promotion decisions lies with the line manager. While human resource professionals may help collect information, serve as a sounding board for decisions, and be a catalyst to ensure that the correct issues are addressed in making a decision, the primary responsibility rests with the line manager. To fulfill this responsibility effectively, a line manager needs to be personally involved in key meetings, make promotion decisions, and monitor results.

Ensure Management Dedication   In a busy organization, some promotion decisions may receive only secondary and fleeting attention. For such decisions to be the right ones, managers with primary responsibility for promotion must devote time to the decision-making process. One company that voiced its commitment to succession planning held an annual half-day meeting focusing on making promotion decisions. In this meeting, pictures and biographies of top employees were flashed on a screen and managers commented on their potential.

By contrast, in some Baxter Healthcare divisions, every quarter, the top managers go off-site for an intensive two-day meeting. Changing market conditions are examined along with the business strategies that will be needed to respond to these new developments. Then each manager who is in a position to affect the ability of the division to implement the new strategy is discussed. His or her current ability to meet business requirements is discussed, and areas for further training and development are identified. As a result of these meetings, Baxter management believes that business strategies are likely to be effectively executed, because key managers have the necessary competencies to do their work.

At General Electric, Jack Welch spends 40 percent of his time on people issues, much of it on promotion decisions. His belief that "strategy follows people" suggests that the time spent selecting the right person for the right job at the right time will have enormous strategic implications.

Ensure Commitment to the Plan   A few years ago, we asked a number of companies to report the percentage of managerial candidates who were promoted "according to plan." Not surprisingly, there was a positive correlation between the percentage staffed according to plan and business performance. Businesses that showed lower performance failed to follow the plan far more often than those with higher performance. Obviously, part of the deviation from plan may have been because using the existing talent pool led to poor performance, and deviating from the plan served to expand the talent pool. However, another part of the problem might have been that expectations raised through the succession-planning process failed to be met, and employees reduced their commitment to the organization.

In either case, it is important to follow through on the succession plan. If employees are not being placed according to plan, it is a sign that either the business is changing more rapidly than expected or the promotion-planning process is not being used effectively.

Another criterion for promotion is whether an employee's division has served as the source of managerial talent within a company. A CEO of a major organization, in describing the performance of the executives who reported to him directly, noted that one woman was technically excellent but that he was unsure of her managerial ability. His main indicator was that few, if any, managers ever grew out of her division. He believed that her commitment to developing further managers was weaker than it should be, and this hurt her opportunities for promotion.

Begin with Employees   The planning of promotions in one company was delegated to a small, exclusive corporate staff. This staff analyzed changing company needs, profiled employee talents, and made matches between company needs and employee talents. It then approached employees with the "good news" that they were being considered for promotion. Such a system worked only with flexible and independent employees.

With dual careers, changing family structures, and employees whose values may integrate work and nonwork activities, however, corporate-driven promotions may do more harm than good. The above company, when confronted with an employee who would not relocate due to personal or family reasons, tended to relegate that employee to career oblivion. After examining its system, the company changed the process for promotion planning and began with employees. Before assessing fit between employee and job, employees were asked about their interest in alternative careers. In candid interviews, employees were told that career paths in the company could take a variety of forms and time sequences. Individuals with other commitments for specific time periods were not placed in the unfortunate position of selecting between a career and their personal lives. The pay-off was outstanding: Employees who might otherwise have been declared career dead were able to make long-term career choices. For example, one manager delayed a relocation for two years because of her children's active involvement in high school activities. However, after the two years, her career opportunities grew rapidly as she was able to be more flexible.

Levels

Distinguish Levels   A colleague proposed that all decisions involving promotion planning be made through extensive dialogue and with few formal procedures. In principle, we agree; in practice, we disagree. We believe that the type of promotion-planning system to be used depends to some extent on the level of promotion being considered.

For senior executives, succession plans should be characterized by more dialogue and less paperwork, by more crystal-ball estimates of the future of the business and fewer definitive statements of exact job titles and responsibilities. For middle managers, succession planning should be characterized by more consistent procedures to ensure quality and equity throughout an organization. For professional employees, succession planning may be further defined to help identify career tracks and let employees know how they can prosper within an organization. While the importance of promotion or succession planning remains constant across levels of an organization, the degree of formality may vary.

Who Is Outplaced: Managerial Choices

Outplacing employees as a means of downsizing corporations has received enormous attention in the past few years as most large companies have reduced the size of their work forces. The way a company reduces its size communicates the values of the company perhaps more than any other area of activity. The extent to which the firm seeks alternatives to outplacement, the processes it uses to implement outplacements if they are necessary, and the attention it pays to remaining employees all send forceful messages to employees and stakeholders.

First, many firms fall into the trap of outplacing employees merely through layoffs. We propose that there are several alternatives to layoffs (see Figure 6-3). At IBM, for example, fourteen steps must be taken before using layoffs as the primary downsizing strategy (see Figure 6-4). These steps communicate two critical messages to employees: (1) IBM will take actions to meet market demands and be competitive; and (2) in the process, IBM will offer employees every opportunity for stability. The buffer work force at Eastman Kodak is designed to provide employment stability for permanent employees. In one slow period at Hewlett-Packard, to avoid layoffs all employees worked nine days and took the tenth day off without pay.

Second, if businesses face the unenviable task of laying off employees, management's behavior and the process used during

Figure 6-3
ALTERNATIVES TO LAYOFFS

Alternative	Description	Potential Problems	Example of Use
Job sharing	Two employees reduce to half time and essentially share one full-time job, pay, and benifits.	1. Difficulty in dividing division of benefits. 2. Only for employees with specialized skills.	Polaroid Corporation: 100 hourly employees. Some worked half days, some one month on, one month off.
Leave of absence	Workers are encouraged to take unpaid leaves with jobs guaranteed upon their return.	Few takers.	Pacific Northwest Bell Telephone
Work sharing	Reductions are made in both hours and pay. In some states workers are eligible for partial unemployment benefits.	Most acceptable to workers in two-income families.	Hewlett-Packard's "nine-day fortnight" policy.
Less paid time off	Reductions are made in paid vacation time or workers are given fewer holiday weekends.	Small effect unless company is large.	Mountain Bell saved 92,150 work days during 1982.
Attrition	Staff reductions are made by leaving unfilled vacancies resulting from retirement, death, or resignation.	1. Important jobs sometimes go untended. 2. Slow and often unpredictable.	Federal government.
Pay freezes	Salary increases are postponed.		Union Carbide postponed salary increases for all employees and some managers.
Pay cuts	Salaries are reduced by a certain percentage.		Natomas Company: Top executives took 10 percent cut.
Demotion	Some jobs are reclassified with concomitant reduction in compensation.	Perceived loss of status of demoted employees.	Boeing Aerospace demoted 250 management employees.
Early retirement incentives	Employees who retire early are offered full pension benefits, cash bonuses, or additional supplementary payments.	Employers have no control over who accepts or rejects incentives.	3M offered early retirement with full pension credit to all of its 20-year employees who were at least 55 years old. 950 employees signed up.
Early retirement incentives and rehiring selected retirees as consultants	Same as above, but part-time consulting contracts awarded to critical personnel who decide to retire.		Union Bank lost a vice president who specialized in personal service to blue-chip customers. She was awarded a part-time consulting contract.
Resignation and rehiring selected persons as part-time consultants	Middle managers in areas such as purchasing, pensions, and planning are encouraged to resign and sign on as outside consultants.	Limited to middle managers in support functions.	Xerox expects program to apply to 25 percent of its corporate management staff. Offers separation bonuses and consultant fees at 95 percent of salary. Fringe benefits are discontinued. Employees are linked through microcomputers.

these periods send loud and consistent messages. Some companies rely on defined longevity standards as their criterion for determining who stays and who goes. Others use job performance as their guide. The candor and openness with which these standards are applied are important. Offering outplaced

Figure 6–4
STEPS IBM TAKES TO SAVE JOBS

Constantly retrains work force, and moves work between IBM plants
Reduces temporary work and overtime
Has employees take unused vacations and encourages leave of absence
Limits student internships in laboratories and other facilities
Limits employee transfer requests to overstaffed plants
Curtails or freezes hiring
Asks workers to move voluntarily to other IBM plants
Sets up early retirement incentives
Brings work that has been contracted out back to IBM plants
Has other IBM plants hire workers away from overstaffed facilities
Transfers employees to other, comparable jobs in the same plant
Transfers workers to lower-grade jobs
Relocates employees to positions at other IBM plants

employees severance packages communicates sensitivity on the part of the company, helps maintain a favorable company image, and reduces the possibility of litigation. Some companies in traditionally volatile industries have formed alliances to share employees across companies; others work aggressively to find new employment opportunities to avoid the trauma of layoffs. During and after layoffs, many companies offer counseling to employees and their families to work through the emotional trauma of career change.

Third, while it is critical to pay attention to laid-off employees, those remaining also require attention. The commitment of remaining employees to the company can be enhanced if management communicates to them what the future work-force reduction might be and how they can help avoid further layoffs. For example, in one company facing layoffs, management spent a great deal of time communicating to the remaining employees the reasons for the reduction, the criteria used to make layoff decisions, and the outcomes anticipated as a result of the reduction. The company also opened lines of communication with open meetings, question-and-answer sessions, and videos. These efforts were designed primarily to shore up the morale of the employees remaining with the firm.

Staffing: Success Indicators

We have seen that decisions concerning who is hired, promoted, and outplaced are critical for business success and that management has a primary responsibility to ensure that the choices made will increase competitiveness, help accomplish strategy, and establish a shared mindset.

To ensure success in the staffing area, we propose nine key questions for management to consider in monitoring staffing activities:

1. What competencies does my business require now and in the future to meet customer expectations?
2. What are the sources for acquiring talent for my business now and in the future? How would I assess our current relationships with these sources? What can be done to develop better relationships?
3. What is the cost versus benefit of hiring employees for one, three, and five years?
4. What is the success rate for attraction (percentage of candidates offered jobs who accepted) and retention (percentage of employees who started and stayed with the company)?
5. How many people are involved in our hiring process? To what extent do we include customers in this process?
6. What percentage of individuals are promoted according to the existing succession plan?
7. What percentage of people are eligible to retire in one, three, or five years? What gaps, if any, exist in the replacement pool for this talent?
8. How much management time and attention are paid to developing back-up talent?
9. What are ways to reduce overall labor costs without a reduction in the labor force?

As managers pose these questions, they can make staffing decisions that lead to a better batting average than the .333 cited by Peter Drucker.

DEVELOPMENT

Development activities help businesses increase their competitive edge by ensuring that employees acquire the competencies required to meet customer expectations. As a vehicle for communicating information to employees about changing business conditions, these activities help firms manage and adapt to change. And by communicating what will need to be done to meet strategic, technological, or financial goals, such activities help businesses implement strategies. Finally, development activities help create unity among program participants about both ends and means.

Development activities have changed radically in the last decade.[9] A number of firms have already redefined their executive development activities to be *competitive weapons* rather than traditional training programs. The Center for Executive Development in Cambridge, Massachusetts, in examining the practices of world-class firms, identified those that offer world-class executive development. These include Aetna, Arthur Anderson, AT&T, Bank of America, Bellcore, Data General, Eastman Kodak, First Chicago, Ford, General Electric, General Motors, IBM, Mellon Bank, Merrill Lynch, Milliken, Tektronix, Travelers, and Whirlpool.[10] To illustrate the essential principles of how these firms use development as a competitive weapon, we offer two minicases.

Whirlpool Corporation

Jack Sparks, the chairman of Whirlpool Corporation, also served as the head of the executive development committee. He identified the management of human resources as a critical success factor. After a thorough assessment and needs analysis, Whirlpool opted to invest in executive education as a means of becoming more competitive.

Rather than purchase an "off-the-shelf" program, Whirlpool management invested resources to customize its executive-development experience. To do so, human resource professionals worked in concert with the executive committee to identify the major strategic challenges that the company would face in the coming year. In its first year, the Whirlpool Executive Program focused on managing change; the second year it emphasized becoming a global competitor; and the theme of the third year was becoming more competitive.

External consultants hired by management were asked first to learn about Whirlpool's unique business challenges and then to tailor their presentations to address those challenges. Each external faculty member spent time with the CEO and other Whirlpool executives to gain a perspective on how the material he or she normally taught would help Whirlpool become more competitive. The external faculty also met as a group to coordinate their separate material into a unified presentation structured around the theme of the week-long program.

Internal facilitators worked with the external faculty to deliver the program. On the first and last days, the chairman and vice chairman reviewed in detail the themes and rationale of the program and committed participants not merely to attend but to apply what was being presented.

The results were dramatic over both the short and the long term. In the short term, participants learned where to focus their attention in the next year and acquired specific tools to make changes happen. For example, out of one program came a better understanding of how to analyze the company's competitors. Participants were more able to position their products against those of the competition and learned how to identify ways in which their products and services met customer needs better than those of competitors. Another program stressed becoming more competitive globally. Here, participants gained an understanding of global competition, pinpointing what it would take to succeed in the world marketplace. The long-term benefit was that with this increased awareness, Whirlpool was able to form an alliance with Phillips and enter over thirty international markets to become one of the largest global appliance manufacturers.

Borg-Warner

When Borg-Warner faced the prospects of a hostile takeover, management responded by implementing a leveraged buyout (LBO; see Chapter 1). The rationale was that the LBO would dramatically focus the business on managing costs and meeting high debt requirements. Management realized that for the LBO to succeed, company executives needed to understand not only what had to be done during the LBO, but why the LBO had been initiated.

The executive development staff at Borg-Warner worked with the senior management team to design a three-day development experience that met the two needs that had been identified. All top managers who would be immediately affected by the LBO attended the program, which emphasized why the LBO had occurred, from an economic and strategic perspective. Specific strategic, financial, and organizational changes that would be required to make the LBO work were identified. The program also enabled managers to enter into dialogue with senior executives to understand the LBO and its implications more fully. Finally, each participant left with a personal agenda for what he or she could do to help accomplish the goals of the LBO.

This development experience not only filled a short-term information need—to understand the LBO. By winning their commitment to the LBO and creating a shared mindset about it, participants learned to respond to the pressures the LBO had created. The success of the program was measured not only in terms of how participants felt about it but on the basis of the company's success in meeting its new business goals.

Similar development experiences have been initiated in a number of organizations. These firms have redefined executive development as a means of becoming more competitive rather than acquiring and transfering information. To make development into a competitive weapon, two primary changes in the traditional approach to development must be effected: traditional training efforts must themselves be redefined, and the use of alternatives to traditional training must be expanded.

Training

Outcomes of Management Development

Management training outcomes traditionally focus on developing conceptual understanding and skill building for participants. Participants attend programs to gain new ideas or to learn new skills in such areas as marketing, business strategy, human resources, or leadership.* While skill building is critical and concepts are central to creating organizational capability, more is required for management development to be a critical factor in building competitive advantage. For development to translate into competitiveness, participants must not only learn new skills but be able to apply them. The skills taught must be more than merely technical ones, such as computer skills, interpreting financial reports, and

---

*We are establishing in this discussion two polarities: development as a competitive weapon and traditional training. To highlight the extremes, we overstate each.

listening skills. Instead, the focus must be on creating business success through integrating personal competencies into organizational capability.

Development as intervention requires and assumes that the outcome of a workshop or seminar directly translates to business performance, so that the lessons learned apply immediately to actual business conditions. Development programs as competitive weapons are less ''charm schools'' and more ''boot camps,'' where new values and approaches to work are instilled (see the horizontal axis of Figure 6–5).

A fundamental assumption behind management development as a competitive weapon is that participants leave not only with knowledge of concepts and skills needed to be competitive, but with an appreciation of how the skills they have acquired can be used within the organization setting. A successful program is

Figure 6–5
OUTCOMES AND LEVELS OF MANAGEMENT DEVELOPMENT

OUTCOMES

	Management Development for Competitiveness					Traditional Management Training
LEVELS	Intervention	Problem-Solving	Team Building	Attitude Change	Skill Building	Conceptual Understanding
Officers						
Executives						
Senior Managers						
Middle Managers						
First-line Supervisors						
Individual Contributors						
New Employees						

measured not by "smile sheets" at the end of a session but by the ability of the participants to identify and implement changes in their areas of responsibility that will put the firm in a stronger competitive position.

The fundamental shift in executive development for competitiveness is redefining *why* participants attend a development experience: NOT to gain new understanding, NOT to learn new concepts, NOT to learn new skills, but to become more *committed*, more *focused*, and more *competitive*. We turn now to the critical issues to be considered if this fundamental shift in mindset about the purpose of development programs is to be accomplished.

Training: Key Success Factors

Participation in Management Development Management training often involves only first-line supervisors or middle managers. For development to lead to competitive advantage, however, employees from every level of the organization must participate in development experiences. For new employees, the focus should be on ensuring that they comprehend and are able to implement critical leadership competencies that are required for progressing up in the business. For first-line supervisors, the focus should be on defining and implementing new models of power and influence to motivate employees. Middle managers should be helped and encouraged to develop personal leadership agendas that establish them as critical sources of support for organizational success. For senior managers, development experiences should provide the impetus for changing how businesses compete by using the development experience as a forum for discussing the future direction of the organization and putting into place the means for moving in that direction.

Unfortunately, many standard, off-the-shelf training courses focus on the types of learning illustrated in the bottom right quadrant of Figure 6–5: conceptual learning and skill building for new employees (orientation) and first-line supervisors (management-skills courses). Many companies emphasize the type of learning represented in the top right quadrant. Senior managers attend development programs as a means of learning new concept or skills. We characterize this quadrant as the "parade of stars" program. In such programs, a parade of outstanding speakers— many from universities or consulting firms—present prepackaged and well-scripted messages, often to the short-term delight of the participants. However, it is up to the participant to integrate these messages into his or her own practices and translate them into action. Like circus audiences, participants watch, are entertained, and leave the seminars feeling good. However, little intervention has occurred and, for the most part, businesses are not more competitive as a result of them.

To make development programs a competitive weapon, a portion of the effort should be allocated to actitivtes in each of the four quadrants of Figure 6–5. At times, concepts and skills must be provided as a foundation for dealing with future changes within a company. However, teaching concepts and skills does not make development a competitive weapon. General Electric's Management Development Institute offers programs throughout the matrix.[11] From new employees to officers, it offers a portfolio of development activities to help employees change their managerial behavior throughout their careers as well as learn new skills and gain insights.

In addition, some companies, including Marriott, IBM, and Motorola, draw external stakeholders into their management-development activities.[12] In one company, 10 percent of all training-course slots are reserved for key customers and suppliers. In another, chief executives of major customers attend three days of a one-week top executive program. By inviting senior officers from customer firms to attend, the development experience is used to build customer commitment and create a shared mindset between the business and its stakeholders.

Ownership of Management Development   Traditionally management development is delegated to, and thus "owned by," human resource departments. Top managers may participate symbolically in short segments, but the human resource professionals design and deliver the courses.

For management development to work as a competitive weapon, however, top managers, particularly the CEO, must assume primary responsibility for the design, presentation, and follow-up of programs. Key decisions on who will staff the program, who will administer it, who will attend, what will be discussed, and how results will be assessed should be made by the persons who have the primary responsibility for the business. With this approach, management demonstrates its commitment to the program—in itself an important part of gaining the commitment of participants—and also ensures that participants understand how management views the business.

At Whirlpool, Borg-Warner, General Electric, Ford, AT&T, and other companies, development activities are the responsibility of top managers. Participants attend programs sponsored, hosted, and delivered by senior executives, not staff specialists. At Aetna, management education is overseen by a committee of vice presidents from line divisions; AT&T's management education is the responsibility of a group of senior officers.

Content of Management Development Traditional management training focuses on generic management principles presented through lectures and case studies. To be a competitive weapon, management development must focus on implementing a business's strategy. In one company, all management-development activities are required to be directly connected to a business strategy. In practice, this means that each seminar—whether on technical, marketing, or managerial skills— is introduced by a module on business context and business strategy. This module becomes the critical element in each program. Such a format helps participants understand *why* a management-development program is being offered, how the course content was determined, and how to apply what they would learn.

Another company tied management development to business strategy by using a customer screen to design the program. Each module had to be directly linked to a customer requirement or expectation. In designing the program, the different principles and activities taught had to be tied to their specific value to customers.

Finally, the content of development programs should be focused, not diffuse. Competitiveness comes from shooting rifles, not shotguns. The managerial behaviors that must be acquired for a business to accomplish its strategies should be identified and then applied to specific situations. When this focus exists, management development accomplishes its intended purpose rather than being a smorgasbord of alternatives. Thus, standardized programs need to be replaced by company-specific ones. Standardized cases need to be supplanted by live cases or cases specific to the participant's business. Participants can write their own cases before the program, then use the material learned in the workshop to assess their own cases rather than being forced to apply principles from external cases.

Presenters in Management Development Traditionally facilitators in management development are training specialists from either inside or outside the business. While these presenters know and understand their own material, they may not be able to relate it specifically to the participants' business.

If management development is to serve as a competitive weapon, senior managers must also play a part in presenting information. At Whirlpool, each external faculty member was introduced by the general manager of the company, who discussed not only what the consultant would say but why it was important. At Eastman Kodak, general managers take an active role in the Kodak Management Program and offer insights into a variety of business issues. At General Electric, senior officers continually attend management-development sessions, so that participants see that the experience is connected with the firm's ongoing business objectives.

When internal managers make management-development presentations, participants understand immediately how the material relates to their business needs. Participants also receive a clear signal that it is politically safe to risk new behaviors. Finally, participant commitment to change is increased when general managers facilitate discussions. One manager summarized the roles of different presenters as follows:

> When outside facilitators present, participants learn;
> When general managers present, participants learn and pay attention;
> When customers present, participants learn, pay attention, and act!

At Marriott Corporation, senior managers use development programs as a vehicle to communicate their goals for the year. In other companies as diverse as the U.S. Postal Service, the Internal Revenue Service, Baxter Healthcare, and Digitial Equipment Company, executives actively participate in designing and delivering management-training programs.

Duration of Management Development   Traditional management-training programs are bounded: They have a beginning and an end. Participants arrive, register, learn, and leave. Programs are often ''off-site'' events quite separate from the firm's day-to-day business activities.

When development is used as a competitive weapon, the distinction between program time and work time is blurred. Program time is also work time. Before attending a program, participants may be asked to do extensive preparation. In different companies, preparation has ranged from reading business plans and speeches to writing a case on a business problem to working with management to plan what will be done in the program to forming a team of program participants to solve a particular business problem. In each case, the development experience is used to meet participants' ongoing business needs rather than merely to gain conceptual understanding.

In addition to preparation, development as a competitive weapon merges follow-up with the program. To ensure follow-up, some companies have made their programs open-ended. In one company, at the conclusion of the formal training, participants wrote memos to their bosses summarizing what they had learned. Participants then shared their memos with other employees in work groups. In another company, participants end the program by entering into formal contracts with each other on what will happen as a result of the program, such as how each participant will interact with other participants. Companies may build in follow-up days as refreshers to ensure that program content becomes practice.

In each case, companies blur the time span of the development experience. Participants work before and after the formal training experience. In a number of companies, the traditional one- or two-week program has been replaced by a series of one- or two-day workshops. At the end of each workshop, participants have a specific practice to implement. Two weeks to a month later, the group meets again to share experiences in implementing the ideas and to acquire new ideas and make new commitments. By so doing, the development experience becomes an integrated, ongoing part of work rather than a discrete off-site event.

Teamwork within Management Development   Traditional management training brings individuals together and hopes that they will have the wisdom, courage, and insight to implement new concepts. For management development to be used as a competitive weapon, existing work teams need to be brought together to ensure support for accomplishing new work behaviors.

Attending seminars in intact teams allows participants to use the workshop to discuss and apply new concepts to on-the-job activities. It also enables them to contract with each other about how they will implement training materials. Teams also shift the focus of the experience from generic concepts to relevant business strategies. In one organization, teams met with senior managers before attending the development workshop. The managers discussed with the team members the company's business plan and identified two or three critical challenges the firm would be facing. Together with the senior managers, the team committed to spend time at the workshop (during evenings and break-out groups) to focus on how the concepts discussed should be applied to the strategic problems that had been identified. At the end of the seminar, the senior managers received a report, based on the material that had been presented, from the team proposing how to meet the business challenges the managers had identified before the workshop started.

Team attendance leads to quicker implementation of new ideas, because social pressure encourages application. Teams offer multiple insights into similar problems, so that a variety of approaches can be explored. Ford and General Electric offered a creative approach by jointly sponsoring a week-long management-training program for teams of employees from both organizations. This experience served to build competitiveness for both Ford and General Electric as employees from each company learned to understand each other and operate on similar management principles.

Linking Management Development to Other Management Practices   Management development is only one human resource practice that can help a business gain competitiveness. To be used effectively, it must be integrated with other human resource practices. Some businesses link development and staffing by ensuring that employees who are promoted pass through selected development experiences. Development through all stages of their careers ensures that employees acquire the competencies that are critical to business success. By linking development to performance appraisal, a firm can ensure that employees receive the proper opportunities to remedy weaknesses identified in their appraisals. Communication becomes part of the development process when senior managers participate and share with employees their thinking on issues affecting the organization. Finally, development sends clear messages to employees about what is expected of them and at the same time helps them to meet those expectations effectively.

Criteria for Development Programs   Based on experience in a variety of different kinds of firms, we have identified 24 questions that can be asked about current or future development programs to help determine the likelihood of their effectiveness in building organizational competitiveness. These questions are listed in Appendix 6–1.

Alternative Development: Using a Variety of Experiences as Part of Managerial Development

In work at the Center for Creative Leadership, development experiences were ranked according to their effectiveness at developing employee competencies.[13] At the bottom were traditional training programs, while at the top was job experience. Task-force assignments, work projects, visits to a university as a recruiter, business trips abroad, and dozens of other "on-the-job" experiences provide employees with the means to generate competencies. Appendix 6–2 identifies a host of job-related activities that may be used for employee development. As more of these nontraining activities are used, employees will increasingly gain competencies that result in strengthening business competitiveness. The long list of activities given in Appendix 6–2 indicates how executives may leverage nontraining development activities as means to building personal competencies into organizational capability.

Development: Success Indicators

Training and development activities may be used to build competitiveness, the capacity for change, the ability to implement strategy, and strategic unity. Managers who oversee development activities can use the following checklist to determine whether their organization's development activities are meeting the needs of the business:

1. Why is the training offered?
2. How will the training enhance strategic, financial, and technological capabilities?
3. What will be the measures of success?
4. What managers are sponsoring the training activity?
5. How does our training benchmark against that provided by competitors?
6. How will training help meet customer needs?
7. Who should attend training activities and why?

8. What alternatives to formal training may be used to ensure that employees develop the competencies required to
do their current and future work?

In one large company, a director of management development with over 30 years of experience claimed that development
work was either feast or famine. He said that such programs either
gain enormous attention, with all employees wanting to participate, or are seen as superficial, with no one wanting to attend. If
development is seen and used as a competitive weapon and the
result for the firm is sustained competitiveness, we believe that
commitment to these activities will become more consistent and
more resources will be allocated in this area.

By putting more resources into both selection and development, a firm generates personal competencies. With new or increased skills, employees are better able to help the business
become competitive by meeting customer needs, adapting to
change, and creating a shared mindset.

APPENDIX 6–1
Key Questions for Designing Successful Development Programs

Preprogram

1. Are senior managers adequately involved in defining the goals and outline of the program?
2. Has the underlying reason for the program been defined? Has the content of the program been linked to the strategic or business needs of the business?
3. Have one or two major themes been identified for the week?
4. Has a framework been prepared for integrating all topics during the week into the major themes?
5. Have facilitators been identified who will add to the program content? Have external facilitators met with general managers to learn about specific business needs?
6. Have specific competencies been identified as outcomes of the program?
7. Have adequate resources been allocated: facility, support staff, materials, and so on? Are the facilities set aside for the program adequate?
8. Has the week been designed for a flow: from general to specific, from concept to application, from organizational to personal, and so on?
9. Have participants been selected on the basis of clear criteria?
10. Do the participants' managers realize the goals of the program?

Program

11. Are line managers involved in presenting and reinforcing material?
12. Are a variety of teaching techniques used to balance the program delivery?
13. Does the program have a balance of concept and application content? Do downtimes focus more on application? Will groups be designed and used?
14. Does the introduction entice participants and tell them the flow of the program over the entire week?
15. Do participants see that they are learning new concepts during the week? Does the program "stretch" the participants and show them what they do not know?
16. Are cases and examples "real time"; from the organization or similar organizations?
17. Will participants have fun?

18. Will the program end on a high with specific implications spelled out for participants?
19. Will symbolic objects or events be used to highlight and reinforce the program, for example, mementos, notebooks, T-shirts, graduation, presentation, roast & boast, and so on?

Postprogram

20. Will there be an evaluation of the results of the program, both short and long term?
21. Will follow-up and implications of the program be required and supported?
22. Are data collected to generate a data base of participants and outcomes for future reference?
23. Has a notebook been prepared documenting what was done for future reference?
24. Will the managers who helped design the program use the material in the future—for example, in talks, meetings, and conferences?

APPENDIX 6–2
On-the-Job Development Activities for Employees

A. Mini-Projects

1. Serve on task force addressing business problem.
2. Plan a new site.
3. Plan an off-site meeting, conference, or convention.
4. Handle a negotiation with a customer.
5. Install a new system.
6. Work with a plant shut-down crew.
7. Integrate systems across units.
8. Supervise a product, program, equipment, or systems purchase.
9. Supervise liquidation of a product, program, equipment, or system.
10. Present a proposal to top management.
11. Go off-site to troubleshoot problems (deal with dissatisfied customer).
12. Visit a campus as a recruiter.
13. Supervise a study team.
14. Run a company picnic.
15. Start up something small (for example, hire a secretarial pool).
16. Run a task force on a business problem.
17. Visit a foreign country on business.
18. Lobby for the organization.
19. Supervise furnishing of offices.
20. Supervise assignment of office space.
21. Make speeches for the organization.
22. Write public relations releases.
23. Serve at the company booth at a trade show.
24. Work with the credit union board or committee.
25. Serve as an executive on loan.
26. Serve on a new project/product review committee.
27. Work short periods in other units.
28. Do a project with another function.
29. Manage a renovation project.
30. Launch a new product/program.
31. Use seed budget on a personal idea/project.
32. Follow a new product/system through entire cycle.
33. Represent concerns of nonexempt employees to higher management.
34. Assign a project with a tight deadline.

35. Manage the visit of a VIP.
36. Serve on a junior board.

B. *Mini-Scope Jumps and Fix-its*

37. Create a symbol/rallying cry for change and implementation.
38. Team build—green staff.
39. Team build—balky staff.
40. Team build—low-competence staff.
41. Team build—former peers.
42a. Team build—individual being developed is expert, subordinates are not.
42b. Team build—subordinates are experts, individual being developed is not.
43. Team build during a fix-it.
44. Team build in a static operation.
45. Team build in a rapidly expanding operation.
46. Size up who to keep and who to let go.
47. Deal with a business crisis.
48. Assign an "undoable" project (last person who tried it failed).
49. Supervise outplacement.
50. Supervise cost-cutting.
51. Design new, simpler effectiveness measures.
52. Assign a person to work on something he/she does not want to do.
53. Resolve a conflict among warring subordinates.
54. Make peace with an enemy.

C. *Mini-Strategy Assignments*

55. Present a summary of a new trend/technique to others.
56. Write a proposal for a new system, product, procedure.
57. Spend a week with customers; write a report.
58. Do a competitive analysis.
59. Write a speech for someone higher in the organization.
60. Write up a policy statement.
61. Study customer needs.
62. Do a postmortem on a failed project.
63. Do a problem-prevention analysis.
64. Study innovation among customers/competitors.
65. Interview outsiders on their view of the organization.

66. Evaluate the impact of training.
67. Construct a success/derailment profile.
68. Write up a contingency scenario.
69. Work on affirmative-action planning.

D. *Coursework/Coaching Dippers*

70. Teach a course or workshop.
71. Teach someone how to do something he/she is not expert in.
72. Teach someone how to do something he/she is expert in.
73. Design a training course.
74. Do a self-study project.
75. Attend a self-awareness course.
76. Train as an assessor in the assessment center.
77. Spend a day with an expert on some aspect of his/her job.
78. Study a new technical area.
79. Study the organization's history/draw business parallels.
80. Assign to work with a higher manager a person who is particularly good or bad at something.

E. *Off-Job Dippers*

81. Become active in a professional organization.
82. Serve with a community agency.
83. Become active in a volunteer organization.
84. Join a community board.
85. Act as a consultant on a problem/issue outside the job.
86. Coach children's sports.
87. Work with a charitable organization.

Source: Center for Creative Leadership, personal correspondence.

7

Reinforcing Competencies: Appraisal and Rewards

People in organizations tend to behave as they see others being rewarded.

Peter Drucker

Once competencies have been generated in employees through selection or development, they must be reinforced. Reinforcement of competencies encourages individuals continually to think and act in patterns consistent with business needs. It also helps employees maintain competencies and acquire new ones to meet changing business conditions.

Two practices work together to reinforce competencies through a performance-management system. Appraisals begin the reinforcement process by setting clear standards and providing feedback to employees. Rewards, which are tied to appraisals, ensure that when individuals meet standards, good things happen. Most people want to do things that are rewarding. When rewards reinforce behavior that is consistent with the organization's goals, individual thought and action contribute to the firm's competitiveness.

APPRAISAL

The appraisal processes seek to focus employee attention on desirable actions—those that increase customer value, help the firm adapt to change and implement strategies, and create unity. Formal appraisal processes also help businesses avoid legal problems when rotating, disciplining, or outplacing employees. The importance from a legal point of view of a strong performance-appraisal system became evident to us when attorneys representing a Fortune 50 firm contacted us to serve as expert witnesses. A senior

135

officer who had been fired from the firm was suing the officers and the firm for $100 million, claiming that his employment contract had been violated. When we probed to learn more about the case, we found that this employee had received performance appraisals designated "outstanding" for two of the three years before he was fired. He claimed that he had not been adequately informed that his behavior was inappropriate, so that he could have changed how he conducted himself. While the company ultimately won the suit—partly because a courageous manager had noted on one of the annual appraisals that this employee was "outstanding" but still needed to improve his cooperativeness—the case remains a good example of the legal problems that may arise when appraisal systems are weak.

In our experience, appraisals have become the "black hole" of management practices. Resources are continually allocated to updating and revising appraisal systems—creating new forms, offering training on using the forms, and ensuring that the forms are completed and filed. Yet these revisions sometimes seem to be undertaken for their own sake, out of a vague sense that "something is wrong here" rather than with a clear focus on how appraisal systems should function to create organizational capability. To make informed choices on designing appraisal systems that work to build competitiveness, managers need to re-examine the three major components of appraisals: (1) setting standards, (2) providing feedback to employees, and (3) managing the process.

Standards

Outcomes versus Behaviors

The first step, setting standards, is to identify the appropriate mix of standards. Standards may emphasize either outcomes or behaviors (see Figure 7-1).[1] Organizations may focus on high outcomes by establishing standards that encourage quantifiable results. Programs for these types of standards are called management by objectives (MBOs) or key result area programs. They establish standards and measure performance based exclusively on work outcomes. When MBOs set standards that are tied to the goals of the organization, they can be effective in motivating employee performance. MBOs work effectively with jobs that have clear outcomes which are within the control of the individ-

Figure 7–1
STANDARDS: BEHAVIOR VERSUS OUTCOMES

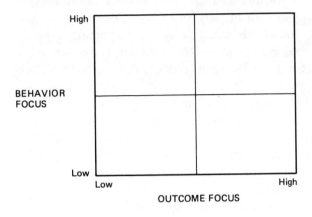

ual. For example, outcome measures can be used effectively with many sales positions. Research on MBOs also indicates, however, that for many jobs specific goals cannot be set. With managerial or research or engineering jobs, for instance, using outcomes alone as standards may not be viable because such jobs are ambiguous and rapidly changing. Setting objective standards requires assessing business strategies and then interpreting how strategies translate into individual outcomes. Outcomes may be rated in terms of quality, quantity, or other measurable results.

Standards defined in terms of behaviors focus less on results and more on process. A behavioral approach emphasizes how work is done rather than what work is done. It identifies the activities an employee can or should perform to reinforce competencies. At McDonald's, a number of behavioral standards have been set for employees: friendliness, courtesy, responsiveness to customers. Each attribute may be defined in terms of what the employee says and does. Employees who demonstrate these behaviors and thereby meet company standards receive favorable appraisals. Behavioral standards derive from examining what individuals must do to accomplish work and then specifying the behaviors that are most likely to lead to business results.

Finding the right balance between outcome and behavioral standards requires examing the type of work that is to be evaluated—the extent to which work outcomes can be defined, the duration of work activities—the extent to which results are short- or long-term, and the degree of individual control over the work.

Characteristics

Whether standards are established on the basis of behaviors or outcomes, researchers have identified four characteristics of effective standards.[2] First, standards must be specific. Setting specific standards, such as what will happen by a certain date and with what resources, makes it possible to accurately measure employee performance against the standards. In defining standards, one expert has empahasized the importance of operational definitions.[3] Operational definitions refer to attributes, quantities, and a number of variables (how much, how long, how heavy, how far, how flat, how smooth, how fast, how thick). The more specific and operational the standards, the more likely employees are to focus on accomplishing them.

Second, effective standards challenge but do not break employees. Research on goal setting has found that when standards are set too low, behavior tends not to be focused because an employee's attention is likely to wander. When standards are set too high, individuals are likely to lose interest in meeting them because they feel defeated even before they start.

Third, effective standards call for the participation of employees. When standards are imposed from above, individuals may resist them. By participating in setting standards, the individual for whom the standards are set has ownership of and commitment to the standards that are established. He or she can also make sure that living up to the standards is possible. Setting standards without employee participation leads to problems. Employees may or may not feel ownership and commitment to the standards when they are prescribed. In one meeting of general managers, a vice president presented the goals for all twenty of the general managers for the following year. Each goal was specific and not unreasonably difficult. At the end of the meeting, the vice president believed that he had done a good job; he even asked all the participants who believed in the standards to stand up to show their commitment, and most of them did so. He was surprised when, at the end of the year, few of his goals had been met. He did not understand that managers needed to participate actively in setting their standards if they were to feel committed to them. He would have achieved better results by inviting participating managers to define the dimensions and degree of the standards being set for themselves.

Finally, effective standards can be self-scored to increase accountability. Self-scoring implies that individuals who participate in setting the standards can evaluate their own performance against the standard. By self-monitoring, feedback on performance is assured, and the individual knows how well he or she is performing. Self-accountability reinforces the standards that have been set, because self-monitoring is usually more immediate, critical, and motivating than public accountability.

Individual versus Group Performance

Standards should focus on both individual and group activities. When standards are set exclusively for individual behavior, we have found that they may encourage counterproductive competition. Such standards may result in the desired individual performance, but may not lead to the kind of performance required by the organization. In an engineering division, individual performance standards were set based on project-completion outcomes and behaviors. The result was that individual engineers began to concentrate exclusively on *their own projects*, doing little to support or help each other. Soon all projects fell behind schedule because individual standards encouraged only individual, not cooperative, behavior.

When the standards for this engineering group were revised to focus on teams, cooperation increased, and engineers began to share information and collaborate to accomplish projects. Team standards may focus on both outcomes and behaviors. Team outcomes refer to project-completion times and quality or quantity of team output. Team behaviors may be measured in terms of cooperation, unity, or participation in team activities.

Balancing team and individual standards requires assessing business and customer requirements. In technologically complex business situations, where the contribution of any single team member cannot be specified without looking at the contribution of other team members, team rather than individual standards are appropriate. A football team, while simple conceptually, is technologically complex. To set only individual performance standards could result in one player doing his job, while the team as a whole falls short of its requirements. In basketball too, team performance has a larger impact on victories than individual performance. It is rare that a winning basketball team also has the leading scorer in the league. The individual performance demonstrated by scoring a lot of points may not coincide with the teamwork required to win games. Standards for organizational performance may also be more critical at managerial than individual employee levels. Managers who have the responsibility of integrating different functions should be appraised according to standards for the integration rather than on the basis of individual performance.

Connect with Competitiveness

Perhaps the most revealing test of whether standards connect with competitiveness is to ask a simple question:

> **If these standards are met, what will the individual contribute to the competitiveness of this business?**

This question has been used as a means of assessing standards in a variety of businesses. Generally, we find that standards set in the appraisal process do not reflect what an individual contributes to business competitiveness. As a result, individual attention is not focused on behaviors that lead to competitiveness but on aspects of the job that the employee enjoys and that are nice, but not necessary to do.

Standards are generally set in one of two ways. First, they are often set by a supervisor or in some other way imposed from above. In an ideal world, these standards are behaviors and outcomes the supervisor believes should be followed to accomplish a business objective. Such, however, is not always the case. Second, standards may be set as the result of a supervisor and employee coming to an agreement about what the firm expects and what behaviors the employee should demonstrate. This method is more effective than imposing standards from above, because an employee feels a greater commitment to standards that have been jointly set. This approach does not guarantee, however, that the standards will be established with business strategies in mind.

To connect standards to competitiveness, we propose a third approach: involving clients inside or customers outside an organization in the *process* of standard setting. In one company, the employee sets standards (both outcome and behavioral) for his or her performance with a customer first, then reviews these standards with his or her supervisor. These customers may be inside or outside the formal organization boundary. By engaging in this two-step process, the employee becomes much more aware of what customers expect, and the employee and the supervisor can share a discussion about how the employee's behavior builds competitiveness in the eyes of the customer or client.

Feedback

What Is Expected? The most important element in providing effective feedback is making sure that employees know what is expected of them. To define expectations, managers and employees need to make explicit choices about the standards that are set, using the criteria discussed above. A useful tool for ensuring that feedback expectations are clear is to require that employees and managers share their views of what the standards are for good performance.

How Am I Doing?   What employees want most from feedback is a clear answer to the simple question, "How am I doing?" Feedback should answer this question in direct, timely, and nonthreatening ways.

One common problem is a lack of direct feedback. When an employee's performance is poor, managers are often reluctant to provide negative feedback for fear they will hurt the employee's feelings and damage their relationship with that person. To help managers overcome this feeling, we have devised a simple process: we ask them if they have ever made a mistake at work. Of course, all of them have. We then ask them who was the first person to learn of the mistake, and they inevitably answer that they were. Most employees who make mistakes are the first to know of them. Receiving feedback on poor performance will not reveal or open wounds, but will help acknowledge and close wounds. When employees do not receive direct feedback from their managers on performance, they assume that either the manager does not know about the mistake or does not care about the employee. Both assumptions are inaccurate and may lead the employee to perpetuate inappropriate behavior. When managers recognize that direct feedback generally doesn't provide new news but makes it possible to discuss old news, they become more comfortable about sharing information with employees. The most common—and the loudest—feedback most managers give is unspoken—when managers don't share good or bad news with employees—which is rarely constructive.

Feedback should be timely as well as direct. The development in the 1950s of an "annual" appraisal process misled many managers into thinking that feedback had to take place only once a year. Feedback should be offered whenever the employee's behavior warrants it. Giving feedback to an employee immediately after the behavior is identifed is a form of intervention that can prevent the establishment of long-standing negative behavior patterns.

Finally, feedback should focus not on the person but on attainment of standards. Performance feedback is descriptive, not judgmental; concerned with behaviors and outcomes, not personality; and deals in specifics, not generalities.

When employees know the answer to the question, "How am I doing?" they are more able to change their behavior and engage in activities that build competitiveness. Feedback enables individuals to begin a personal change process to adapt to organizational changes. It helps them focus attention on creating a shared mindset within an organization and on ensuring that their work practices are consistent with business strategies.

Process

Purposes Appraisals may serve multiple purposes. First, they can be used to review *performance*. Appraisals as performance reviews emphasize the extent to which an employee has accomplished standards within a given time period. Generally, performance appraisals are used to allocate rewards based on attaining certain objectives. To make sure that rewards are allocated fairly, the performance-appraisal process must be systematic, equitable, and consistent. Employees at all levels should receive the same kinds of performance appraisals that assess merit and allocate resources.

In addition, appraisals may be used to discuss an employee's potential and to establish development plans relating to future career opportunities. *Potential* appraisals highlight how an individual's strengths may be enhanced for career and organizational success. For potential appraisals to be effective, future job requirements need to be specified, career opportunities defined, and development experiences planned for future career opportunities.

Performance appraisals highlight the past; potential appraisals lay the foundation for the future. The former allocate rewards based on merit; the latter offer opportunities for growth. Both types of appraisal are necessary to build competitiveness by creating a unified sense of goals and purposes of an organization.

From them employees understand how the past and future may be integrated into a unified direction for both themselves and the business.

Who Does the Appraisal? Traditionally, appraisals are done by an employee's immediate supervisor, who is likely to be the best source of information concerning the extent to which an employee performs tasks and meets standards. Supervisors, however, are not the only source of valuable appraisals. More elaborate appraisals have been designed at some companies to ensure that employees receive feedback from many people who are familiar with the person's performance, such as peers, subordinates, a higher supervisor, and clients. When more participants are included in the feedback process, the employee receives a wider and more accurate range of information. In addition, individuals who participate in the feedback process are likely to feel an obligation to the individual and be more committed to helping the employee reach career goals.

At General Electric,[4] multiple raters are used for appraisal. Peers provide information about how the individual relates to those at the same level. An employee's ability to collaborate, work in teams, and play by the rules may be perceived more clearly by peers than by supervisors. Subordinate appraisals help an employee learn about his or her leadership style, use of power, and ability to delegate.

Peer reviews also serve to mediate disputes when employees receive what they perceive to be unfair appraisals. At General Electric, Borg-Warner, Control Data, and Honda, peer reviews have been established for employees who believe their work performance has been misjudged or that they have been mistreated in some way. At General Electric, the peer review committee is selected from among names chosen by the aggrieved employee from a pool of employees who have volunteered for peer review work. Each panel member receives twelve hours of training on the legal and ethical issues of reviews. Employees who have been wronged have found the peer review system appropriate for sharing and resolving grievances and disputes, while managers have found it provides an appropriate system of checks and balances to their appraisal efforts.

A valuable information source is the employee's client or customer. In one company, customers were formed into focus groups to help define standards that would be important from their point of view. When the time came to perform appraisals, the customers were included in the data-collection process. Customers filled in evaluation forms, indicating the extent to which they perceived the employee was meeting the standards the customers had helped establish. Involving customers in the appraisal process provides the employee with feedback and builds customer commitment to the employee as well.

Positive and Negative Reports   For employees, the onset of appraisal time evokes feelings of uncertainty and fear, because the focus is on a formal annual review. We believe that appraisal should be an ongoing process whereby employees know what is expected of them and how they are doing. If an employee is surprised at the results of the formal review, the appraisal process has not worked effectively.

To make sure that appraisal serves as a tool for building competitiveness, the process needs to focus on both the positive and the negative. The negative side of appraisal, the one that receives the most attention, should be modified so that it is grounded in the *employee's* choices to engage or not engage in productive work activities. Too often, in a performance review information flows only one way—from the manager to the employee. For the appraisal to build competitiveness, it should help the employee see how his or her choices are affecting business performance. To redefine negative feedback as an employee-driven rather than as a manager-driven process, a number of firms have instituted a system called positive discipline. In positive discipline, employees who come in late, do a sloppy job, or mistreat a colleague first get a verbal reminder rather than a reprimand, and next get a written reminder. If the maladaptive behavior persists, the employee is given a ''decision-making leave day''—a day off, with pay, during which the employee is expected to think about the job and decide if he or she really wants it. If the answer is yes, then the employee must agree, either verbally or in writing, that performance will change. If the employee fails to revise work habits, the company may argue that the employee has chosen to leave the company. This technique has had favorable results at Tampa Electric, Frito-Lay, and dozens of other companies who have found that when employees are forced to accept ownership for their behavior, they are more likely to change than if the appraisal is imposed from above.

Managers need to give equal attention to positive reviews. In one company, a management team committed itself to matching every incidence of negative feedback with positive feedback. These managers initially found that they had trouble coming up with positive comments: They were more practiced at delivering bad news and sharing with employees what had gone wrong. After extensive work, however, they found a number of positive reinforcement tools. They simply said "thanks" to employees for good work, wrote letters of commendation to employees and their families, found ways of publicizing superior employee perform- ance (for example, internal and external newspaper stories), and talked about successful employees in management forums. Such examples of positive reinforcement balanced the traditional nega- tive image of the performance appraisal and encouraged em- ployees to focus on key business activities. In addition, in their one-on-one meetings, these managers emphasized giving positive rather than negative feedback. By so doing, they made the ap- praisal process uplifting rather than degrading for employees. While the management team kept no quantifiable indicators of success, it found the mindset shifting in the work unit from one of "fear of failure" to one of "support for success."

How Often?   Traditional wisdom suggests that appraisals should be done quarterly or semiannually. This logic stems from the idea that as employees receive feedback, they learn what the organiza- tion expects of them and can make behavioral changes, if re- quired, to meet customer demands. In one company, managers who did monthly stewardship interviews found that employee performance improved and stayed at a very high level. The monthly interview helped catch performance issues before they became serious and provided employees with ongoing feedback on their job performance. Research on this company found that the personal monthly interview actually saved managers time, because problems were identified before they became serious enough to require a great amount of attention.[5]
When the span of control includes twenty or thirty man- agers, however, as is the case in many companies, allocating the needed amount of time to each employee in formal appraisal settings is a problem. In these cases, the traditional approaches to appraisals must be modified. In the dynamic and flexible organi- zations that will emerge in the 1990s, control through objectives and standards must be complemented with control through shared mindset—that is, employees will have to be taught the

principles of job performance. With these principles, employees can then establish by and for themselves the specific standards that will lead to higher performance. Employees who learn such principles thoroughly are liberated to enact those principles in ways that empower them to make decisions for the benefit of the organization. This approach to appraisal represents a dramatic shift. It refocuses appraisal from standards to values, from management by objectives to management by mindset, from system-driven appraisal to shared dialogues, from observing and controlling employee behavior to teaching principles and letting employees act for themselves. It also shifts the focus on appraisal for its own sake to integrating appraisal with staffing and development practices. Employees trained to share a set of principles will require less formal appraisal.

Management procedures for handling performance appraisals should be based on the underlying culture of the business. If the business relies on formal procedures and on rules as control mechanisms, frequent meetings between manager and employee become important. If the business relies on a shared mindset that can be generated through staffing, development, and appraisals emphasizing principles, meetings need not be so frequent and should focus on values rather than practices.

Normal Curve versus Percentile   We all remember teachers who graded on a curve rather than on achievement alone. Managers face the same decision in designing appraisal systems. Normal curve standards imply a ranking process among employees; percentiles imply standards against which employees are judged.

Rank systems have been used in businesses with high success. At Exxon, every employee is ranked against other peer employees. These rankings are done by multiple managers who know a number of the peers being ranked. The discussions provide managers with valuable insights on how their employees are perceived. Employee bonuses and incentives are based on positions in the rankings. In addition to ranking individual employees, groups of employees are ranked to ensure that when an entire group is outstanding, the whole group is ranked above another group, so that the lowest-ranking individual in the higher-ranking group may receive more favorable reviews than the highest-ranking individual in the lower-ranking group. Ranking systems work best when employees are exposed to multiple managers who may comment on employee behavior, when retaining only the top employees is critical to business success, and when enough trust exists within the ogranization to ensure that employees who are not ranked at the top feel security and stability.

Assigning employees to percentiles offers all employees opportunities to accomplish standards. Percentiles focus on a defined set of skills; when employees engage in activities that result in skill acquistion, they can move into higher percentiles. The percentile process for appraisal allows all employees opportunities to progress. It works best when specific sets of skills can be identified as crucial to the business, when employees can undertake well-defined actions to learn and demonstrate competence in these skills, and when the increased skill demonstrably translates into increased customer value.

The Appraisal Interview   While we have encouraged businesses to make the appraisal process an ongoing one, the appraisal interview is important. The appraisal interview represents a significant emotional event for both employees and managers. To make it a positive experience, efforts can be made to ensure that the session focuses on problem-solving rather than evaluation.

Appendix 7–1 outlines a process for making the appraisal interview create a climate of trust and mutual respect rather than fear. We recommend that managers begin by highlighting positive aspects of the employee's work before proceeding to no more than two items of concern, and then ensuring that appraisees have a chance to comment. Appendix 7–2 identifies some common problems associated with the performance appraisal and suggests behaviors that can be used to avoid or overcome them. With proper preparation, managers can learn how to go beyond superficial dialogue and focus the employee's attention on building competitiveness.

Building Ongoing Relationships   If appraisals are to become tools for competitive advantage, they must be based on relationships of trust. To build trust each party must be able to rely on the other and believe that what the other says will happen *will* happen. Both parties to the appraisal must have confidence that the other will carry out obligations. Trust can exist only if there is approximately equal commitment to the agenda and if the actions agreed on are doable. Trust is also built if relationships have a personal as well as a work basis. The extent to which the manager and the employee share hobbies, habits, and outside work activities and are able to talk about common interests is a further factor in trust-building.

Building relationships of trust comes through a focus on the "... abilities" over time. *Dependability* assures that each party can rely on the other and believe that what the other says will happen will, in fact, happen. *Predictability* helps each party develop confidence that the other party will carry out obligations. *Workability* assures that the actions between the two parties require approximately equal commitment and that actions by each party are doable. *Likability* helps build relationships on a personal as well as a work basis.

By creating an ongoing relationship of trust, both the manager and the employee benefit. Standards can be more effectively shared, set, and supported, and feedback becomes more meaningful.

Appraisals: Success Indicators

Our discussion of appraisals reduces to a simple point: appraisals may be used to build competitiveness. To ensure that appraisals contribute to organizational capability, managers should ask the following specific questions:

1. How do the standards in the appraisal system reflect what customers expect from the business?
2. To what extent do the standards set tie individual performance to the organization's strategic, technological, and financial goals?
3. What is the appropriate mix of outcome versus behavioral standards?
4. What percentage of employees receive feedback on their performance through appraisals?
5. How talented are managers at delivering feedback to employees?
6. How much trust exists within the business?
7. How effectively are appraisals used to assess performance and build potential?
8. How do employees feel about the fairness, integrity, and openness of the appraisal process?

REWARDS

Rewards work with appraisals to reinforce employee competencies. The premise underlying the use of rewards to create a competitive advantage is that self-interest leads people to act in ways that further their own ends. People are willing to devote time and energy to activities they see as likely to result in outcomes favorable to themselves.

Almost any business has employees who lack motivation. These individuals are slow to complete assignments, take extra time at lunch, never volunteer for extra duty, are the first to socialize about nonwork topics, and are likely to leave work early. Almost every manager has at least one such employee. In most cases, when we visit with the "unmotivated" employees, we find that they demonstrate a lot of commitment and motivation outside work. They may be active in local community or church organizations or in sports, may coach children's activities, may be leaders in the PTA or scouts, or be enthusiastic travelers. To label such individuals unmotivated in inaccurate. The fact is, their motivation is directed toward off-the-job activities. The challenge of using reward practices to reinforce and motivate behavior is to find a way of focusing individuals' energy on meeting business goals.

Rather than mislabeling employees as unmotivated, managers need to design reward practices that motivate individuals to dedicate time and energy to business as well as personal goals. Rather than hoping for employees to be motivated to work, reward systems can and should be designed to make work activities function to promote people's self-interest.[6] The three essential components of an effective reward system are setting *criteria* for rewards, using *financial* rewards, and using *nonfinancial* rewards. When most of us think of rewards, we think of financial ones such as bonuses, benefits, stock options, free tickets or memberships, and so on. However, when we assess elements of a job that are most rewarding, we often think of nonfinancial rewards such as community status, the interest inherent in the work itself, a creative work environment, the sense of accomplishment, access to laboratory equipment, career opportunities, promotions, titles, and so on. We believe that equal attention should be given to nonfinancial rewards when managers design reward systems.

Reward Criteria

A host of reward practices may come and go, but reward criteria persist.[7] Assessing reward practices against the criteria below enables managers to design creative reward systems that motivate employees. The eight criteria listed here are indicative rather than inclusive. As the questions raised by consideration of each criterion are asked about possible rewards, reward practices should more effectively build competitiveness.

Availability

This criterion poses the question: *To what extent are there enough rewards available for accomplishing the desired outcome?* Managers must recognize that some rewards are limited and thus, although valuable, can be only partially effective. For example, a salary increase may be a short-term reward, but over time, as the additional money is assimilated into personal and family spending patterns, it may not be enough to ensure long-term motivation.

Different individuals need different rewards. What may be enough for one person will not suffice for another. The availability criterion requires assessing individual needs and determining what amount of reward will seem significant to a given individual. The reward of traveling to an exotic site to present a paper or attend a conference may be much more rewarding to an employee with few opportunities to travel than to one with many travel opportunities. In general, the more available the reward, the more likely it is that an employee will be motivated to meet business requirements.

Performance Contingent

The performance-contingent criterion poses the question: *To what extent are rewards tied to individual, team, or organization performance?* By establishing definite criteria, managers ensure that rewards are allocated only when standards are met and goals are accomplished. As we have seen, a variety of choices exist in establishing outcome or behavioral standards for individuals, teams, or organizations. Dozens of companies—including AT&T, Avon, General Motors, Rubbermaid, and Wal-mart—have converted to pay-for-performance programs based on the simple principle that when performance increases, pay increases.

Asserting that performance contingencies exist is not enough. Rewards need to be allocated differentially, based on the extent to which individuals meet standards. The performance-contingent criterion implies *equity*, not *equality*. Individuals receive rewards according to the work they have accomplished, not merely because they belong to an organization or a group. Access to company recreation facilities and participation in benefit plans are examples of rewards that are often viewed as entitlements rather than rewards. Saying that performance is contingent on meeting standards is a first step; actually differentiating rewards based on accomplishment is a more challenging second step. In general, the more performance contingent the reward, the more likely an employee will work to meet the standards necessary for business success.

Timeliness

The timeliness criterion with respect to rewards raises the question: *To what extent are rewards immediately linked to performance?* Businesses that rely exclusively on rewarding employees through locked-in annual salary increases probably fail to meet this criterion. Performance does not occur in twelve monthly increments but in daily, weekly and monthly increments. Rewards that are flexible and immediately tied to performance meet the timeliness criterion. Awards that are distributed immediately after an outstanding performance meet this criterion. Those distributed six months or a year after outstanding performance, because the approval process is so lengthy and complicated, do not meet this criterion. When the time between performance and rewards is long, individuals forget that the performance resulted in the reward. In general, the shorter the time between performance and reward, the more an employee sees the connection between the two, thereby encouraging behavior consistent with meeting business requirements.

Durability

The durability criterion poses the question: *To what extent are rewards likely to be effective over time?* If a reward results only in a short-term increase in motivation, it fails to meet the durability criterion. Salary increases are a good example, as we have seen. More durable rewards induce behavioral changes that last over time. A promotion, a favorable assignment, or increased job responsibilities, for example, tend to be more durable: the recipient is more likely to feel rewarded on an ongoing basis. In general, the more durable the reward, the more likely the individual will maintain commitment to a new behavior over time.

Reversibility

The reversibility criterion asks the question: *To what extent can rewards be rescinded or taken back?* Often rewards intended for performance become entitlements and cannot be rescinded. When this happens, the reward system becomes less effective. One company adopted the practice of paying a small base salary, with a large annual incentive intended to allocate rewards based on overall company performance. For eight years, the company had reasonably good performance, and each employee received the same annual bonus. After eight years of annual incentives, the company's profits declined, but when management attempted to reduce the annual incentive, according to the formula created nearly a decade earlier, employees nearly revolted. Employees had come to assume that they were entitled to the incentive no matter what the overall company performance was. The reward had become nonreversible, not because the program itself was wrong but because for eight years, regardless of company performance, each employee had received the same bonus. Had management linked the annual incentive payment more specifically to business performance, when the business had a particularly bad year, employees could more readily have accepted the reversible nature of the reward.

Too much of a good thing may be a bad thing. Too many benefits offered over too long a period of time may come to be seen as entitlements, not earned rewards. The struggle companies have had in revising medical benefits indicates how difficult it is for many rewards to be made reversible. Employees do not want to give up their medical benefits, yet they do not see these benefits as directly linked to their work performance.

Reversibility of rewards is important because it increases flexibility in how rewards are allocated. When rewards are reversible, those earned in one time period may or may not be earned in the next. Each project or time period begins the reward cycle anew. In the academic setting, the reversibility criterion holds true. For a faculty member, each paper submitted for publication is accepted on its own merit by a panel of reviewers who do not know the author. Just because one manuscript is accepted for publication does not guarantee that others will be. Each manuscript is judged on its own merits. The reward of having a manuscript published may be reversed with the rejection of the next manuscript. As a result, there is constant pressure on faculty to publish. In general, the more reversible the reward, the more appreciated it will be and the more likely committed behavior continues. In this way, reversibility ensures that rewards are used as tools to build competitive advantage.

Visibility

The visibility criterion raises the question: *To what extent are rewards visible to many employees?* Low-visibility rewards, such as cash awards that only the employee and his or her supervisor know about, may not generate much commitment, because few people have observed that a certain behavior is likely to be rewarded. A promotion, on the other hand, is a visible reward that often attracts wide attention. Individuals who were not promoted spend a great deal of time trying to figure out what led to the promotion, in an effort to improve their own future chances. In general, the more visible the reward, the more likely it will be to generate employee behavior consistent with building competitiveness.

Visibility also has drawbacks. At times, it may create a perceived inequity in the system. When an employee receives a large reward that others believe they too deserve, the employees who were not rewarded may reduce their commitment. Publicly announcing salary increases may cause dissention as well as motivation. In such cases, managers must be willing to live with the discontent aroused and to talk honestly with employees about why they were not equally rewarded. While this problem has led many managers to deliver less visible rewards, we would still argue that in general the more visible the reward, the more it will induce employees to identify valued behaviors and to work toward developing them.

Shared Mindset

The share mindset criterion highlights the question: *To what extent do rewards create and maintain a shared mindset inside and outside the business?* The importance of shared mindset for organizational capability was discussed extensively in Chapter 4. Reward systems can help build a shared mindset by consistently sanctioning similar activities and values. Reward practices that contradict rather than complement each other send mixed messages to employees. In one business attempting to generate employee creativity, for example, management awards were given to creative employees, but promotions were given to employees who did not take risks. As a result, employees received mixed messages, and creativity was not reinforced.

Using reward practices to build shared mindset requires an understanding of the core values of a business. It then requires a continual assessment of all reward practices to ensure that they continually support the shared mindset and are consistent with each other. In general, the more consistently rewards reinforce a shared mindset, the more effective they are at building competitiveness. For example, in a business in which the desired mindset is customer service, a reward that encourages behavior that focuses on customer service is the publication of positive letters from customers about an employee in the monthly newsletter. The customer letters reward employee behavior consistent with the customer-service value and encourage other employees to do likewise.

Customer Value

The customer-value criterion raises the question: *To what extent do rewards enhance customer value?* Reward practices should encourage employee behaviors that help to provide perceived customer value. To ensure that reward systems reinforce such behaviors, managers may want to have customers involved in the design and delivery of rewards. Businesses have invited customers to present employee awards, formed customer focus groups to review the standards set in the performance-appraisal process, and solicited customer comments on employee performance, using those comments to measure performance and allocate rewards.

Recently, we experienced three outstanding examples of focusing on customer values in rewards. When we directed a one-week workshop at the Chaminade in Santa Cruz, California, we were given 100 fake gold coins to share with participants. Workshop participants were asked to give these coins to employees who gave outstanding service. We learned that Chaminade employees could accumulate gold coins and turn them in for financial bonuses. Northwest Airlines has recently focused its rewards on customer values by giving its frequent travelers "service coupons." When a Northwest employee performs outstanding service, the traveler is encouraged to send in a service coupon. Employees receive bonuses based on service coupons sent in about them. At Fairfield Inn, part of Marriott Corporation, when guests check out they are asked the extent to which they found the check-in staff helpful and whether their room was clean. This customer data can then be tied directly to employees responsible for these actions. Keeping a strong link between rewards and behaviors that enhance perceived customer value is thus another way to use rewards for competitive advantage.

Summary

Before allocating rewards, criteria for defining the effectiveness of the rewards must be specified. We have identified eight criteria against which rewards may be assessed. When reward practices meet more of these criteria, the practice is more likely to be a means of building organizational capability and competitiveness.

Financial Rewards

Base versus At-Risk Salary

The most fundamental financial reward is the base salary. Base salary reflects a combination of seniority, hierarchical position, and value to the business. It is often associated with nonfinancial rewards such as office space, support staff, greater discretion over time and resources, and opportunities for more flexible and enriched assignments.

As organizational hierarchies become less rigid, the traditional base salary is being replaced by increasing amounts of salary "at risk." At-risk salary comes in a variety of forms, generally tied to some form of incentive based on the performance contingent criterion, as indicated by individual or business performance. Reebok chairman Paul Fireman receives 5 percent of any pretax corporate profits exceeding $20 million. Walt Disney chairman Michael D. Eisner has received over $2.5 million in cash bonuses on top of a $750,000 salary, because an incentive clause in his contract provides for an annual bonus of 2 percent of the company's net income over a 9 percent return on equity.

Increased amounts of total compensation at risk may occur throughout the company, not only at the CEO level. General Motors traditionally rewarded white-collar employees with lock-step annual pay increases tied to seniority, position in the organization, and inflation rate. Most employees received high performance ratings and were given the standard salary increase. Under a new compensation system affecting over 100,000 employees, GM now ranks employees against each other, using a distribution system whereby employees are ranked into the top 10 percent, the next 25 percent, the next 55 percent, and the bottom 10 percent. Pay increases are then pegged to these rankings. Traditionally, the company allocated a fixed amount (for example, 8 percent) for base-pay raises. Now the company divides this total pool into three parts. One part (about 2 percent) goes to base-pay increases, a second part to salary increases as determined by merit (about 2.5 percent), and a third part to lump-sum or management awards (about 3.5 percent). In addition, profit sharing, which traditionally existed at the executive level for the top 5,000 officials, has been opened to all employees. The logic behind this shift is to increase an employee's at-risk incentive to increase commitment and performance. In the short term, GM executives are finding that managers are paying more attention to changing business conditions, listening more to managers in other divisions, and trying to find ways to build a total business success. In the long term, GM executives hope that this incentive system will help shift the mindset to more collaboration across business lines. At the GM Saturn plant in Tennessee, the contract with the United Auto Workers provides that 20 percent of pay will be in the form of performance bonuses.

When Avon Products increased the commission base of its sales force, the immediate effect was an increase in earnings for each salesperson. Since each salesperson earned more, the company found that overall results increased 15 percent with the new system. While we do not suggest that Avon's success is solely due to a changed incentive policy, the new system certainly gave employees a greater financial incentive to perform. At Great Atlantic & Pacific Tea Company (A&P), corporate and individual store performance was on a strong downward trend through the early 1980s. To halt this trend, managers collaborated with the United Food and Commercial Workers (UFCW) Union to attempt an experiment with 60 stores in the Philadelphia area. Workers took a 25 percent pay cut in exchange for an unusual promise: If a store's employees could keep labor costs at 10 percent of that store's sales—by working more efficiently or by boosting store traffic—the employees would receive a cash bonus equal to 1 percent of sales. They would get a 0.5 percent bonus if labor costs were 11 percent of sales or 1.5 percent if labor costs were 9.5 percent of sales. This approach expanded to over 300 stores and has been credited with the company's 80 percent increase in profits between 1984 and 1986. Stores where the practice was implemented saw a 24 percent increase in sales in two years, while labor costs in these stores fell from 13 to 11 percent (with an industry average of 12 percent).

Modifying base-salary systems to include at-risk pay may help focus employee attention on activities that lead a business to be more competitive. It cannot be overemphasized, however, that to implement an effective at-risk pay system requires understanding not only the reward systems but the appraisal practices that establish standards and provide feedback. Emphasis must also be placed on selection and development practices that ensure employees have the competencies necessary to do the work and on communication practices that ensure the sharing of information with employees.

Types of Financial Incentives

Many types of financial incentives exist. Some directly provide the employee with cash. Bonuses based on performance against budget, quality, or other standards may be used as immediate financial incentives. Management awards have become popular in some companies as a means of providing employees with an immediate cash reward for completion of a project or activity. While the number of companies delivering cash awards has increased, only 7 percent actually use such rewards at present.[8] In addition to management awards, lump-sum payments have become popular as a means of rewarding performance without putting base salaries further out of line and committing the company to long-term payments. Cash distribution through profit sharing and stock options has also been widely adopted. Ford employees, for example, received an average of $3,500–$4,000 a year in the late 1980s as profit sharing. Ford management attributes some of its success throughout the 1980s to the fact that employees see how their performance as individuals makes the company stronger in the marketplace, and how improvement in the marketplace translates into personal financial gain. At Rubbermaid, employee bonuses are based on both profits and increase in book value of the company. Hourly workers are also included in the profit sharing, which may account for the company's having received over 12,600 suggestions for cost cutting and improvement in housewares in one year alone.

Financial incentives may also take indirect forms. Companies may offer financial incentives through increasing the number of vacation days; offering more health, child care, elderly care, or life insurance benefits; providing free health exams; providing discounts at company outings or on company products; giving Christmas presents; providing automobile benefits; and other indirect forms of cash. Often, though, these forms of financial rewards come to be seen as entitlements that the company cannot take away, but for which it receives little increased commitment. In many companies aware of the hidden costs of these benefits, salary check stubs highlight the amount paid by the company to the pension fund or for health care. Highlighting the amount the company commits to these financial benefits at least makes the employees more aware of what is offered. Ideally, these rewards should be more tightly linked to performance and enhancing customer values. Receiving more of the indirect financial incentives could be tied to better meeting individual and company standards.

Maintenance of Equity

A major challenge of a financial system is to maintain equity. Equity suggests that each individual perceives that his or her effort and performance justify the financial rewards received. Inequity occurs when an individual believes that someone else's rewards are not justified ("John made more than I did but did not deserve it"). If the perception is based on justifiable facts ("He is paid more than I am, but we do the same basic job with the same results"), then the inequity will persist until it is rectified.

Maintaining external equity requires understanding the market for individuals with different skill levels and consistently rewarding employees with the market. One compensation consultant informed us that he found "90 percent of U.S. companies want to be in the top 75 percentile for pay." Most companies want to be known as leaders in compensation. To ensure external equity, managers may rely on informal or company-sponsored surveys of benchmark firms—businesses in the same industry, geographic location, or size. In addition, many firms have turned to national data bases that provide criteria for benchmarking compensation practices. Regardless of the process used to achieve it, assuring external equity keeps employees focused and committed.

Internal equity must also be managed. Problems here may arise among individuals or departments. The airline industry, which institutionalized internal inequity by hiring new pilots on a separate pay system than older pilots, found that the internal inequity led to a lack of commitment on the part of the pilots who were being paid much less than their older counterparts. Employees who believe they are underpaid in relation to others, or older employees who see younger workers being offered more pay than they received to attract them into the company, are bound to feel resentment. Lump-sum payments, one-time management awards, and other financial measures have been used to resolve issues of financial equity. We propose that more creative solutions can also be effective. In a large law firm, new attorneys were not hired at the same price as older ones. To provide equity to the new attorneys, the law firm offered them more flexibility in their time commitments, more support for additional training (for example, they could take time off during the work day to attend classes), and greater job autonomy than some of the higher-paid attorneys. Internal equity was maintained through nonfinancial incentives.

Nonfinancial Rewards

Prestige

Within any organization, employees receive prestige rewards. Common prestige rewards include a larger, better-located, or better-furnished office; a parking space; access to executive clubs and dining rooms; the right to fly first class; a private secretary; favorable mention in a company publication; a multifunction telephone; an expense account; access to a company vacation resort; and so on. Such rewards have more meaning within the company than outside it and often have more social meaning than actual meaning. Office size and location send well-defined messages about internal status. In a company in a cold climate, parking in the basement of the office building means status as well as not having to walk in the cold.

Because individual behavior is shaped by the desire to gain prestige rewards, these rewards become valuable levers for influencing behavior. In most companies, prestige rewards are not used in accordance with all the criteria we suggest. While these rewards are visible, durable, and reversible, they are not tied to performance or customer value, nor are they used to create a shared mindset. By not using these rewards aggressively, managers may be missing opportunities to motivate and shape employee thought and action. Our suggestion is modest: Learn to use prestige rewards as well as financial rewards to shape employee behavior. Allocating office or parking space or titles based on performance or the enhancement of customer value by employee behavior is another way in which rewards can become tools for reinforcing competencies.

Work Content

When asking employees why they initially took a job, the answers almost always focus on the financial and prestige elements of the work: salary, title, career opportunity, quality of the company, and so on. When asking employees why they left a job, the answers almost always focus on the content of the job; "I wasn't doing what I really wanted to do";"I wasn't able to use my skills as well as I should have been"; "I got bored with the job and needed a greater challenge." The content of a job may be an employee's greatest motivator.

Job content has been studied extensively, and jobs have been categorized as "enriched" jobs, autonomous work-unit jobs, or self-designing jobs.[9] Some of the critical elements of an enriched job have been identified:

- □ *Autonomy*: More enriched jobs have greater job autonomy, giving the employee more responsibility for making decisions that affect work outcomes.
- □ *Feedback*: More enriched jobs have greater and more immediate feedback on how successfully job expectations have been met.
- □ *Skill variety*: More enriched jobs ask employees to perform a variety of skills and tasks rather than one skill over and over.

□ *Task significance*: More enriched jobs offer employees the opportunity to see the significance of the job that is being accomplished by understanding the broader context for the work being performed and the value of the work for a customer.

When jobs contain more of the above characteristics, employees are more likely to find them rewarding and motivating.

Managers may work to structure and design these elements into a job (see Chapter 9 on flexible organizational arrangements and the importance of teams). When they do so, the work itself becomes a major reward—and meets many of the reward criteria established above. Designing systems that create enriched jobs may be one of the most essential contributions a manager can make to building competitiveness.

As indicators of the success of reward systems, managers may pose the following questions:

1. To what extent do the rewards we offer meet our reward criteria?
2. To what extent do the financial and nonfinancial rewards meet customer expectations from the product or service we are delivering?
3. To what extent do the financial and nonfinancial rewards help implement the financial, product, and technological strategies of the business?
4. To what extent do the financial and nonfinancial rewards help create and sustain a shared mindset within the business?
5. To what extent do the financial and nonfinancial rewards help the organization adapt to change?
6. How effectively do the reward practices integrate employee and organizational needs?

These questions should help managers focus on reward practices and ensure that the individual competencies reinforced are those that are most directly tied to building competitiveness.

APPENDIX 7-1
Steps in the Performance-Appraisal Interview

1. PREPARATION.

2. INTRODUCTION.

3. DETERMINE TOPIC(S) EMPLOYEE WANTS TO DISCUSS.
   A. Employee brings up area of concern.
      1. Ask questions to explore causes.
      2. Obtain employee's solution(s).
   B. Employee brings up area of positive performance.
   C. Employee does not offer topic.

4. DISCUSS CONCERNS NOT MENTIONED BY EMPLOYEE.
   A. Describe employee's specific performance.
   B. Describe the expected standard of performance.
   C. Ask employee to identify cause of situation.
   D. Ask employee for his/her suggested solution.

5. DEVELOP WRITTEN ACTION PLAN(S) FOR CARRYING OUT KEY SOLUTIONS OVER SPECIFIC TIME PERIODS.

6. GIVE SPECIFIC FEEDBACK FOR ANY POSITIVE PERFORMANCE THAT HAS NOT ALREADY BEEN DISCUSSED.

7. SUMMARIZE INTERVIEW AND DISCUSS RATINGS.

8. SET FOLLOW-UP DATES.

9. THANK EMPLOYEE FOR INTERVIEW.

APPENDIX 7-2
Common Problems and Responses in Performance Appraisal

Situation	Response
Employee is defensive or argumentative.	Listen and rephrase the employee's point of view before making your points.
Weaknesses are severe and perhaps noncorrectable.	Document weaknesses.
	Work on one or two problems at a time.
	Tell employee that behavior must be changed or she/he must consider leaving.
	Do not attack the person personally, but focus on the job-related skills or lack of skills.
	Ask employee if she/he is really happy at the company.
	If appropriate, help employee prepare to leave the organization.
	Make it the employee's choice and in the employee's interest.
The employee won't talk.	Ask open-ended questions that cannot be answered with a yes/no; for example, "how?"
	Don't try to fill in silence with your talking; wait patiently for the employee to answer.
	Say, "You seem to be uncomfortable discussing this. How can we make this easier for you?"
Issues that need to be raised are very personal (for example, hygiene, personal habits)	Bite the bullet: If it affects work, it must be discussed.
	Say, "This is not easy for me to bring up, but I want to help you to do your best, and the way you dress is interfering with your opportunities for success."

8

Sustaining Competencies: Organization Design and Communication

> Simply doing more of what worked in the Eighties—the restructuring, the delayering, the mechanical, top-down measures that we took—will be too incremental. More than that, it will be too slow. The winners of the Nineties will be those who can develop a culture that allows them to move faster, communicate more clearly, and involve everyone in a focused effort to serve ever more demanding customers. To move toward that winning culture, we've got to create what we call a "boundaryless" company. We no longer have the time to climb over barriers between functions like engineering and marketing, or between people—hourly, salaried, management, and the like. Georgraphic barriers must evaporate. Our people must be as comfortable in Delhi and Seoul as they are in Louisville or Schenectady. The lines between the company and its vendors and customers must be blurred into a smooth, fluid process with no other objective than satisfying the customer and winning in the marketplace.
>
> John F. Welch, *Fortune*, March 26, 1990, p. 28

Sustaining competencies ensures that they become part of the fabric of the organization, and therefore endure over time. By implementing programs and processes that sustain competencies, management overcomes the tendency to look for quick fixes through popular programs and instead lays the groundwork for continuous improvement.

The key to sustaining competencies lies with two management practices. *Organization design* includes the processes by which responsibility is allocated, roles are defined, control and accountability are established, and decision-making authority is delegated. *Communication* also sustains competencies by ensuring that each individual in an organization has a clear understanding of what should be done, as well as why the tasks identified are important. When employees have more information about why things should be done, they are more likely to lend their support.

164

Most efforts to build organizational capability start with great fanfare but fade as employee commitment wanes. At the personal level, self-improvement programs, such as exercise and weight-loss programs, often fail because the individual commitment that is required cannot be sustained. A similar phenomenon occurs within organizations. Many promising programs are announced with high expectations, but quickly dissolve because of lack of employee commitment over time. As we will demonstrate, the strategic use of organization design and communication can prevent such fade-outs.

ORGANIZATION DESIGN

The titles and reporting relationships within an organization send clear messages to employees about the firm's priorities and may significantly affect performance and commitment. One company that wanted to institute a program dedicated to continuous improvement had two false starts before demonstrating the full commitment of senior management by giving the individual in charge of the program the title of vice president and having him report directly to the general manager. Other organizations have found that when they remove several levels of management they become more flexible, provide employees with more autonomy over their work decisions, and can be more responsive to customer needs. Or a higher level of individual commitment may be attained through structuring an organization into teams. By involving appropriate employees in the process of organization design, these individuals may come to share a mindset about the means and ends of the organization they are designing. Finally, by sharing decision-making responsibilities, individuals may be more committed to implementing strategies and adapting to change; strategic unity is thus established among both employees and customers.

Many managers seek an *ideal* organization structure. But Nirvana does not exist. We propose that in lieu of seeking a single, ideal structure that can endure forever, management should establish a *process* for ongoing organization design. The appropriate outcome of organization design is not an organization chart but a stable process for continually modifying the organization and clarifying reporting relationships, responsibilities, and control systems.

A stable design process is especially important in light of the trade-offs that management will need to make in the process of redesigning the organization. For example, should internal efficiency or responsiveness be the primary criterion for the new design (see Figure 8-1)? An organization's efficiency refers to reducing costs, through economies of scale, lower overhead, or increased productivity. Centralizing an organization's activities generally reduces the unit cost of the company's product or service. An organization's responsiveness is its effectiveness in meeting unique customer needs. Generally, a highly decentralized organization is better able to meet these needs. Thus, businesses often shuttle back and forth between centralized and decentralized structures as they try to apply these different criteria. The challenge, however, is neither to centralize nor decentralize but to gain the benefits of both approaches by doing both simultaneously—being, as one manager said, "the most centralized autonomous organization in the industry."

Other paradoxes that have to be juggled in deciding on an organization structure involve the following choices:

☐ *Flexibility versus stability.* Organization structure must simultaneously encourage flexibility of individual thought and action and organization responsiveness while at the same time ensuring stability and consistency of individual thought and action as well as of organizational procedures.

Figure 8–1
CRITERIA FOR ORGANIZATION DESIGN

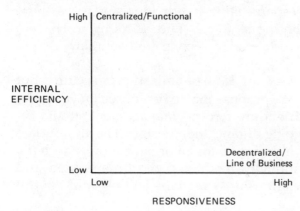

□ *Big versus small.* Organizations must at the same time draw on the benefits of size (economies of scale, large distribution systems, widespread brand identity) and maintain the individual commitment and flexibility of a small, dynamic organization. General Electric's chairman, Jack Welsh, has proposed that GE become the ''biggest little corporation in the world'' through its efforts to be simultaneously large and small.

□ *Domestic versus global.* Organizations face the dual challenges of maintaining market share and consistency in a domestic market while branching into global markets. To do so, organization structures must maintain existing manufacturing and distribution systems while complementing them with strategic alliances and global organization structures.

No one organization structure will fit all situations or provide an ideal resolution to the conflict of competing demands. We would propose that the process of responding to paradox is more important than finding a perfect solution: Paradoxes will continue to exist long after any design has outlived its usefulness. Once management accepts that the process of organization design is a fluid, ongoing one and implements the procedures that make it most effective, the ability to adapt to change—and thus to compete successfully—will be enormously enhanced.

The sections that follow address the three main questions of organization design: (1) What should be the *shape* of the organization—for example, how many levels, what roles exist, what reporting relationships, what division of labor and so forth? (2) What type of *governance mechanisms* should be established to shape employee behavior? (3) What *processes* are needed for the continual reassessment of organizational planning?

Shape

Organization Operating Mode

An organization structure should define responsibility and roles; help employees respond to customer demands; and communicate to employees and stakeholders the goals of the organization. Five types of structures can be identified: functional, product, matrix, product-management, and customer-management modes (see

Figure 8-2
CHARACTERISTICS OF ORGANIZATION MODES

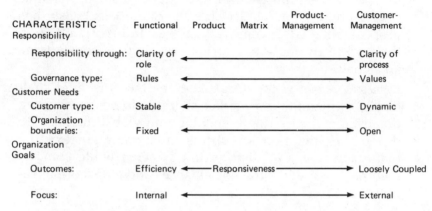

ORGANIZATION TYPE

CHARACTERISTIC Responsibility	Functional	Product	Matrix	Product-Management	Customer-Management
Responsibility through:	Clarity of role				Clarity of process
Governance type:	Rules				Values
Customer Needs					
Customer type:	Stable				Dynamic
Organization boundaries:	Fixed				Open
Organization Goals					
Outcomes:	Efficiency	Responsiveness			Loosely Coupled
Focus:	Internal				External

Figure 8-2).[1] While all five exist in businesses today, we believe that the *customer-management organization mode* will become prevalent in this decade as business conditions change and the pressure to meet customer expectations increases.

Classic Functional Organization[2]   In this traditional organization structure, responsibility rests with the top manager, to whom all questions flow up and from whom all decisions flow down (Figure 8-3). Each functional area has its unique expertise and economies of scale, reporting relationships, and responsibility.

Such a structure has many advantages. It is the least complex, encourages economies of scale, and assigns clear accountability for functional errors. It is useful when controlling costs is an important objective and the organization needs to centralize decisions to ensure control. The functional structure works best with stable customers who expect exactly the same product to be delivered over and over. The primary disadvantages are that it becomes unwieldy when there are more than one or two product lines. It also does not lend itself to growth or flexibility, which means that change or innovation cannot be handled effectively.

Classic Product Organization   In this type of organization, the focus is on development of new products. Each new product or product group is given autonomy. For each new product or product group, a functional unit is established for design, develop-

Figure 8-3
CLASSIC FUNCTIONAL ORGANIZATION

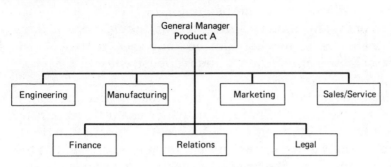

ment, and delivery (Figure 8-4). Between 1955 and 1975, the majority of the Fortune 500 companies shifted to a product organization.[3] In the most extreme form of this structure, the corporate office becomes merely a bank that allocates capital to the different product lines.

The advantages of this organization system are that it allows for a high degree of customer responsiveness, is relatively simple, assigns clear accountability to the product manager for each product, and encourages the growth of product lines. Its drawbacks lie in its fragmented focus, with functional expertise split across product lines, low economies of scale, and inability to adapt to a cost-controlling environment.

The challenge is to learn how to combine these traditional structures to reap the benefits of each. Since the early 1970s, organizations have attempted to define alternative organizing

Figure 8-4
CLASSIC PRODUCT ORGANIZATION

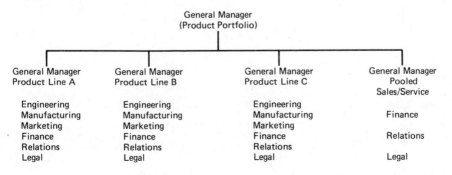

modes that are both efficient and responsive (see Figure 8–1). The three alternatives considered below are options for resolving the paradoxes we discussed at the beginning of this chapter. Since these types of organizations are more recent, the clear distinctions between them are somewhat blurred, but each represents an attempt to achieve both efficiency and responsiveness.

Classic Matrix Organization[4]   In the classic matrix organization, a functional manager and a product manager share the reporting responsibility for performance (see Figure 8–5). Some functions, for example, finance, legal, and human resources, are kept at the general-manager level. The product general manager has responsibility and accountability for product design and delivery and for drawing from the functional organization resources to meet goals.

The advantages of the matrix organization are that it focuses simultaneously on economies of scale and product. It is not so costly as the product-organization mode and is better suited to product development than the functional organization. It allows for resources to be shifted across product lines and is helpful in situations where scarce engineering or other technical expertise needs to be strategically allocated among a number of projects or programs. The drawbacks are that it is complex and requires voluntary problem resolution at the general-manager level, which

Figure 8–5
CLASSIC MATRIX ORGANIZATION

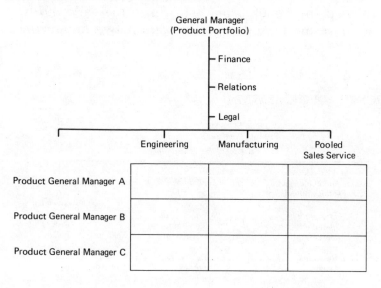

may slow down decision-making. In addition, maintaining a balance of power between the product and functional managers is difficult and time-consuming and must be renegotiated with each management change. Finally, each product manager may have a different marketing focus and different customer contracts.

Product-Management Organization In the past few years, some companies have adapted existing matrix organizations to a product-management organization mode (see Figure 8–6). In the product-management organization, the marketing manager becomes a product manager with responsibility for pulling together product teams. Responsibility is not shared with a functional manager but remains with the product manager, who heads a team of people from each function and is the advocate for the product assigned to him or her. The product manager has the ultimate responsibility for every aspect of the product's design, development, and delivery and is accountable for the product's success or failure.

The advantages of the product-management organization are similar to those of a matrix organization: the balance of a strong functional focus with a marketing focus; ease of adding or subtracting product lines; and costs somewhere between a pure functional and a product organization. More companies are turning to the product-management structure as they look to global organization. In these cases, the product manager has global responsibility for product design and delivery. Country managers work

Figure 8–6
PRODUCT-MANAGEMENT ORGANIZATION

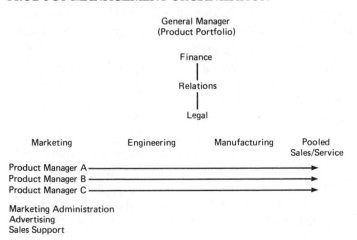

General Manager
(Product Portfolio)

Finance

Relations

Legal

Marketing   Engineering   Manufacturing   Pooled
Sales/Service

Product Manager A
Product Manager B
Product Manager C

Marketing Administration
Advertising
Sales Support

as technical support for the work within the country.[5] The draw-backs are that there is often functional inequality, the role of the product manager is demanding and complex, and the development of a cooperative team requires attention to management processes that not all product managers are equipped to give.

Manufacturing organizations have been using the product-management mode with some success. At Outboard Marine Corporation, most Evinrude and Johnson outboard motors now come from five small, focused factories in North Carolina and Georgia. Each plant, with fewer than 500 employees, specializes in one phase of manufacturing and assembly. At Spruce Pine, North Carolina, for example, Outboard Marine casts engine blocks with a rare "lost-foam" technique that yields smaller yet more powerful engines than conventional methods, and at much lower costs. The blocks are then trucked to Brunsville, North Carolina, for the addition of pistons, fuel systems, and other equipment and then on to either Rutherfordton, North Carolina, or Calhoun, Georgia, for transmissions. As a result of this product-management focus, the 150-horsepower Evinrude retails for about $5,000 compared to $6,000 for the Yamaha.

Customer-Management Organization   The primary difference between the customer-management and the product-management structure is illustrated in Figure 8–7: focus. The focus of an organization may range along a continuum from exclusively internal to external. The primary focus of functional, product, and matrix organization modes is *internal*—on how employees are organized to respond to customer needs. An *external* focus, on the other hand, begins with how individuals outside the organization respond to what happens inside and how those inside connect to what happens outside. The product-management organization is a step in this direction. The customer-management mode goes further, with the organization structured around its customers.

When AT&T was first deregulated, it organized around products, not customers. As a result, separate sales teams called on customers for long-distance business and for telephone and computer equipment. The result was confusion among customers, who heard two separate AT&T sales representatives presenting potentially conflicting sales pitches. In reorganizing, AT&T turned to a customer-management organization, ensuring a single contact point for each customer. The single contact could

Figure 8-7
FROM PRODUCT-MANAGEMENT TO
CUSTOMER-MANAGEMENT ORGANIZATION

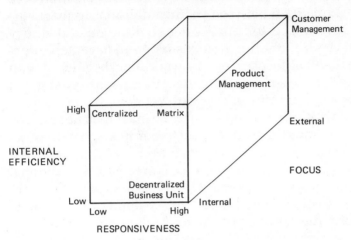

represent all AT&T products and had the ability to work with the different product managers. IBM has also set up separate sales offices organized along customer lines, with one for financial and brokerage customers in New York, another for General Motors in Detroit, and another for Ford in Dearborn, Michigan. Organizing around customers ensures commitment. A customer manager, who integrates the resources required to deliver what the customer needs, works with the product manager, who integrates internal resources for product development.

The customer-management organization may be characterized by three fundamental management processes. First, in a customer-management organization, the focus is on *flow, not function*. A customer-management organization does not begin by describing business functions but by understanding the flow of work through an organization continually being driven by customer needs. Employee roles are defined by the flow of work required to meet customer requirements rather than by a functional analysis. A flow management process emphasizes the work activity chain which must be followed to transfer organizational inputs into customer outputs.

In an electronics firm, the shift from function to flow management process was significant. With a more traditional functional focus, product managers were accountable to sell products. Because the firm had a number of products sold to the same customer, it would not be unusual for a single customer to experience multiple sales representatives, each representing a different product. At best, this created confusion; more often it created conflicts and competition between product divisions to meet customer needs; at worst, customers became so disoriented that they chose another vendor. Shifting to a customer-management organization, management focused on the work flow, beginning with a definition of customer requirements. Since most customers want to have easy means of working with vendors, the firms need to build a flow within the firm to meet the customer needs. The electronics firm organized around a customer-management organization and assigned a customer manager to work with the customer. This customer manager was more than a traditional account representative who primarily made sales calls. The individual had total accountability for meeting customer requirements and had a profit and loss responsibility based on customer performance. The customer manager, in many cases, actually has an office in the customer's facilities and becomes, to some extent, an active member of the customer organization. The customer manager is responsible for ensuring that the flow of products and services within the firm meets the needs of the customer. He or she has the obligation of reaching back into the organization and drawing out resources to focus on customer needs.

The focus on flow over function is characterized in Figure 8–8. In this figure, the customer stands at the head of a work-flow organization design. The customer manager has the obligation of diagnosing and responding to customer requirements. He or she then must have the ability to look into the matrix of organizational functions and products to match customer needs with organization competencies. In making this match, he or she must be able to manage a constant flow between organization competencies and customer requirements.

Valmont, a maker of metal poles (for example, lighting poles) and irrigation equipment, has recently organized around ''strategic business clusters.'' The intent of the strategic business clusters highlights the importance of flow over function. The business cluster managers have the responsibility for identifying key customer requirements, then pulling resources from within Valmont to meet customer needs. The business cluster managers are senior executives who know Valmont's business competencies, who have the respect of Valmont functional and product managers, who have accountability to make sure that customer sales increase, and

Figure 8–8
FLOW OF CUSTOMER-MANAGEMENT ORGANIZATION

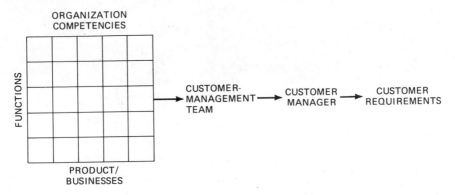

who are organizationally equivalent to Valmont general managers. The strategic business clusters system has allowed Valmont to focus its resources on key accounts to ensure that, like a funnel, Valmont's resources efficiently flow to customers.

Second, the customer-management organization depends on *dynamic teams rather than fixed hierarchies.* These teams are simultaneously stable and unstable. The customer manager ensures stability. This individual becomes a means of ensuring continuity between the organization and customers. The customer manager should not be rotated often because the relationship between the firm and each customer depends on the stability of this relationship. While the customer manager is stable, the team also requires adaptability consistent with changing customer requirements. The customer manager has the obligation of extracting resources from within the organization to focus on customer needs. Since customer requirements vary, composition of teams may also vary. This dynamic team may be conceptualized as a star (see Figure 8–9). Each point of the star represents a set of competencies that may be identified, extracted, and integrated into a customer-management team to satisfy the requirements of the customer. Over time, these teams may change composition as customer requirements change. With changed customer requirements, new team members may be added or taken away.

In the electronics firm which has implemented this organization, a customer manager is assigned who knows and is respected by her customer. She has the obligation of maintaining an ongoing relationship with key employees throughout the customer organization, so that she can understand, define, and predict customer

Figure 8–9
CUSTOMER-MANAGEMENT ORGANIZATION

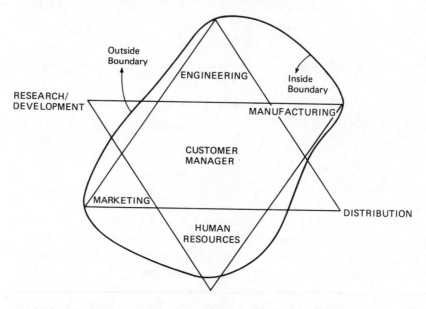

requirements. She also has the obligation of extracting resources from her firm to meet those requirements. The team she manages changes composition, depending on the changing requirements of her customer.

Another example of the process and importance of dynamic teams in a customer-management orgranization comes from the commercial construction industry. A project manager in the commercial construction industry is the equivalent of a customer manager. His job is to manage a project completely by identifying the requirements of the owner and architects, then by forming a team which has the collective competencies to make sure that the project is accomplished. Over time, the composition of the team changes. When a project arises in a new city, the project manager may have to create a new team with resources from the local work force. His job is to secure resources and create a team that will meet the demands of the project.

The third characteristic of the customer-management organization is a *permeable rather than fixed boundary*. At the beginning of this chapter, Jack Welch discusses the boundaryless organization, which is characterized by a permeable boundary. The permeable boundary implies that the boundaries of what is inside and outside the organization may be blurred and porous. The permeable boundary occurs in two ways. First, the customer manager and customer-management team experience a dual role, of being part of their home organization while spending an enormous amount of time in the customer organization. The boundaries between the two organizations are nearly invisible because it becomes difficult at times to identify who is formally part of which organization.

In some divisions of Hewlett-Packard, engineers spend as much time in customer offices as in their own, and product design is based largely on customer input. In General Electric's aircraft engine division, a permanent team is assigned to Boeing in Seattle. This team ensures an ongoing flow of information between Boeing and GE. The team leader is responsible for integrating the diverse groups from GE to focus on Boeing's needs. Customers may also be involved in nonproduct decisions. The customer-management structure provides for customer input in decisions involving policy, staffing, and performance appraisal, and in information sharing with employees.

In addition, there is a permeable boundary around the customer-management team itself. Customer requirements may be satisfied with competencies that reside exclusively within the organization, and the customer-management team has only its own organization members. Or, as would likely be the case, some customer requirements may call for competencies outside the current boundary of the organization. In this case, the customer manager has the obligation of going to other vendors to draw on the resources to meet the customer requirements. The boundary of the customer-management team is permeable because ownership of resources is less critical than ensuring that customer needs are satisfied (see Figure 8–9, where the points on the star represent resources to meet customer needs and the line represents resources inside and outside the organization boundary).

In the electronics firm, for example, the customer manager discovered a unique application problem facing the customer. As the customer manager looked inside her organization, she did not find the competencies to meet these requirements. As a result, she formed a strategic alliance with a software firm that had the required competencies. In this customer-management organization, the boundary between the electronics firm and its customers was permeable—shifting constantly to ensure a flow of products and services to meet customer requirements.

In the construction industry, the project manager has a similar obligation. If his organization has full-time employees who possess the comptencies to deliver the project, he can draw exclusively from those resources. But, as is more commonly the case, his organization does not have all the competencies to deliver a large and complex project, so his job is to contract for those resources. This contract may be a one-time agreement, a joint venture, a licensing arrangement, or some other form of creating unique organizational arrangements to meet customer requirements.

As relationships between firms and customers persist over time, the amount of services that may be shared between organizations and customers increases. Initial participation in the customer-management team may include individuals with competencies in product, technology, service, or engineering. As customer relationships evolve, organizations may provide additional service by adding to the customer-management team individuals with competencies in staff functions (for example, human resources, finance, business planning). In one organization that wanted to install long-term service-based relationships with key accounts, the organization offered customers access to its outstanding human resource practices. By including customers in a firm's human resource practices, a greater bond, or commitment, ensued.[6] A customer manager has the responsibility to assess which existing resources may be extracted to service customer requirements.

In customer-management organizations, customer managers have ultimate responsibility for representing the business to its customers. As such, they have the obligation of organizing and facilitating the teams. Product managers continue to have the obligation of integrating diverse functional areas into specific products, which may then be further integrated and adapted to customer requirements. However, because the customer-manager organization is designed around teams, it is a leaner organization with employees focusing directly on customers through teams. The ability to form and merge teams with internal and external membership and to concentrate on customer needs is critical to the success of the customer-management structure.

Examples of the customer-management organization exist in a variety of industries today. In large law firms, senior partners are assigned to key customer accounts. The partners seek to meet the needs of these accounts with resources drawn from both inside and outside the firm. At times, a lawyer who manages a key account will recognize that the client's needs are beyond the scope of the firm, so the account manager will subcontract a source from outside (go beyond the circle in Figure 8–9) to meet the client's needs. Film producers also function with a customer-management structure. Their job is to make a film, blending resources from different studios. In both of these areas, the customer manager—the law partner and the film producer—is accountable for meeting the needs of the customer. Some of the resources designed to meet customer needs are drawn from within and some from without the organization, and the teams formed to reach the objective are temporary.

A customer-management organization is conducive to greater organizational capability. We envision more companies shifting away from functional, product, and matrix organizations to product- and customer-management structures. As these shifts are made, the requirements for flexible organizational arrangements increase (see Chapter 10). The boundaries between an organization and its customers become less significant, as discussed by Jack Welch, and the ability to focus and integrate resources to respond to customer needs increases.

De-layering

Organizations are finding that traditional spans of control are changing dramatically. The traditional rule of thumb has been that spans of control encompass from five to seven individuals. At Xerox, General Electric, and Reynolds Metals Company, the average span of control doubled from the beginning to the end of the 1980s. At Du Pont, plant supervisors once had a span of control of about fifteen employees, but that number has been increased to an average of about forty today. Some Japanese firms, such as Fanuc Ltd., currently have spans of control that include up to sixty employees.

As spans of control increase, the pattern is to move decision-making down to the individual most responsible for the work assignment. Reducing management layers in an organization increases individual responsibility and accountability and should also increase organizational flexibility and responsiveness. Middle managers who served a control and watchdog function have been removed to empower individuals to respond more quickly to customer needs. At General Motors, the response time for creating a new car was reduced over the decade of the 1980s to forty-eight months. At Toyota, the time from concept to production remains eighteen months. This difference can be explained by the fact that, despite reorganizations, General Motors still has as many as fourteen management layers compared with only five at Toyota. Designed to minimize error, the GM system also stifles initiative and innovation.

The impact of reducing management layers is both short and long term. Over the short term, the result is immediate profits. At Mercury Maine, a division of Brunswick that makes boat motors, a management layer was removed just below the division level, with the responsibility of this layer consolidated at the corporate level. The outright cost savings was $6 million a year. In addition, at the corporate level, the headquarters staff was reduced from 550 to 220 by eliminating some jobs and reassigning employees to plants. The total one-year savings for the corporation was $20 million. Hartmarx Corporation, a maker of men's business suits, centralized the administration of its 330 specialty stores through consolidation and computerization of purchasing decisions. As a result, about 300 regional and divisional employees were eliminated, saving the company about $12 million a year.

The longer-term impact of de-layering is even more significant. With increased independence, employees are likely to feel commitment to the firm, as evidenced by an increase in their suggestions. At Corning Glass, for example, reducing management layers resulted in the implementation of many employee suggestions that saved the organization money. The long-term effects of empowering employees by removing layers of management will be to make organizations more flexible and dynamic, thus rendering them more competitive.

Decisions concerning reducing management levels must be based on a realistic assessment of industry trends, of the need for flexibility to meet customer needs, of whether the managerial competencies exist to handle increased responsibility, and of whether processes are in place to ensure that de-layering empowers rather then offends employees. Removing layers of management that have long been built into an organization requires both skill in controlling individual behavior and courage.

Strategic Alliances

As the boundaries of an organization become more open to customers, they also become more open to alliances between suppliers and competitors that enable the organization to become globally competitive. As one researcher[7] has suggested, the shape of organizational structures must adapt to dynamic global industries. In lieu of vertically integrated firms, organizations will form networks of alliances in countries around the world. Such alliances are formed in an effort to reduce product-development time, gain entry into global markets, and share and acquire technology, so that allied firms can be more responsive to customer needs and expectations. Acquisitions, internal ventures, joint equity ventures, minority investments, cooperative agreements on licensing or manufacturing, research and development consortia, or joint bidding and subcontracting arrangements are some of the forms these alliances might take.

The customer-management organization recognizes these alliances as a means of acquiring resources to meet customer needs, and such strategic alliances have already been formed within various industries. Studies have shown, however, that in the majority of cases the alliance lasts only three years and fails to meet the objectives of either firm. To succeed, alliances need to have patient capital, managerial support, balanced partner inputs, sufficient operating autonomy, and a dynamic organization structure and control system.

Governance Mechanisms

Governance mechanisms are the organizational processes through which competencies are sustained and employee behavior is shaped. Depending on business circumstances, different governance mechanisms may be appropriate. One researcher has defined three distinct approaches to governing employee behavior: market, bureaucracy, and clan (see Figure 8–10).[8]

Market

A market governance mechanism involves offering employees specific incentives for accomplishing clearly articulated standards. Employee behaviors and attitudes are shaped by the organizational practices of setting goals and reinforcing them through rewards. When clear performance expectations can be established and monitored, when performance can be directly linked to organizational outcomes, and when the organization focuses on short-term transactions, the market system may be the most appropriate

Figure 8–10
SITUATIONS FOR GOVERNANCE MECHANISMS
(Ulrich, Quinn, and Cameron, 1989)

	Means of Governing Behavior	Organizational Characteristics	Task Characteristics	Individual Characteristics
Market Governance	Explicit incentives	Clear goals Short-term transactions	Measurable Link individual performance to organizational outcomes	Short-term goals
Bureaucratic Governance	Rules and procedures	Stable systems	Performance standards easy to monitor	Lack of long-term professional competence
Clan	Values or norms	Long-term transactions Teamwork	Individual performance difficult to measure	Self-monitoring Professional

for governing employee behavior. In the classic case, market mechanisms influence the behavior of salespeople, whose results can be clearly measured and monitored. Unfortunately, in more dynamic and changing organizations, market controls fail and need to be replaced with other mechanisms.[9]

Bureaucracy

Bureaucratic governance makes use of organizational policies and procedures to shape employee behavior. In situations where performance standards can be monitored closely through personal inspection and where employees lack the professional competence to perform without being monitored, management may rely on policies and rules to govern behavior. As we have seen, however, the traditional, rule-controlled bureaucratic organization is being replaced by less hierarchical, more networked organizations. While the bureaucratic approach may be effective in stable environments, it may not allow for enough flexibility to be able to respond to change.

Clan

Clan governance mechanisms shape and sustain employee behavior through a shared mindset. Shaping employee behavior through development of a shared mindset is workable when long-term contracts and relationships exist between employees and employers. Over time, employees learn the norms and expectations of employers, and employers learn to trust employees to act in accordance with the organization's values. Clan governance also operates well with professional employees in changing and ambiguous job settings. As technologies, organizational boundaries, and employee demographics all change rapidly in the 1990s, market and bureaucratic governance mechanisms will fail to sustain personal competencies, so that organizations seeking to survive will adopt the clan approach to influencing employee behavior.

A primary means of ensuring clan governance is to structure an organization around teams. Teams establish shared values and mindset among team members and at the same time exert informal pressure on members to meet team standards. At Ford, "Team Taurus" was so successful that management realized that employee performance could be better motivated by peer pressure than by bureaucratic rules, and the team concept has been adopted in many Ford divisions.

Champion International, the fourth largest U.S. paper producer, has also turned to the clan approach to foster increased employee productivity. In one plant, teams on the assembly line are in charge of production. For example, the team assigned to a particular machine establishes the norms for production and performance. In addition to setting performance standards, the teams have devised ways to increase production with existing equipment. As a result of employee input, Champion estimates that it will save $100 million over three years.

In these cases and in dozens of other companies, clan governance mechanisms as instituted through teams have replaced market and bureaucratic controls. By working in teams with shared mindsets, employees face social pressure, which sustains commitment to job assignments. When customers are made part of such teams, their commitment is also strengthened.

Processes

Traditionally, the chief outcome of the organization design process has been an organization chart that establishes reporting relationships. In a changing and turbulent business environment, where the organization chart may be outdated before it is published, the outcome of organization design must be a stable and understandable process for making organizational decisions.

The process we propose here consists of five sequential steps that serve to establish a stable process for making organization design decisions. It may be applied to a business as a whole or to subgroups (for example, engineering, marketing, human resources) within a business.

Step 1—Specify Key Tasks to Be Done

Key tasks are work activities that are critical to the accomplishment of a business's goals. Identifying key tasks forces an examination of the activities performed within an organization. It also encourages a discussion of why some tasks are performed. We recommend that for initial analysis no more than ten key tasks be identified. In one large organization facing reorganization, a management team identified these ten key tasks: research, design engineering, manufacturing engineering, quality assurance, manufacturing, purchasing, distribution, finance, sales and marketing, and human resources. While each of these key tasks could be subdivided, they represent an array of the activities performed within the organization (see Figure 8–11).

Step 2—Define Optional Areas Where Tasks Can Be Performed

The following options exist:

- □ *Headquarters:* Tasks can be performed by a central staff at the corporate office.
- □ *Geographic:* Tasks can be performed by a staff who live in one geographic area where the business employs a large number of people.
- □ *Group:* Tasks can be performed by a group-level staff which has responsibility for many businesses.
- □ *Division/Business Unit:* Tasks can be performed by a division or business unit within the company.
- □ *Outside:* Tasks can be subcontracted through alliances or bids from outside vendors.

By identifying the key tasks and the options for where they can be performed (see Figure 8–11), management can create a responsibility matrix that provides a process for deciding how work will be allocated. One axis of the matrix includes the key tasks; the other, the locations where those tasks could be accomplished.

Figure 8-11
FRAMEWORK FOR ORGANIZATION DESIGN
PROCESS: RESPONSIBILITY MATRIX

WHERE WORK CAN BE PERFORMED

KEY TASKS	Corporate	Geographic	Group	Division/ Business Unit	Outsource
Research					
Design Engineering					
Manufacturing Engineering					
Quality Assurance					
Manufacturing					
Purchasing					
Distribution					
Finance					
Sales and Marketing					
Human Resources					

Step 3—Define Criteria for the Responsibility Matrix

Once the matrix in Figure 8-11 is established, managers need to set criteria for ensuring that responsibility for each work activity is appropriately allocated. The primary question is: "For our business to have a competitive advantage in the eyes of our customers, where should this work activity be done?" This question forces a dialogue about customer values for each work activity. Would the customer prefer that costs be lowered, which might result in centralization of the activity for economies of scale? Would the customer prefer to pay a higher price but receive customized service and personal contact? The answer to these questions will help establish where work should be assigned.

Step 4—Assign Tasks to Specific Locations

In discussing each row of the responsibility matrix, managers can help clarify roles and assign accountability and responsibility. The primary question at this stage is: What level in the organization will have *primary responsibility* for accomplishing this task? In one organization, this decision was called assigning the "R." The discussion about assigning responsibility is a key component of the organization design process, because current practices are defined and desired ones are debated.

For example, in the company just mentioned, most "R's" were in the corporate column, because this company was largely centralized. In the dialogues about reorganization, the decision was made to keep certain activities—for example, research, quality assurance, purchasing, and distribution—at the corporate level, because top management, employee representatives from each level, and customers all believed that economies of scale in these activities would increase customer value. Using the same criteria, other activities, including design engineering, manufacturing engineering, and manufacturing, were assigned to specific groups, while marketing and sales, finance, and human resources were given primarily to the business units.

Step 5—Prepare Reporting Relationships and Establish a Process for Re-evaluation

One dilemma of companies focusing on a *process* for organization design has to do with time. It is easy to get so locked into endless debate about the ideal outcome that no decisions are ever made. But the essence of the process we advocate is that it is based on the assumption that there is no single right answer and that there must be ongoing reassessment. Dialogue and debate, however useful, must be halted at some point and a new organization design implemented. When that time comes, everyone involved in the process should be heartened by realizing that over time the responsibility matrix (Figure 8–11) will need to be re-evaluated and redefined if necessary. Their decisions will not be cast in stone.

In the corporation mentioned above, the dialogue lasted about three months and involved both internal employees and external customers and suppliers. The management staff, armed with the input, then met privately to make the decisions about what work would be allocated at what levels. The statement announcing these decisions did not focus on the new reporting relationships or on where work was to be done but on the *process* used to come up with the decisions. The announcement also made clear that reorganizing was a way of life, that the process of evaluating where work would be allocated would occur again, and that no one should get too comfortable with the present reorganization because everything would change again. A year later, management re-evaluated the organization design and after further discussion decided to move more activities from the corporate to the group level. For example, since each group was developing unique products, the management chose to move the research activity to the group level.

Organization Design: Success Indicators

Organization design is a key component of building organizational capability. To ensure that the design of an organization contributes to its competitiveness, the following questions should be asked:

- □ To what extent does our organization design reflect customer values?
- □ To what extent does our organization have the right number of layers to meet both efficiency and responsiveness criteria?
- □ Compared to competitors, what are our organization costs and benefits?
- □ To what extent do we control individual behavior through shared values?
- □ To what extent do employees share the values of management?
- □ To what extent do we use appropriate mechanisms (for example, employee involvement, teams) to allocate decision-making responsibility?
- □ To what extent do employees understand the *processes* used in arriving at an organization design?

COMMUNICATION

Communication processes sustain personal competencies and build organizational capability. When employees understand what customers perceive as valuable, they are more able to provide what is required. In some organizations, such information is treated as confidential and is not shared beyond a limited cadre of marketing, sales, and senior managers. In businesses where employees lack information, customer value can never serve as a criterion for employee behavior.

Effective communication also creates strategic unity. Communication processes ensure that consistent, credible, and continuous information flows through an organization. When such information is shared, employees begin to share a mindset about the business's ends and means. Finally, communication processes help overcome resistance to change. One common barrier to successful change is a lack of information about the positive outcomes of the change. Many managers of a company attempting to enter the European market resisted the change because they were not comfortable with the idea of moving to Europe. They believed their quality of life would be affected, their children's education would suffer, and they would be cut off from the rest of the company. To overcome this resistance, the managers were given thorough information on the benefits of a global perspective for broadening their horizons, on the quality of the schools their children would attend, and on how contact could be maintained with U.S. headquarters. This information enabled managers to see their assignment to Europe as potentially beneficial to themselves, their families, and their careers.

Managers spend more time communicating than they do in any other single activity.[10] A recent study indicated that the quality of a company's performance corresponded directly to the effectiveness of its internal lines of communication. The researchers found that 79 percent of middle-management employees in high-performing companies were satisfied with the amount of internal information they received, compared with 69 percent at low-performing companies. Among professional employees, such as computer programmers and accountants, at these high-performing companies, 65 percent said they were satisfied, compared with only 34 percent at less successful companies.[11]

Establishing effective communication processes is not easy. At times, employees must hear the same message many times over before they fully understand it. Maintaining the consistency of a message is also difficult. Many people have experienced the classroom exercise in which a story is told to one person and then shared with person after person until twenty people have heard it. Usually the final version bears little resemblance to the original story. To maintain effective communication, three issues must be addressed: (1) *what* information is shared, (2) *who* shares and who receives the messages, and (3) *how* messages are shared.

What to Share

Why versus What

Most information shared in an organization focuses on *what* should be done—for example, *what* program, activity, or behavior is expected of employees. We suggest that unless there is understanding of *why* activities should occur, resistance will persist about what should be done. Until employees understand the *why*, they do not accept the *what*. In a Farm Credit Bank in the mid-1980s, a number of farm foreclosures were necessary because the farmers failed to pay bills. For many months, anger and resistance ran high among the farmers, and the loan officers who had to communicate the bad news of foreclosure faced animosity and opposition. The situation, at times, became quite ugly. Farmers wanted to keep their land; loan officers wanted to fulfill their duty. The bank president concluded that for a period of time there should be a hiatus, during which time loan officers would only share information on the farmer's performance in paying back the loan. This information, given to the farmer weekly, compared the loan performance with district averages, bank averages, and national averages. The farmers were also given information about how the bank was affected by low-performing loans. After two months, the loan officers were instructed to ask the farmers for advice on how to proceed with their duty as bank employees to collect on outstanding loans. While not all farmers appreciated the actions the loan officers had to take, most understood *why* foreclosure had become necessary. The animosity changed to acceptance (not necessarily agreement) of the inevitability of foreclosure.

In an insurance company with a portfolio of management-development programs, the president required that the first module of every such program explain *why* the program was critical for business success. His logic was twofold. First, if each participant understood why training should occur, each would be more committed to acquiring the skills being taught. Second, if no clear and logical reason for offering the program could be given, the program was canceled.

In both cases, the principle is the same: sharing information on *why* activities should occur elicits more commitment than merely sharing *what* should be done. We have found that most communication efforts focus 80 percent on what, not why. We propose that 80 percent of communication efforts should be devoted to why, and acceptance of what will then follow.

More versus Less

Management of a large U.S. manufacturing company seeking a strategic alliance with a Japanese firm met to prepare a proposal for the venture. After a conclusion was reached, a senior executive was dispatched to deliver personally the confidential message to the Tokyo firm. By personally handing the message to executives in the potential alliance he had fulfilled his obligation to maintain confidentiality. Imagine his consternation when later that afternoon at a public forum before all headquarters employees, the president of the Japanese firm read the proposal to all employees. This case illustrates the choices that need to be made concerning how open to be with information. While we do not argue that all information should be publicly shared, we believe that many firms have a misplaced fear of sharing too much information. Information is too often marked confidential and shared with only a few of the people whose work it will affect.

Without accurate information, employees tend to create and act on rumors. With too little information, employees often attribute unintended meaning to the scanty information they have received. A firm that was considering closing a manufacturing facility did not share information with employees for fear they would leave when they learned the plant was going to be closed. Because business was poor and because employees learned through informal channels that changes were being considered, rumors ran wild. Employees came to believe that the company would not only close the plant but would not offer opportunities at other plants nor any outplacement services. The result was that many high-quality employees who could find employment elsewhere did so. With falling productivity and morale, the plant had to be closed months earlier than had been anticipated.

Another company handled the same kind of situation quite differently. Management announced that a plant would have to be closed and set the date for this event two years into the future. Managers met with all employees to explain why the closing was necessary. They also communicated their desire for employees to stay to the end and offered those who did stay opportunities for movement into other facilities, outplacement services, severance packages, and a major financial bonus for staying to the end. Ironically, during the two years prior to the plant closing morale and productivity were the highest the plant had experienced in a decade.

Often information that is designated confidential becomes empowering when it is openly shared. Competitor analyses, market-share data, and performance-against-plan information may be shared openly with employees. In the meter-reading department of a utility company, a manager decided to communicate openly the performance of department members. He posted a simple communication device: on a weekly basis, for each employee, he posted three colors—red for above average, green for average, and black for below average. After two months, the overall performance of the department had improved by 5 percent and after six months by 15 percent. Merely communicating more openly about the performance of the group led to greater employee awareness and commitment.

In an effort to increase the sharing of information, many managers use public forums with "no holds barred" questions. Such forums may occur in a variety of employee gatherings: training programs, employee meetings, dinner speeches, or staff meetings. One manager began such a session after an employee dinner by asking individuals at each table to write three questions anonymously—the tougher the better. He promised to answer as best he could. After responding to some difficult questions, a dialogue began with employees where information was shared honestly and openly. The atmosphere of candor was created in part by the manager's acknowledgment that he did not have all the answers. At a planning meeting in another company, with about 40 senior officers present, the chairman asked some probing questions. After about 30 minutes, one manager who had been asked a tough question replied, "I am sorry, I don't know the answer, but I will try to find out and get back to you." The chairman stopped the meeting and asked everyone in the room to stand and applaud. In most planning sessions, he explained, managers would try to bluff their way through answers, a practice that could only be counterproductive and obstruct openness. Now, he said, maybe people could begin to admit that they lack information and to set about getting it.

In a business that had been performing poorly and in which employees knew action would be coming that affected them— cutbacks in people and resources—an executive stood before a group of senior managers and said, "I have been in a number of meetings the last few days to discuss how we can tighten our belts in this difficult situation. I want to assure you that if you could have been in the meetings I was in and knew what I knew, you too would feel confident that we can respond to the challenges ahead of us." Response to his comments was not overwhelming. Skepticism reigned and remained. In our later discussions with this manager, we asked why other employees could not have been involved in the same meetings, why they could not have received the same information he and the other executives shared, and why the employees could not have found the same confidence through sharing more information.

Good and Bad News

Sharing more information implies sharing the bad news as well as the good. Theodore Pincus, Chairman of Financial Relations Board, the nation's largest financial public relations firm, argues that when managers communicate with investors, they should be candid:

> Does candor pay off? It is axiomatic that more information reduces investment risk and, other things being equal, lower risk should translate into a higher P/E multiple. I call this increase in the multiple a credibility premium, and I can cite plenty of companies that have earned it because they candidly discuss their plans and goals.

Walter Kissinger, Chairman of the Allen Group, an auto-parts company on Long Island, New York, provides candid assessments of his company's performance in annual reports and statements to shareholders: "Why not place our successes and mistakes out in the open? When senior management is willing to be held accountable, it also sets a good example for our operating people inasmuch as this is what we demand of them." Allen's financial performance is 14.9 percent return on equity, and it is ranked nineteenth among 41 auto-parts dealers. But Allen's 1986 price-to-earnings (P/E) ratio of 16 ranks ninth among these 41 companies; its decade-long P/E ratio of 13 places it fifth in the competitor group. Fifty-eight institutional investors hold 55 percent of its stock. In these and other companies, management recognizes that sharing both good and bad news develops trust among employees, investors, and customers and helps to build a stronger and more competitive organization.[12]

Ideas versus Values

Being more open implies sharing personal values and commitment as well as facts and ideas. Often management views only objective, rational facts as information. But by appealing to employees' emotions as well as intellect, managers may achieve more positive results and build a greater capacity to change. Winston Churchill—perhaps one of the most effective communicators in recent history—often reflected his personal feelings and emotions in his speeches. Churchill often referred to his family, his values, and his personal commitment to his nation's destiny. These personal references made the information he was sharing speak to not only the head but the heart. By integrating ideas and values in their communication efforts with employees, managers can increase capacity for change.

Who Should Share Information

Our point about sharing information is relatively simple: the more people who share information, the more consistent and prevalent the message will be. Information may obviously be communicated to employees by management.

In addition, companies may communicate information through customers, suppliers, investors, and other stakeholders. Stakeholders, for example, may present information at training programs and management forums. One company's newsletter dedicated one column a month to interviews with customers and another to interviews with suppliers. These features helped employees throughout the business learn more about suppliers and customers. In an attempt to upgrade company performance, all executives at Jaguar were required to listen to two hours a week of tape-recorded 800 phone calls. Such calls generally involved customer dissatisfaction with the product. Listening to these complaints significantly enhanced the commitment of managers to improve both the product and customer service. After a General Electric aircraft failed and the pilot heroically landed the aircraft, the pilot visited the company and pleaded with employees to improve the quality of their performance. At sales meetings with Baxter Healthcare, patients whose lives had been saved by Baxter products met with sales personnel and encouraged them to sell the products.

Another valuable source of information is other employees. At Whirlpool, representatives were selected from different manufacturing facilities to tour Japanese factories. After their visits, these hourly employees prepared videotapes, seminars, and discussion groups for employees in each of their plants. Through these communication processes other employees were helped to understand competitors and the need for higher quality and productivity.

Using many people to communicate—managers, customers, suppliers, investors, and employees—helps reinforce personal competencies within an organization. Multiple sources of information ensure that similar messages are shared and understood and that actions and thoughts are continually focused on business goals.

Who Should Receive Information

Just as information can be shared among multiple sources, it can also be received by multiple sources. In additional to sharing information with employees, we suggest that communications should include families, members of the community, and other stakeholders. By ensuring that many people receive information, the organization creates strong ties with different groups, which leads to greater commitment. Communicating with families through picnics, letters to the home, special announcements, and meetings involving the entire family helps build a stronger commitment to the business. In one division of Marriott, annual senior management meetings include spouses or significant others. The rationale is that work affects more of an employee's life than the part spent in the office. Spouses are encouraged to ask questions and participate in the meetings. Special sessions are designed for spouses, so that work challenges can be better understood, the needs of the spouse can be openly discussed, and stronger ties to the company can be built.

How to Share: Use a Variety of Tools

In recent research, a variety of communication tools have been identified that range from low to high along a richness continuum (see Figure 8–12).[13] Rich communication tools, such as interactive

Figure 8-12
COMMUNICATION TOOLS AND THEIR CONTEXT

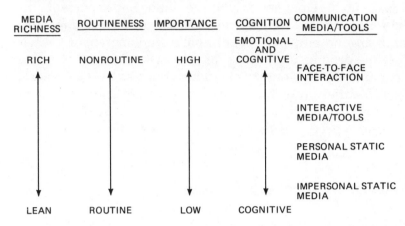

media and face-to-face interactions, allow for rapid feedback and create a personal relationship. Lean communication tools are less personal and allow for no feedback. A traditional view of communication is that "rich" tools, such as customer focus groups and one-on-one interviews, are always better. We disagree because we believe that the key issue in selecting a communication tool is to match the tool to the situation. Different degrees of richness are appropriate, depending on whether the information being communicated is routine or nonroutine, whether it involves facts and ideas alone or emotional content, and whether or not it is important. Since richer communication tools require more resources and energy, their use should be reserved for situations where the job cannot be done as well by merely sending a memo or posting a notice.

Apart from matching the form of the communication to its content, variety is also important. For example, in most companies bulletin boards are cluttered with dated notices that no one pays any attention to. One company put bulletin boards in key locations such as elevators, lobbies and lunchrooms. Bulletins were posted for 24 hours and then removed. Within weeks, this traditionally ineffective means of sharing information became useful. Employees began to notice new items and made sure they read them before they disappeared.

Using outside media to communicate inside can also achieve excellent results. Articles in local newspapers, case studies, or advertising messages focused on persons or groups outside the company also communicate within the company. Dow Chemical's advertising slogan, "Dow lets you do great things" sends a favorable message about Dow not only to the public but to current and potential employees as well. Hewlett-Packard's advertising campaign built around employees continually thinking about "What if . . . " while driving, showering, or otherwise engaged communicates commitment not only to customers but also to employees.

When a variety of communication tools are used, personal competencies are nourished and sustained because employees learn what is expected of them and have these perceptions continually confirmed.

Communication: Success Indicators

Our conclusions about communications are not radical: more is better than less; open is better than closed; two-way is better than one-way; explaining why is better than just telling what; many senders are better than one; many media are better than few. These simple principles contain profound implications for building competitiveness because they sustain personal competencies and increase organizational capability. When attention and resources are committed to communication practices, personal competencies are sustained: Employees know what is expected and work to fulfill those expectations.

The following questions can be asked to determine the success of communication practices:

- □ To what extent do employees know why some business activities receive more attention and resources than others?
- □ To what extent is information shared among employees, customers, suppliers, and other stakeholders?
- □ To what extent are communications consistent with the strategies and goals of the organization?
- □ To what extent do we use a variety of communication tools that match the message being communicated?
- □ To what extent do our communication tools sustain personal competencies and a shared mindset among employees and stakeholders?

The answers to these questions will give managers a clear sense of how effectively they are using communication processes to create a shared mindset and thereby enhance the competitiveness of their business.

9

Influence Management for the 1990s

To convince you need to persuade. And in order to persuade you would need what you lack: Reason and Right.

Miguel de Unamuno, 1936

When John F. Kennedy was trying to influence his party's delegation to nominate him as its presidential candidate in 1959, he ran into powerful resistance in the form of former President Harry S. Truman, who, it was rumored, opposed Kennedy's candidacy on the grounds of his Roman Catholicism. Of course, Truman could not go public with such opposition. Instead, he chose to criticize Senator Kennedy for his youthfulness and immaturity. Truman said publicly, ''[We need] a man with the greatest possible maturity and experience. . . . May I urge you to be patient?'' In a public response, Kennedy offered the following rebuttal: First, he already had fourteen years of Washington experience, far more than Truman had when he took office. Kennedy expressed his willingness to let his party be the judge of ''my experience and ability.'' But, ''if fourteen years in major elective office is insufficient experience,'' he said, ''that rules out all but three of the ten names put forward by Truman, all but a handful of American Presidents, and every President of the twentieth century—including Wilson, Roosevelt and Truman.'' And, he continued, if age, not experience, had been the criterion, a maturity test excluding ''from positions of trust and command all those below the age of forty-four would have kept Jefferson from writing the Declaration of Independence, Washington from commanding the Continental Army, Madison from fathering the Constitution . . . and Christopher Columbus from even discovering America.'' Kennedy demolished the age argument with such force that his supporters were grateful to Truman for providing such a highly publicized opportunity for him to demonstrate his mettle.

197

This example illustrates several key points about influence. First, Kennedy did not have positional power with which to overrule Truman. Second, he was able to transform a perceived liability (youthfulness) into a perceived asset. This is an ability managers will increasingly need to acquire to meet the problems that will arise in the next decade. Additionally, Kennedy was able to associate his own agenda with powerful positive symbols (Jefferson, Washington, the Constitution). By so doing, he took his listeners down the path that led to the decision he wanted. Next, he was able to use contention to express his own purposes while at the same time neutralizing Truman's opposition. Finally, by undermining Truman's influence, he was able to strengthen the political power of his own supporters vis-à-vis Truman's backers.

Kennedy's tactics for managing influence illustrate a variety of approaches that will be required in the new organizations of the 1990s. The forces at work (globalization, the consolidation of Europe, the Asian impact, new requirements for quality and service, the proliferation of information, environmental pollution, and so on) will create a need for organizations both to coordinate multiple specializations and to adjust rapidly to shifting markets, competition, and technology. What this will mean for day-to-day operations is much more extensive interaction among engineering, sales, manufacturing, human resources, finance, and so on, all of whom will influence each other's decisions more directly than has hitherto been the case. For example, manufacturing people will need to be present as engineers are engaged in the design process; human resource managers will need to play a role when negotiations are underway with suppliers or when innovative work arrangements are being considered.

Managers will therefore have to expand both their range of influence and the repertoire of influence strategies at their command—direct confrontation, collaboration, compromise, and so on. Managers who believe that the influence skills they learned in the 1980s—when their organizations were de-layering, downsizing, and refocusing on quality—will be sufficient for the 1990s are not likely to prove effective.

Discussing influence has some unique properties. Unlike the topics of other chapters in this book, influence is not a special property of the highly capable organization. All organizations have or use influence. Influence is a process. It permeates the productive and unproductive. The point is that the kind of influence used can have consequences for the outcomes of organizations. Its discussion here is critical because up to this point we have argued that in order to establish competitive advantage it is necessary to:

- ☐ Develop a common mindset.
- ☐ Build new human resource practices.
- ☐ Establish a capacity for change.
- ☐ Develop leadership at all levels of the organization.

Such requirements rely on a wide variety of influence strategies. Three general strategies are discussed in the following section, while recommendations for expanding the range of such strategies are developed throughout the rest of the chapter.

INFLUENCE IS MANIPULATION

Several choices confront those who would influence others. A core question is, "To what degree am I willing to act in such a way as to *manipulate* people into doing something they otherwise might not do?" This question is at the heart of influence. The choice is not whether to be manipulative, because to influence is to manipulate. In its positive sense, manipulation was practiced by Moses, Christ, Mohammed, Buddha, and Confucius, as well as many other respected leaders. Martin Luther King manipulated city councils into changing their bus-seating arrangements. The American reformer Saul Alinsky manipulated slum landlords into rehabilitating their properties. By the same token, Japan manipulated the United States into letting it sell "small economy cars" in the United States, which then gave Japan dealers and service centers as a base for expanding into sedans. Whether we like it or not, no organization can survive and remain competitive without using influence. Every manager must learn both to exert and to receive more influence. Indeed, the goal for improved organizational capability is to raise the total amount of influence used up and down the organization and between the organization and its customers, suppliers, and distributors.

THE NATURE OF INFLUENCE

The process of influencing people can be described as one in which the *influencer gets others to make choices consistent with the influencer's goals.* The influencer uses decision paths (usually referred to as channels) to direct the choices of the persons to be influenced.

The person being influenced makes decisions on the basis of perceptions of the surrounding environment. There are two possible channels for getting a person to make the choice the influencer desires.

First, we can change the *situation* in which the other person is placed.[1] In the light of this changed situation, the individual may decide on a course of action that he or she would not otherwise have chosen. In other words, through rearrangement of the components of the situation itself, the structure of the situation is changed, and this restructuring results in different action.

When Jack Welch, the chairman of General Electric, informed his business heads that he would not retain any core business unless it could be first or second in its market, he literally changed the situation of the organization from being a purely profit-driven business to one that could exist only if it had a dominant market share.

Alternatively, we can attempt to change the other person's *intentions,* not by restructuring the situation but by communicating with the individual in such a way that his or her perceptions of the situation change. In the light of a changed perception, the person may change intentions and decide on a new course of action—the one the influencer hoped to bring about.

For a supplier and original equipment manufacturer consciously to shift the nature of their relationship from all that is implied by a vendor–buyer contract to a partnership alters dramatically the possibilities of the relationship. Under the partnership arrangement, they may, for example, choose to share customer market requirements or do mutual research and development. They shift their intentions from one in which the buyer negotiates on cost only to agreeing to pool their resources for mutual profit.

A good example of a situation channel in organizations is the budget process. Whoever must concur on a budget plan is situated in the decision path or channel. On the other hand, convincing manufacturing that its product no longer meets customer demand is an example of using the intentional channel or decision path. In the past, hierarchical organizations have tended to rely much more on the situational channel. The adaptive organization of the 1990s will need to use both.

Given these two channels, there are three basic tactics of influence. The first is *contention*, in which the influencer is assertive and does not cooperate with the other person. This is a power-oriented mode in which one uses whatever source of power is available. Second is *cooperation*, in which an attempt is made to find some expedient, mutually acceptable arrangement that to some extent at least meets the needs of both parties. The last type is *collaboration*, in which an attempt is made to arrive at an outcome that fully satisfies both people and that as a result may increase the total amount of influence possible.

If we juxtapose the two dimensions of influence, we find that there are six different influence positions (see Figure 9–1). Each represents an alternative way of influencing others in the organization, and each has different consequences for maintaining influence. Given the fact that the manager must wield influence if he or she is to participate in the corporation's strategic, innovative, and leadership activities, the question becomes how to do it. The discussions and examples that follow will provide insight into the pros and cons of each approach.

CONTENTION

The contentious approach to influence means that the influencer is assertive and does not require cooperation from others. When a judge issues a sentence, there is no requirement that the defendant agree. When a senior executive orders a cutback or issues a proclamation that from now on employees who travel will use a certain airline, the decision is not open to discussion.

Figure 9–1
INFLUENCE POSITIONS AND STRATEGIES WITHIN AN ORGANIZATION

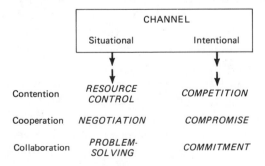

People tend to believe that using a contentious approach to influence people is necessarily counterproductive. But contention may increase clarity of goals, force the consideration of alternatives, and increase flexibility. Some organizations intentionally build contention into their structural arrangements for precisely that reason. In the 1990s, contention strategies may be necessary to confront organization members who are not facing up to the radical changes taking place in the business environment. At other times, the outmoded management practices of the last two decades may need to be changed by radical, confrontative means. When cycle time is at stake, dramatic measures may be required to keep the organization competitive.

Chapter 4 discussed the importance of mindset as a cornerstone of organizational capability. One might automatically assume that the development of a mindset can best be accomplished through collaboration; and indeed, collaborative approaches usually result in commitment. There are, however, several examples of leaders establishing mindset through more contentious approaches. Almost all the revolutionary leaders of this century have established their power by first capturing the military and then the educational system. Certainly Fidel Castro did not evolve his style of government by collaboration. In business, one CEO developed a set of principles to constitute his mindset for the organization. He then sent the list to every business head and manager through first-line supervisor with the directive that they spend twenty minutes discussing the principles at every extended staff meeting off site and at all employee meetings. He also required that they send him notes of any discussion. He then responded to every question raised and revised the principles four times based on the feedback. Notice that he gave no one the option of ignoring the principles (contention) but did give them some opportunity to influence him with their remarks.

Another CEO, in an effort to establish a mindset, began by asking each of the ten individuals reporting to him to write a vision for the company. After discussion and extension, a joint vision statement evolved. The process was repeated with the next 150 top managers, with the vision revised with each iteration. Finally, a task force integrated all of the input, and the document was published in draft form. The designation "draft" stayed on the vision statement for the next two years in order to invite further discussion and revision. This is a much more collaborative approach, which resulted in the same end. Generating the initial document took somewhat longer, but support for it grew rapidly.

These two examples illustrate the central theme of this chapter—managers must learn how and when to use the full range of influence tactics.

Resource Control

Power has been defined as using resource control as a basis of influence. As two writers on the subject express it:

> Power is regarded as the capacity of an actor (person, group, organization, nation) in a particular situation to manipulate via the structural channel. That is, power is the manipulator's ability to restructure the situation in such a way as to get others to act as he desires.[2]

While this description fits our view of resource control, it is too limiting because it ignores other ways of obtaining power. In a classic research article two experts in the field have documented that *expertise* (being perceived as having unique knowledge) or the ability to act as a point of reference can serve as an alternative source of power.[3] The critical thing about resource control is that it is a *capacity*. One does not have to use the capacity to have it. The mere recognition that someone possesses a capacity affects how others behave and react. A subordinate is aware, for example, that the boss has the capacity to fire him or her whether or not the boss ever exercises that power.

The sources of resource control for the manager are control of alternatives and use of authority. In alternatives control, the target of influence must not only achieve a desired outcome of the influencer but must do so by using the means specified by the influencer. The target is not free to choose alternative paths to the same goal. In many ways, this is the most restrictive use of contention because it requires the target to perform specific behaviors in a specified manner. It also requires that the influencer closely monitor specific behaviors. For example, a senior manager interprets the ''hiring freeze'' as limiting the manager's choices. An alternative is for management to require costs to be reduced but leave it to the manager to decide how. In a federal housing agency, the chief legal counsel once influenced Congress to require his signature on mortgages for public housing units costing over three million dollars. Every contractor in the nation knew this lawyer had the capacity to veto their projects, and they had no alternatives.

To use another example, consider the process of performance appraisal. It is usually treated as a source of legal documentation and has been successfully used by employees to sue employers who have dismissed them when their ratings were all good or excellent. Most organizations require that an employee's performance rating be "up-to-date" when the employee is being considered for promotion or lateral transfer. Some organizations use performance ratings as the basis for deciding on rewards such as bonuses. So, in theory, performance appraisal could be one of management's most important tools.

In practice, however, the performance review is often regarded with derision. Busy managers, who see it as a bureaucratic requirement, seldom do it except when required, hardly ever use it as a tool to shape performance, and allow the integrity of the appraisal to be undermined by system concerns. The latter include limiting the number of excellent ratings possible or believing that other managers are "easy" raters, and therefore one's own department will "look bad" if ratings are lower overall. Human resource managers may collude in this situation by assuming that their responsibility in the matter is purely technical— as long as the form itself has been well designed by their department, they have fulfilled their obligation.

Now examine what happens when management takes a more contentious approach to performance appraisal. In several organizations, it is part of the company's philosophy that the appraisal be used as a primary tool for shaping performance. The position taken by the head of human resources is that the appraisal process, since it is a major way of managing people, should be as tightly controlled as processes relating to dollar resources. Using this idea, such organizations audit the process. Both written records and the actual face-to-face appraisals are reviewed. A manager found to be subverting the process can be severely reprimanded, just as would happen if he or she were found to be mismanaging the budget. In Chapter 6, we stated that the standard set for appraisals should, when achieved, contribute directly to competitive advantage.

A human resource manager in this setting is expected not only to provide expertise (that is, to make sure the appraisal form is technically sound) but also to exert direct influence on the political process associated with appraisals through the audit. This individual is also expected to influence the culture of the organization by changing the perception of the appraisal process from one that is derided to one that is genuinely respected. Maintaining the integrity of the process is difficult, however. One organization that has a policy of rank-ordering performance frequently finds examples of managers who rotate their subordinates through the rank order.

From an influence point of view, the dissolution of the appraisal process may stem from allowing too many alternatives (including not doing it) in a process that is critical to the organization and to the individual being appraised. To control alternatives, several practices have been developed. First is the aperiodic audit process mentioned above. Second, the appraisal is opened to input from others. For example, several companies require that peer and subordinate appraisals be included in the individual's record. In matrix organizations, proportional appraisals can be given according to the matrix cell in which the individual spends the most time. In one high-performing manufacturing plant, members of the core manufacturing team complete appraisals of one another. Another company devotes time each year to reviewing its top 300 managers in an open forum. Prior to the session, each manager must be reviewed by one officer other than the individual's own boss. Each year's recommendations are compared to those of the previous year to ensure that development recommendations have been carried out. All of these processes serve to limit the alternatives of the single manager appraising a single individual.

A major computer company based in the Northeast has learned to use resource control actually to foster innovation. The head of research and development invites anyone, at any time, to submit proposals for innovative ideas. He funds ideas that relate to technology, organization, service, and so on. This manager characterizes the typical initial conversation about a new idea as follows:

EMPLOYEE Bill, I have this great idea and I need $50,000 to try it out.

BILL That does sound like a great idea. I'll give you $5,000 and you use it to convince me that the other $45,000 would be a good expenditure. And by the way, you will need to work up your idea on your own time until we see how feasible it's going to be.

Bill uses his capacity to control resources in an effective, even contentious, way. He supports the new idea, but he pushes the idea promoter to stretch himself to prove its viability. Does the employee really believe the idea is a winner? Will the employee go the extra mile to promote it? Bill's feeling is that he must be confrontational, that providing easy resources will not be doing the person with the idea a favor. Bill argues that this is precisely what an outside banker would do. His contentious strategy quickly sorts out winning ideas from ideas being posed for other than achievement reasons. Does he turn off some good ideas? Probably. Is he managing the new idea process effectively? Undoubtedly.

There is no reason to expect that our competitors will ease the pressure in the next decade. In fact, there is every reason to expect that they will get tougher. Therefore, we must be tough on ourselves, which means employing rigorous influence processes such as resource control and other contentious strategies. We will need to confront poorly formed ideas and status quo operations that are no longer responsive to the changing environment and to exercise resource control in order to implement mindset development, performance appraisal, head count, and costs.

Once again, however, if only contention is used, or if it is the predominant mode of influence, we can expect rigidity and stress to result due to the tension that often accompanies contention.

An unusual application of contention has been used by Cummins Engine Company. In one of its plants, an operating team (which gets directly involved in new hires) has created a videotape which must be viewed by all job applicants. The tape challenges the prospective employee as to whether that person is ready for the tough conditions on the plant foor. In the tape, actual workers describe why it is demanding to work at Cummins—and what makes working there worthwhile. This confrontative strategy screens out persons who might otherwise find out after only six months of employment that they cannot succeed in the Cummins environment.

Two conditions must prevail in order to use contention or confrontation paths effectively. First, these influence paths must be practiced in a larger organizational climate of mutual trust. Individuals must know that the organization cannot continue to exist if such poor management practices are exercised. At the same time these practices must be confronted without jeopardizing the individual's career. Over twenty years ago, a social psychologist's study of high- and low-performing college basketball teams demonstrated that there was much more confrontation about poor play as well as more recognition of good play between players on teams that performed well. Second, contentious strategies of influence must never be the only type or even the dominant type of influence used.

For the manager who wants to be in a position to wield influence through resource control, the question becomes, how can a resource-control base be built? The managers we interviewed cited the following strategies as having been successful:

- Write the first draft; that is, when a new course of action needs to be determined, be the first to outline the action plan. This tactic forces others to influence within the alternatives you have created.
- Develop unique data bases and knowledge relevant to competitive advantage—for example, future trends, population changes, reward systems.
- Demonstrate an ability to increase the corporation's flexibility through managing complex change.

Use human resource systems of selection, performance management, and so on to acquire, develop, and retain tomorrow's leaders.

Competition

Whereas resource control is the situational form of contention, competition is the intentional one. It is an attempt on the part of the influencer to change the intentions of the other person through forcing the recognition that the person cannot win. Usually competition arises naturally as individuals perceive that there are a limited number of resources to be divided in a win–lose process.

Anyone who has introduced managers to the prisoners' dilemma exercise in which groups are given the opportunity to compete or collaborate knows that about nine out of ten groups will choose to compete.

Competition among employees is not harmful in itself. When it enters into reward systems, career succession systems, and status symbols, however, it has the potential for taking energy away from industry competitors and focusing it inside the organization. When this happens, very destructive behavior can occur. One company, which produces corrugated material for containers, posts records of each shift's run on the corrugator machine and fosters competition between shifts. It has continued this practice in spite of numerous incidents in which one shift has let a machine run past an obvious maintenance point, knowing the machine would break down on the next shift (especially when the next shift was yesterday's record winner).

The use of competition as an avenue of influence inside organizations should be strictly curtailed. It is a well-developed, highly destructive force within most organizations today. Marketing will find ways to compete with sales, manufacturing with engineering, labor with management, and so on. Companies often spend considerable dollar resources just to contain competition between groups within their organizations. One bank gathered its top managers, from its comptroller to its tax-audit staffs, at an off-site workshop for a week just to hammer out jurisdictional disputes.

If the energy that comes from the natural proclivity of individuals to be winners can be redirected toward industry competitors, the competitive instinct can be turned into a competitive advantage. For example, one manager collected information about other internal divisions and similar divisions in other companies to set her staffing levels, making sure that her levels were competitive. Her staff picked up her initiative and began to display to their subordinates comparative industry data on productivity.

Part of the reason for the development of internal competition is that the line of sight is much clearer to other departments or functions within an organization than it is to the parallel segments of competitor firms. Knowing this, some managers have chosen to increase competition by improving their line of sight to their competitors. Some examples follow.

The president of one firm compared last year's sales with those of his chief competitor. He was able to determine that, if he included the entire supply of products, his competitor's products would have to cost 20 percent less than his to produce in order to maintain the same margins. Therefore, he argued, when the entire sum was determined he had an $8 million cost problem. He used this figure to confront his entire work force. In one year the cost differential was reduced to 5 percent and in two years to 0 percent. Being confronted with an $8 million dollar figure was much more effective than citing 20 percent.

The manager of a manufacturing plant reduced the line-of-sight problem by purchasing his competitor's parts, which he displayed along with data about costs and quality, so that each unit of the organization was constantly confronted by the competition.

A third company hired an outside firm to do a competitive analysis of buying practices. The firm discovered $140 million in "opportunities." A list of these opportunities was posted in the purchasing department and reviewed on a periodic basis. This is, again, a confrontation of data.

When a manager considers it necessary to be in contention with another individual or division, using control of resources or authority will be more effective in the long run than applying competitive strategies. If forced to compete, the most effective strategy is to think of the competitor as outside the company and use the same tactics one would employ with a real competitor. Sometimes internal competition can be used effectively when it is more symbolic than real. At Domino's Pizza headquarters, the name of the region with the slowest average monthly delivery times is posted in the central elevators, which are used by all company executives. That regional manager obviously takes quite a ribbing from his or her peers.

The important consideration regarding competition is to work vigorously to keep it pointed outside the organization rather than within it. It is an influence tactic familiar to most of us, although how to direct it may not be so apparent.

COOPERATION

Douglas Hume, when asked why he continued to serve as ambassador to the United Nations replied, "Because the potential to reach agreement on all the important human issues of peace, hunger, and shelter is there." While he may never have achieved that full potential, his logic is to be admired. The same potential needs to be acknowledged in organizations. If there are rigid barriers between functions or divisions in an organization, cooperation can be used to overcome these hierarchical separations and restore flexibility.

To decide that one wishes to influence through cooperation and coordination is to acknowledge that the organization is a setting in which people must achieve both the corporation's goals and their own, even though there may be trade-offs involved in achieving both. Lee Iacocca refused to consider restoring wages and salaries at Chrysler unless they were offset by productivity gains. This is the idea of coordination and cooperation. In the 1990s, organization will have to break down functional rigidities in order to reduce cycle times in product development. This effort will call for much more extensive cooperation across functional barriers, which will require that managers acquire greater skills in influencing through cooperation.

It may be taken for granted that people will cooperate across divisions and functions. And yet, based on data we have collected on cooperation across divisions, the general pattern is almost always the same:

> Division managers believe their division is more cooperative with other divisions than do the subordinates of their division.

> Subordinates of division A believe they are more cooperative with division B than division B believes they are.

Cooperation is most likely to break down when influencers lose sight of the fact that their goals are interdependent with those of their targets. This situation has been characterized as "the leak's in your end of the boat" phenomenon. Cooperation often takes longer and may make the task more difficult; yet, it is essential to influence because it forces recognition of the interdependence of goals between influencer and target.

Figure 9–1 identifies two positions of cooperation: *negotiation* and *compromise*. Negotiation is the art of orchestrating resources, while compromise involves trading off resources.

Negotiation

Formal negotiation between labor and management is perhaps the best known use of influence, and one in which managers play a significant role. The tactics used in labor negotiations—building agreement about what can be placed on the bargaining table, representation, breaking the agenda down into subparts—are relevant to other types of negotiations, such as those relating to any form of resource allocation.

In an aerospace division that was undergoing major change as a result of two years of deficit operation, a steering committee was established to guide the change effort. The managers of marketing and engineering moved quickly to negotiate a charter ensuring that the committee would not become involved in either of their areas. The human resources manager found herself inundated with recommendations for change in her area because she had not foreseen the consequences of the marketing and engineering negotiations. Actually, as the effort turned out, many productive changes were made in the human resources division, but long-term changes were needed also in marketing and engineering. At first, the human resources manager found herself so overwhelmed that she could not respond to the steering group. An outside adviser showed her how to turn every request for change into an opportunity to negotiate. For example, the steering group requested that she make available a variable-cost health benefit program. She agreed to this if the plan were restricted to those employees whose performance ratings merited it. This allowed her to move on another objective of hers, which was to shift more rewards into contingencies related to performance, while still cooperating with the steering group. She became an expert negotiator. Her principle became: every request is an opportunity to negotiate a higher level of employee performance.

Compromise

Compromise involves the conscious coordination of intentions: The two parties agree to make trade-offs, often to correct an unequal distribution of resources in the interest of productivity. Compromise is usually an ongoing process, whereas negotiation is generally periodic. Many people feel a psychological resistance to compromise, perhaps because it sounds like a weak or less than *macho* resolution. But where resources (human, dollar, and information) are in short supply, regular compromise may be the most viable influence strategy. The best (and the worst) examples of cooperation often occur in the scheduling of plant floor time to meet the demands of multiple orders or mixed product lines. In such cases, the influence process varies greatly from plant to plant. In some companies, the scheduler rules the plant floor; in others, there is a conscious attempt to develop opportunities for negotiation and compromise among machine operators. Most of the new, so-called greenfield, experimental facilities, such as Westinghouse's College Station, Texas, plant and Digital's Enfield, Connecticut, plant, have chosen to let the autonomous plant floor teams directly negotiate and compromise about the use of scarce resources.

This practice results in the teams directly controlling issues that in other settings require personnel administrators. Autonomous teams may also manage such matters as employee sick leave, tardiness, vacation periods, release time, overtime, space needs, and customer complaints. When these areas are considered to be the domain of formal management–labor negotiations, the cost to the organization is much greater. One auto plant, unable to generate internal resolution of such matters, must pay for one full-time steward for every 1,000 employees and a plant-wide steward supervisor for an annual salary expenditure of more than $1 million, plus the lost time of thousands of employees involved in grievances.

The risk of cooperation is that agreement will be reached too easily, without rigorous attention to real differences, real alternatives, or cost-saving choices. Cooperation that involves sharing resources requires trust—not an easy commodity to build or maintain. For this reason, most efforts at cooperation evolve into formal negotiations that substitute written agreements for handshakes.

If competition is the natural tendency of growing up in a competitive society, cooperation may seem like an "unnatural act." People may need more help to learn to cooperate. And yet, where cooperation prevails, stringent controls may be reduced and the overhead costs of win–lose arrangements described above may be eliminated.

COLLABORATION

In conflict resolution parlance, collaboration is defined as that type of influence in which two equally strong parties aggressively pursue their goals (agendas) by redefining future outcomes to permit mutual satisfaction. Collaboration is not compromise. Collaborators do not trade off their goals; rather, they orchestrate outcomes and often find ways to multiply each other's resources.

Ideally, matrix organizations are intended to create situations that foster collaboration. Too often, however, managers perceive the matrix in a competitive, win–lose manner. This perception is one of the most destructive forces working against the matrix structure. Here too, we see that traditional ways of administering the performance appraisal contribute to a lack of collaboration within an organization. Consider, for example, the case of the individual matrixed between a program manager and a manufacturing manager. Obviously, such an individual will experience conflicting demands from the two bosses, but if the employee knows that performance ratings, salary increases, promotional opportunities, and so on all come from the manufacturing manager, how the conflict will be resolved by the employee is quite clear. But by developing a process of joint appraisal, the two managers are forced to collaborate in order to get the most from the human resource they jointly control. The same argument can be made for dotted-line relationships between corporate and divisional staff.

Collaboration as a path to influence can take the form of either *problem-solving* or *commitment* (see Figure 9–1).

Problem-Solving

Problem-solving in an organization is the systematic process of logically analyzing, making decisions about, and taking action on concerns and issues. One area in which problem-solving is needed but is almost universally lacking is the pervasive staff meeting.

Most organizational training programs designed to improve the effectiveness of meetings focus on building organization and time-management skills. While time management is important, the effectiveness of the staff meeting depends more on mutual problem-solving. In three different companies, we have seen divisional staff meetings reduced to half the time they would usually take when they became problem-solving sessions. In these companies, employees spent four hours learning to use two new tools. One session focused on problem-solving skills and the other on learning to assign responsibility quickly. The problem-solving format permitted the division to specify, for each agenda item, whether it was for information only or was a matter requiring problem definition, a decision, implementation, evaluation, or the exploration of alternatives.

Once managers found that work could actually be accomplished in meetings, they became more productive. More important, the problem-solving approach created a norm that problems were opportunities to collaborate, not just chances to criticize.

We recently helped a company shift its relationship with five key buyers from vendor–buyers to partners. The suppliers listed several aspects of the company's normative climate that made it difficult for them to enter into a partnership. One of the most difficult was that the company treated problems of supply, quality, inventory, or transportation as occasions to blame individuals, whereas the supplier organizations viewed problems as opportunities to apply rational problem-solving. As one supplier put it, "When a problem arises all our engineers, manufacturers, schedulers, and so on, jump in and try to solve it. At your company you try to find which person or function to blame." Again, blaming assumes that someone wins (the blamer) and someone loses (the one at fault). Problem-solving works on the assumption that by combining resources all parties can win.

Commitment

The final influence position—commitment—has been written about widely in the management and sales literature. Commitment is achieved most readily when one has a set of important goals (an agenda) and is willing to engage others in the process of reaching those goals. Essentially, there are two very different approaches to eliciting commitment from others.

First, about 80 percent of people will commit to an idea on the basis of factual information. These people expect to be convinced through data about population trends, the aging of the work force, the cost of a wrong hire, and so on. On the other hand, 20 percent of people are likely to be convinced by a portrayal of future possibilities. These individuals are more interested in what *will* happen rather than what *has* happened. They can be persuaded by the quality of images and alternatives that are presented. Naturally, persuasive arguments contain elements of both. Managers often believe they have communicated successfully when they have merely presented the facts. But in many instances, meaning is created only when facts are compared and contrasted; commitment is created when the influencer, on the basis of facts, can convince others that there can be a better future. Facts can be separated from the self. Meaning never is. Facts can be presented in a vacuum. Meaning, by definition, is always contextual.

In organizations, meaning emerges from the individual's understanding of the rational and social context. How many times have you heard someone say, "That's a good idea, but it will never work here"? In other words, while the idea has technical merit, because of the political and/or cultural conditions in the company, it will not work here. As with any generalization, there is probably an element of truth in such a statement. The influencer may then face the complex challenge of having to change the political or cultural conditions in order to achieve a goal. By and large, individuals will usually resist committing themselves to anything that seems inconsistent with existing values and norms, but if they can be persuaded to feel that what is proposed will change such norms for the better, their resistance can be overcome. In the new organizations of the 1990s, which will be much more network-based than hierarchical, mutual influence will have to be based on a shared commitment.

LEADERSHIP AND COMMITMENT

When leaders attempt to influence others, they begin with an agenda—their own personalized plan. They try to get others to "buy into" their agendas, never missing an opportunity to "rehearse" their agendas with others. They develop a set of contingencies that allow them to redefine operational requirements into opportunities for implementing their agendas.

The leader's agenda or personal plan can be a source of integrity or a vehicle for meeting power needs. It is what distinguishes influence attempts which are undertaken as ends in themselves from those undertaken as a means to achieving a clear purpose. While many types of purpose may exist, those that are desirable promote human well-being at the same time that they foster organizational competitive advantage:

> Leaders who are successful seem to understand the importance of making work meaningful for themselves and the people who work for them. The pattern that emerges is one of a constantly shifting set of issues that surface as the organization sails into uncharted waters. Some managers avoid the issues or put them in the "too hard" basket; other organizations don't renew. Others not only welcome the issue but take some pains to dig them out and turn them into causes. Their organizations have a chance. A few leaders are able to find adventure and nobility in the causes. Their companies will probably stay fresh. Some are able to turn organizational causes into individual commitment. Their organizations will almost certainly regenerate.[4]

Ultimately, the quality of leaders' agendas and the methods they use to influence others toward the ends they have identified determine whether organizational performance will be exceptional, mediocre, or merely coercive.

The extensive literature examining the subject of leadership has been consistent in identifying one basic qualification of outstanding influencers (leaders). Those who influence have a mission. (Sometimes they are referred to as "maniacs" with a mission.) Whether they make them explicit or not, leaders have visions of what the future can be. They are able to project a future reality that captures others' enthusiasm and energy. Indeed, one definition of charisma is that charismatic leaders can convince others that their reality *is* reality.

Tom Peters' videotape, *A Passion for Excellence*, recounts the story of Air Force General Bill Creech, who in the 1980s saw more clearly than others that the ineffectiveness of a wing command was not due to F-15 pilots, but to the lack of ground support, which had been known to take hours to find a replacement part. Creech concentrated on improving ground support and was able to reduce part-replacement times to minutes. He used recognition to motivate the ground crew—he invented the "roll by," a parade of support trucks to parallel the "fly-by" of planes. Persons who worked for him reported that he was single-minded about his agenda. Creech was convinced that effectiveness was in the hands of the support crew, and he influenced others to implement his agenda. To gain competitive advantage, managers must develop agendas that clarify:

- □ The specialization's contributions to strategic direction.
- □ How to support increased innovation through the redesign of rewards, work design, and so on.
- □ How the process of continuous renewal can become basic to planning.
- □ How core management systems can become the basic tools for implementing strategy (see Chapters 5–7).

INFLUENCE IN TOMORROW'S ORGANIZATION

As organizations move away from total reliance on hierarchies, in which influence is primarily based on the authority of position, to organizations with several overlapping structures such as networks, matrix arrangements, and hierarchies operating simultaneously along with permeable boundaries which accept customer and supplier ideas, the range of influence strategies employed must be very diverse.

No manager who clings to a single influence style can be successful. The days are gone when it could be said, "He's autocratic as hell, but he gets the job done!" Or, "I don't know how he is so effective and still so low key." Or, "He is the consummate politician!" Rather, what will be required is the use of a variety of influence approaches depending upon setting and resources. In effect, the successful manager will employ influence contingently, using the strategies that follow:

1. There will be a growing need to employ contention as the way to influence the organization to face up to changing customer needs and demands for quality and service. This is really what Jack Welch, CEO of General Electric, refers to as the mirror test. One side of the mirror needs to reflect what your customers really think of your products and services. The other side must reflect your own style, contribution, and value-adding behavior.

2. Take every bureaucratic "no" as an opening for negotiation. Every organization has certain legal constraints imposed on it from the outside. Even more constraints, however, come from the organization's own policies, procedures, and systems. Sort out those that are the law and negotiate those that appear to be the law. You will not receive increased sign-off authority, learning opportunities, or other resources as gifts: You must negotiate. Recently, one organization informed its management that it must downsize by 15 percent. All but two of the managers began developing the slate to be dismissed. The remaining two immediately approached senior management with a plan to reduce costs by 20 percent, partly through layoffs, partly through outsourcing, and partly through other types of savings. In other words, these managers were able to "get the right agenda" on the table. Not only were their plans accepted, but the other managers were asked to do the same.

3. Compromising organizational rules for the sake of the customer must become a more prevalent form of mutual influence. In their new-found zeal to control inventories, companies often do it so well that customer replacement

parts are greatly delayed. One medical equipment supply company learned this the hard way after installing inventory ceilings on its service organization that resulted in downtime of major diagnostic equipment costing customers millions of dollars. The company realized that in order to keep customers' needs in the forefront, it had to compromise on "ideal" inventory ceilings.

4. Persuasive problem-solving converts mistakes into learning opportunities. The success of one aerospace company was based on its reputation for being able to find new ways of overcoming seemingly insurmountable technical problems. Unfortunately, this reputation led to a culture in which no one would admit the existence of problems until they became dire and required huge resources to resolve. In the turnaround, one key lesson for managers was the early detection and admission of problems and willingness to persuade others that a difficulty was brewing. Persuading and assisting others to transform problems into opportunities in an influence strategy that will lie at the heart of the renewing organization.

5. With all that has been written about it, commitment is still an elusive influence strategy. All seem to agree that it cannot be legislated. One person's commitment is another's burden. Compliance, on the other hand, is relatively easy to obtain because people's jobs and salaries can be put at risk (comply or leave), but it requires monumental efforts to monitor and excessive overhead to manage. In the 1990s and beyond, most organizations are likely to evolve into loosely coupled, network-based, highly decentralized operations in which audits, controls, and quality assurances are self-imposed. All these conditions will make the organization that tries to rely on compliance a noncontender. Organizations that make commitment a main source of influence will be the major contenders. To add value in the future, managers must know how to get others to commit to their goals. This will require visions that give meaning and (sometimes) adventure to work life. It will mean creating conditions in which people can sign on for goals they believe to be meaningful, rather than just complying. It may mean that informal contracting will become more the norm than formal job descriptions. Such contracts could be for shorter durations than

the standard job contract and could include expectations about what the rewards will be when the outcomes are obtained.

Extending the influence process so that all employees *know more* and *care more* is yet another component of organizational capability. Employees need to understand why their organization has chosen a particular strategy, mission, or direction. They will have to care more so that every customer is satisfied. Well-informed, committed employees are more productive, take more initiative, and thereby help to create a competitive advantage for the company.

10

The Capacity for Change

All is flux, nothing is stationary. There is nothing permanent except change.

Heraclitus, c.460 B.C.

Creating the capacity for change is a core component of organizational capability. In a study of over 1,000 managers, researchers found that the ability to manage change was the most important discriminator between high and low performers. In the eyes of the 8,900 managers who completed data about these 1,000 individuals, the ability to manage change was a major determinant of how effective these managers were.

We have emphasized throughout this book that the capacity for change must exist in any organization that hopes to remain competitive in a rapidly changing world. We have also demonstrated how the effective use of management practices can contribute to employees' ability to cope with change and effectively meet its challenges. In the remaining chapters, we focus on how to build processes into the organization that will ensure that each time a change occurs, it can be dealt with successfully.

The phases of successful change management are fairly straightforward and well documented. The first step is to define clearly the current state of the organization; the next is to determine what has to be done and create a coherent plan for change. Then comes deciding *how* to do it and, finally, obtaining results. By our definition, a company has a capacity for change when it has learned how to reduce the time it takes to move through these phases successfully (see Figure 10-1). In this chapter, we will look at the processes and competencies involved in diagnosing the current system, planning for change, and managing the transitions.

Figure 10-1
PHASES OF SUCCESSFUL CHANGE MANAGEMENT

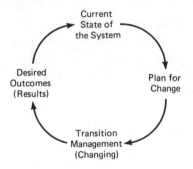

A CHANGE MANAGEMENT CASE

Place yourself in the situation of general manager (GM), Jim Bern. It is April 1984. Two months ago Jim was appointed "acting" GM of the DSD division, which employs 1,500 people. The division used to be one of the technological jewels in a company that prided itself on being "high tech." The division provides state-of-the-art technology in detector or warning devices which can operate in satellites, aircraft, missiles, or tanks.

One year ago the GM Jim replaced had proposed and won a contract to design, develop, and manufacture a new device for a foreign government. However, when he and his team went to the country to negotiate the final contract, they returned with a contract for $33 million rather than for the $55 million DSD had bid. This was particularly distressing because the company had planned to use the money from the contract to build the manufacturing capability for these devices and would not have made any profit on the $55 million. When the company began questioning the GM about what had happened, he left.

As is often the case, this incident was only the proverbial tip of the iceberg. For years the engineering department had a history of producing technologically sophisticated prototypes that turned out to be too costly to manufacture. Thus, the U.S. government found that while this division would typically come in with the best technology, it would consistently be over budget and behind schedule. The penalties that resulted erased profits. The manufacturing department believed that it was taking all the blame for the engineering department's mistakes. In fact, on several key devices, an 80 percent rejection rate by the quality-assurance department was not unusual.

The group vice president at corporate headquarters, to whom Jim reports—and who told Jim that his appointment was only temporary because a search was on for a more experienced replacement—is seriously concerned about the situation. Within the first six months of Jim's tenure he replaced the head of engineering and the comptroller and created a new position that focuses exclusively on the $33 million contract. He also "strongly suggests" that Jim use a consultant who has helped with the change processes in other parts of the company.

The division is structured in a matrix, with the traditional functions—engineering, manufacturing, sales, marketing, and so on—on one axis and programs and platforms on the other.

A cultural audit to determine the norms and values embedded in the division had just been summarized, with feedback to Jim and his direct reports. The audit identified prevalent division attitudes as follows:

- Being late is OK, and expected in meetings.
- Stall for information, work out the details later.
- Don't assume responsibility when a problem arises, and if it's not your problem, don't help.
- If you want to get promoted, screw up.
- Don't ask questions—pretend you understand.
- If you don't want to commit, stall by saying, "I'll get back to you." Plan to meet requirements, but don't initiate.
- Shipping predominates over quality and cost.
- Win the contract without regard to real costs or profitability.
- Individual work is more important than group work.
- Don't worry about keeping promises on dates and deliveries.
- Rules can be bent to get the job done.
- Employees are a commodity.
- Trying hard, even when unsuccessful, is all that counts.
- Surfacing the problem (late in its occurrence) is more important than solving it.

Finally, Jim has just completed the sale of his house in Oregon and moved into the much more expensive Boston area only to learn that Corporate plans to solve the problem of the DSD division by selling it.

UNDERSTANDING THE STATE OF THE SYSTEM

Jim Bern has found himself in what change agents refer to as the *current state*. The term hardly seems adequate when one considers the compexity of the DSD situation. But it does provide a neutral description of the place at which everyone begins the change process. The overall change process can be characterized as beginning with the current state, moving through a transition state, and arriving at a desired state.

The competencies necessary for getting started in the change process are *creating meaning* and *problem identification* (see Figure 10-2),[1] two skill sets that enable a manager to determine the current state that needs changing. Creating meaning—alerting the organization to the larger meaning of such "symptoms" as loss of market share and customer dissatisfaction—helps awaken the organization to what is happening in its environment. Recent research has identified this as an important competency of transformational leaders. Problem identification is the process through which the relevant data are analyzed, the problems of the business are brought into sharp focus, and the information is clearly communicated to top management and employees. Only when problems have been clearly identified can an organization start to work on solving them.

To illustrate, let us return to Jim Bern in 1984. Although it may seem surprising, not many people besides Jim believed there

Figure 10-2
CLUSTER: CREATING MEANING AND PROBLEM IDENTIFICATION

Creating Meaning	Problem Identification
Clarifies business goals.	Identifies relevant data for problem-solving.
Puts specific problems in context of larger system.	Identifies problems central to business success.
Summarizes data so that others understand key issues.	Diagnoses the client's problems.
Forecasts potential obstacles to success.	Clarifies roles and responsibilities.
Creates frameworks for defining problems.	Uses effective verbal communication.
Articulates outcomes of change.	

was anything systematically wrong with DSD. The generally held view was that the former GM had either goofed or taken some cash under the table and negotiated a poor contract. (To attribute poor organizational performance to a single individual—a mistake that is frequently made—serves to blind the organization to its underlying problems. Certainly the former GM must bear some of the responsibility for what happened, but his actions were part of a much larger organizational pattern.)

Fortunately, Jim was smart enough to see that DSD had much larger problems with Engineering, Manufacturing, and the general norms of the division. Late in 1984, Jim also found out that the finance department had not imposed adequate inventory controls, which forced him to write off $20 million in both 1984 and 1985. A key to turning DSD around, therefore, was giving new meaning to the nature of the problems facing the division. For example, there was a need to transform the attribution about the $33 million contract from, "It was the former GM's fault" to "DSD's approach to contract pricing is not adequate; therefore, a better pricing system is needed." There was a need to change Engineering's view of itself as a group of esoteric technical geniuses and to make it realize that it had to learn how to design manufacturable devices. There was a need to install better information and financial systems and controls, to build a new set of operating norms emphasizing timeliness, commitment, taking responsibility, and confronting problems at an early stage. People in the organization needed to become aware that DSD's key customers (the federal government and foreign governments) no longer believed that DSD would deliver operational detection systems as promised. (Indeed, DSD lost two major proposals in the next year because of its growing reputation for unreliability.) Jim also recognized that DSD's matrix structure was matrix in name only. All the power still resided in the functions. The programs were not able to distribute rewards, nor were they seen as opportunities for career progression.

What Jim needed, and indeed what DSD needed, was a way to build a coherent, meaningful picture of the situation as it stood and identify the changes in both attitude and structure that would have to be made to solve the problems.

Some experts believe that this ability to create meaning is at the center of leadership and that every organization needs this approach from time to time. One manager, a vice president of Federal Metals Group, put it this way: "I believe that managers are not just collectors of data, administrators of information, or even managers of knowledge. We are all of those, but above all, we are managers of *meaning*, articulators of identity, both for ourselves and for our organizations.''

Several models exist for developing meaning. One approach that many companies are now endorsing is a total quality approach. Given this approach, the problems Jim has with Engineering can now be redefined as a lack of attention to customer requirements. That is, Engineering builds what it wants to build rather than conforming to customer specifications. In fact, in 1985, the DSD engineering group built a forward scanning infrared device that worked perfectly—except that it was too big to fit into the nose of the fighter plane it was designed for. Looked at in this light, the manufacturing function is a ''customer'' of Engineering: designing products that can be manufactured is a component of quality.

Jim could also have interpreted DSD's problems in terms of competitive advantage. Once again the customer is invoked: Every DSD function should supply more value to the customer than its competitors do. Pricing must be competitive, and manufacturing must have higher levels of reliability and productivity than competitors. When this approach is adopted, every meeting, every performance review, can be viewed as an opportunity to outperform one's competitors by insisting on efficiency, quality, and reduced cycle times.

What Jim actually did (with the help of the consultant imposed on him) was to work from the assumption that all organizations are composed of three overlapping conceptual systems—the *technical*, the *political*, and the *cultural*.[2]

The technical system encompasses the basic knowledge about external reality upon which various functions operate. For the engineer, this knowledge may be polymers, silicon, wings structured of composites, and so on. For the marketing manager, it may be information bits, buyer motivation, tools for analyzing market share, and so on. For the human resource manager, it may be demographic trends, a health cost containment program, and so on. Resistance to change arises from the technical system because of the basic habits people form in their disciplines. To change suggests that they may lose control or even that their basic knowledge is worthless.

As organizations develop, a political system evolves consisting of the influence positions, coalitions, and structural arrangements that individuals have created to manage power. Resistance to change develops naturally from this system since change may result in a loss of influence and power.

An organization's culture is its pattern of basic assumptions—invented, discovered, or developed—as it learns to cope with problems of external adaptation and internal integration. Culture may screen out certain external events as being trivial, and it may restrict the range of acceptable behavior within an organization. Culture may also be a source of competitive advantage for a company. Precisely because it has the values, beliefs, and norms of an organization embedded within it, an organization's cultural system may be a source of resistance to change.

Jim sorted the disparate aspects of DSD into three to six key factors within each system. With this approach, he created meaning for others in DSD with such statements as the following:

- Within the technical area we must develop a better system for pricing proposals and implement a system for ensuring design-to-production.
- Within the political area we must redistribute power across the matrix—become more market than engineering driven.
- Within the cultural area we must develop and commit to a new set of values that emphasize the primacy of the customer, timeliness, the rewards of responsibility.

Now Jim was positioned to portray the division's entire set of problems and the interrelationships among them and to identify which problems most needed to be addressed. He also helped to create meaning by contrasting how things worked at present—from a technical, political, and cultural standpoint—with how they might work better in the future. Jim needed to create a *vision* of what a desirable future would look like. Notice the two different kinds of meaning involved. First, Jim had to help the system determine what was most important to fix; second, he needed to portray what the system would look like when fixed.

For Jim Bern, it was easy to identify what was wrong and to use the conceptual tool of the technical, political, and cultural view of change. It was not easy for him to formulate a vision of how things would look when they were fixed. Put another way, Jim's strength was his analytical ability. His ability to use his intuition to visualize the future was much more limited. He needed help from others to formulate such a vision. Although both abilities are needed, few managers possess both, so that they need to draw on the resources of others to compliment their own competencies. In a study of over 1,000 managers, we found that high-performing managers clearly are stronger in these two competence areas than their low-performing counterparts.

One additional challenge still faced Jim in the current state. He needed to help his staff tackle and solve problems systematically, as he himself was learning to do. This meant teaching them how to *analyze* and *define* the problem, *develop* alternatives (plan the intervention), *test* new ideas, *implement* new practices (manage the transition process), continuously *assess* improvement, and *recycle*.

To continuously assess improvement also forces the organization to *recycle*; that is, reanalyze, redefine, and develop new alternatives, based on changes and improvements that have already occurred. Recycling is essential to continuous renewal. To do this successfully, the division needed an umbrella concept—in this case, the technical, political, and cultural model discussed earlier. If Jim Bern had chosen to analyze the situation of his division in terms of quality or competitive advantage, such concepts might also have worked. The important thing is to have a conceptual framework that both ensures an analytical approach and encourages discipline in the management of change.

Intervention Planning and Transition Work

By the fall of 1984, Jim Bern had pretty much accomplished state-of-the-system analysis, had planned the needed changes, and was ready to begin the transition process that he hoped would turn DSD around. With its attempt to sell the division, corporate management delayed his efforts to get started. About 30 days in the fall were consumed with the sale negotiations. Finally, just about when Jim decided he must move ahead with the transition activities regardless of the sale, the company discovered that it could not sell the division as intended: The only prospective buyer was unacceptable to the foreign government with whom the $33 million contract had been signed, because the interested buyer manufactured systems for an enemy of that country.

It was a courageous act on Jim's part to decide to go ahead with the risky change activities he had planned, not knowing whether he would be sold with the division, given another corporate assignment, or dismissed. By January 1985, Jim was ready to launch his intervention change plan. The plan called for three actions: building his own team of top managers, putting 10 percent of his key managers through an intensive five-day workshop which focused on the problems of DSD and the potential future of the division, and creating a parallel change structure (a steering group) to guide the overall change program. Of the three elements, Jim provided outstanding leadership with both his own top team development and with the workshops. He did not work as well with the steering group because of his tendency to forge ahead with any change he wished without involving them. The steering group ultimately dissolved because members perceived themselves as not having a central role in the change process. On the positive side, this forced line management to accept more responsibility for the change. The negative consequence was that the change effort became more spotty and more top down without the guidance of a steering committee composed of a diagonal slice of the organization.

The plan also specified what would change and how it would change. Indeed, any manager must face the larger question of what really changes in change. Too often change has meant reorganization or attitude change only. Figure 10–3 defines the targets (the what) of change: the *task, structure, system, and processes.* Any change in one of these core elements will require two concomitant changes. First, the technical, political, and cultural subsystems, as illustrated by "TPC" in Figure 10–3, will need to be realigned, and there will be a need for *individual development* to support the change being targeted.

When Jim realized he would need to build his own team of top managers, he also identified the tasks he and his team would need to accomplish:

- □ Clarify goals—what tasks need to be done.
- □ Clarify roles—what structures need to be established.
- □ Manage differences—develop individual conflict-resolution skills.
- □ Establish procedures—improve key processes (long-range planning, budgeting, and so on) and systems.
- □ Establish trust—by accomplishing the tasks cited above.

Similarly, the second and third elements of Jim's plan would systematically leverage change in each of the targets of change. By putting the top 10 percent of his managers through an intensive

Figure 10–3
TARGETS OF ORGANIZATION CHANGE

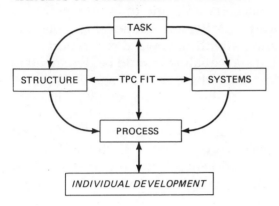

off-site workshop, Jim intended to get them to attack each target of change. Indeed they did. They initiated efforts to improve quality, manufacturing, and customer relations. The managers changed the structure of the division by inserting stronger cross-functional product management teams. They changed systems by deciding to link variable rewards to superior performance (the Great Performer Program), and they planned improvements in the scope, accuracy, timeliness, and availability of their information systems. Finally, they streamlined many cumbersome processes related to long-range planning, meeting effectiveness, cost analysis, and so on. At the same time, the off-site workshop provided ample opportunity for individual growth through individualized feedback.

To improve the overall technical system, the managers developed a schematic plan outlining the tasks and decisions needed for DSD to go from idea to proposal to prototype to manufacturing to customer delivery and service. They rearranged the political system from powerful, isolated coalitions of hardware and software engineers to cross-functional product teams. They addressed the problems of the cultural system by initiating processes emphasizing honesty, cycle time reduction, integrity, and efficiency.

The competencies necessary to implement such a plan (or for that matter, any transition plan) include constructive problem-solving, open expression, use of reasoning, consistency, and co-operativeness. There are also specific skills needed to establish the kinds of relationships required for building coalitions, networks, and task forces.

Jim Bern's plans consciously set out to establish such relationships. His focus on building his own top team of managers
and using workshops to concentrate on the division's problems
ensured that he could work directly on relationship issues of
trust, credibility, and openness with his own direct reports and
increased the likelihood that such qualities would be developed in
the 150 managers attending the subsequent off-site workshops.
The 150 managers attended workshops in groups of 30, with each
function and each program represented in each workshop. Each
workshop also continued the problem-solving started in the first
phase by focusing on five major core problems. Each problem was
carefully defined prior to the workshops, and one manager was
assigned to track the problem through the course of the workshops.

Each workshop group was divided into teams, and each team
was given the freedom to explore the core problems from the
technical, political, and cultural perspective. It took eight months
to complete the set of workshops, and during that time each
problem moved to a different phase of solution in each workshop.

The workshops were given very high ratings by the participating managers, especially in the areas that focused on building networks and coalitions.

The relationships built during the workshops did much to
break down the old norms described earlier in this chapter. The
important point to emphasize is that use of relationships is critical
to management. In the case of DSD, these relationships became
primary vehicles for overcoming rigid blockages to communication between division functions. Personal deals and contracts
could be established across functional lines, which were critical to
solving such problems as design-to-production, total costs, and so
on. In DSD, the breakdown of meaningful work relationships had
brought the division to the brink of disaster.

Managing relationships in the transition phase of change can
also be viewed from the technical, political, and cultural perspective. For example, the technical requirements for effective work
relationships can be summarized: openness and confronting
problems, tasks, and so on. From a political view, relationships
can be categorized as egalitarian, hierarchical, collaborative, and
so on. Desirable cultural norms can also be identified: mutual respect, honesty, integrity, and so on.

Note that with DSD, corporate management's first inclina-
tion was to rid itself of the problem division (a solution used

frequently during the 1980s). All this would have done would have been to transfer the problems to another company. The next company would then have put in new management, which might have resulted in relationship changes or might not.

In the decade of the 1990s, more corporations will need to learn how to enhance their competitive advantage by managing change as Jim Bern did rather than by incurring the costs associated with removing unprofitable divisions. Many of the transition management skills needed have to do with innovation; they involve addressing the questions, What can be done to create a rich environment for innovation? How can individuals be rewarded for taking risks to do something new? These issues are discussed more fully in Chapter 11, but here is how Jim Bern tackled the problem of innovation.

In conjunction with his consultant and his human resource staff, Jim developed what was to become known as the Great Performer Program. The program consisted of two phases.

First, 4 by 5 foot posters of outstanding performers such as Martin Luther King, Jr., Charles Darwin, Luther Burbank, Albert Camus, John Kennedy, and Mother Teresa were displayed throughout the division. Each poster gave a two-paragraph description of the person's accomplishments. In the second phase, people from DSD were nominated as Great Performers by their peers or managers, and a cross-functional task force decided who was to receive the designation. Posters of the individuals selected were displayed and each person received a pin and a cash award. Over 200 Great Performer awards were given out between 1985 and 1987, resulting in millions of dollars of savings to the division and—just as important—a work force that focused its energies on innovation.

Jim Bern knew intuitively that he could not build enthusiasm, support, and commitment for his change efforts if all he could say was, "We have to fix our problems." He had to develop a vision of what DSD could be (and as noted earlier, this was personally difficult for him). He had to capture the imagination of a work force that had long been floundering in defeatism and destructive work patterns. He had to convince his superiors at corporate headquarters that DSD was worth saving, that it would make an important contribution to the corporation's technology, and do so profitably. He had to believe in something that did not as yet exist, and he had to sell his ideas to others as though it would exist. In the years between 1985 and 1988, Jim had his top team develop the vision for DSD. Then he used every gathering of any group of employees as an opportunity to review the vision, to get ideas on how to build the vision further, and to evaluate plans, goals, and performance reviews against the standards implied in the vision. He had his consultant develop a leadership assessment form that measured managers' current performance against the vision of the DSD manager of the future.

Stabilization

One might wonder whether this section dealing with stabilization belongs in a discussion of the planning of change. Clearly it does. For the change effort to be successful, the same people who initiated and led it have to stabilize it.

Much has been written about the long-term impact of stress. To manage the stress that is the inevitable concomitant of change, periods of relative stabilization built into a longer-term process of change are essential.

For Jim Bern, the first intimation that he needed to stabilize came when his consultant provided information that some of his most valued managers were spending an inordinate amount of time worrying about whether they would be removed in the next 30 days. During 1985, as already mentioned, Jim's supervisor had replaced the director of engineering and the comptroller. A new director had been added to the staff to manage the $33 million program. Next, the director of manufacturing was replaced. Shortly afterward, the director of sales was made subordinate to the director of marketing. A new director of quality assurance was appointed. The personnel director had received a poor performance rating from Jim and was doubtful of her long-term employment at DSD. As these changes occurred at the top, similar personnel changes were cascading down through the organization. While most of the managers believed these changes were necessary, they did not know whether they too would soon be asked to leave.

Jim Bern believed he had made all the necessary personnel changes at the top by late 1985. His managers, however, were still worrying about whether they were going to be employed in 10, 20, or 40 days. It was natural, of course, for the managers who had been present in 1984 to worry about their jobs because they had been part of a very dysfunctional division. This worry created the dynamic for them to examine their assumptions, style, and behavior as managers. Those who remained made major changes in order to cope with a changed DSD. But the same dynamic persisted, undermining even the good managers' confidence.

A time comes when every manager needs confirmation that the changes that have been put into place are working. One difficulty is that typically this need will appear before the organization has had a chance to see the bottom line turnaround. DSD was operating productively by late 1985, but the bottom line would not reflect this until 1987 because of write-offs in both 1985 and 1986, that should have been written off before 1984. Thus, by early 1986, Jim Bern had to help his managers (and himself) understand that the changes were working. Once again, he had to create meaning in a situation in which facts alone were not sufficient. What he did to create such meaning required the use of symbols and metaphors. Once his consultant helped him identify the need for such stabilization, he took action.

Jim had already installed a goal-setting process in 1985. By 1986, the second round, most of the bugs in the process had been worked out, and he decided to use this process to introduce stability. The goal-setting process was an iterative, top-down, bottom-up process, which began in October 1985, cycled down and then back up through management, and was concluded in extended top staff meetings in late January 1986. At the end of the cycle, in January 1986, Jim, because of his awareness of the need for stability, brought together his top team in an off-site workshop for the last day of goals discussion. At the end of the discussions, Jim stood up and acknowledged the hard work that had gone into the planning. He then used the following analogy:

> I know that it has been like playing on a losing team here for the last few years. Our wins have been few, our losses many. We have been rapidly dropping members off the team and adding new ones. For the players on this team, it must seem as though we have been in preseason for two years and that every few weeks or months we keep trying to find new players. I know that some of you go home at the end of the week wondering whether you will make next week's cut. With this event, I want to declare preseason over. Each of you has proven your willingness to change, and you have proposed goals which, if accomplished, will turn this organization around. I have asked my assistant to prepare a charter which has our mission, goals, and values for 1986 described on it. I want each of you to sign it, as I will, in order to symbolize to you that I

consider this the varsity team for 1986. I do not plan to make any personnel changes among you (unless there is gross impropriety) until we have had a chance to see if you accomplish your goals, which will be at least a year from now.

The signing of the charter gave the managers a year's time in which to prove their competence and also acknowledged their efforts to date. The positive tone of Jim's presentation and his acknowledgment of the top team were difficult for Jim to do. He was almost obsessed with the idea that if he let up on the pressure for change people would begin to slack off. It took a considerable amount of coaching to get his agreement to take this step. Afterward he was glad he had.

Many of the managers developed a similar process with their subordinates. Stabilization of the top team did not mean a reduction of changes in other areas. In the same year, DSD changed its manufacturing process so dramatically that its nondefect yields went from 20 percent in 1985 to 89 percent in 1986 to 98 percent in 1987.

Identifying changes that are congruent with the desired state and acknowledging and rewarding such changes are crucial to stabilizing the new behaviors of managers. To make changes more durable and more stable over time, it is necessary to introduce policies and human resource practices that reinforce the changes desired. For example, if management wants to support the introduction of new products as a regular part of senior managers' responsibility, it needs to find a way to reward such behavior. For example, 3M has done this by basing a portion of each year's executive bonus on the performance of products less than five years old which were introduced by that manager. Its executives have consequently increased their support of new product development.

Stabilizing change requires isolating the new behavior and figuring out how to maintain it by using the appropriate reward, recognition, or other policy. One company, which is moving toward the widespread use of temporary systems such as networks and coalitions, has developed a structured process for forming such arrangements. Here members of the network or coalition manage part of the performance-appraisal process for fellow members. Another company has institutionalized the process of discontinuing major products by holding a "wake" for the product (usually a wine and cheese party complete with eulogies) and celebrating the new appointments of those transferring to another product line. Again, this reduces much of the stress associated with not knowing what will happen to the product line and the people associated with it. Still another company uses executive promotion announcements to describe how the promotion fits into the technical, political, and cultural change plans of the division.

A steering committee that regularly communicates what has been effective in a change effort encourages stabilization by creating a sense of accomplishment, direction, and gain.

Ultimately, as changes occur that are indicative of the desired future state of the organization, the manager who wishes to sustain such changes periodically examines the core human resource practices (selection, development, evaluation, rewards, communication) to see that they support the changes. Information system flows may also be redesigned to support change. Using semiautonomous work teams in the manufacturing process is much more likely to succeed if each team is supported by continuous feedback on orders, quality, product changes, warranty costs, service experience, and so on.

Renewal

Stabilizing the change process (a paradox in itself), while helpful, is not enough. Each newly stabilized change must be periodically examined and, if necessary, destabilized (a further paradox). It is worth repeating the lesson from history that John Gardner gave us in the 1960s.

> How curious, then, that in all of history with the immensely varied principles on which societies (and organizations) have been designed and operated, no people has seriously attempted to build a society or organization which would take into account the aging of institutions and to provide for their continuous renewal.[3]

The truth of this statement was confirmed for another researcher when 80 percent of the companies he had classified as excellent in 1980 no longer met the standards six years later, leading him to write about the importance of renewal.

The essence of renewal is learning how to learn, not once but many times. In DSD's case, an interesting puzzle remains regarding renewal. Jim Bern and some of the managers had learned the importance of renewal. However, the company soon rewarded Jim and several of his direct reports by promoting them to positions carrying larger responsibilities elsewhere in the company. The latest reports from insiders indicate that DSD is showing signs of regression due to these departures and due to lack of learning about how to continuously renew. Unknown at this point is whether Jim and the managers will carry their learning to other parts of the organization. Also, what DSD had learned about renewal seems not to have transferred to corporate management. So the question remains, how can we know when an organization has learned?

Yet renewal requires learning how to learn. The capacity for change will become a competitive advantage only when an organization can manage change more rapidly than its competitors. How can we learn how to do business differently, based on what we have already learned? How do we build in the continuous loop that forces us to learn from experience? As one expert has pointed out, this loop is what distinguishes the computer from all former machines. Suddenly we are faced with a machine that not only learns from its mistakes and successes but also anticipates how to use such learning to increase success rates in subsequent situations. The requirement for renewal in the process of managing change is precisely the same. Making organizational capability renewable means not just gaining a short-term competitive advantage on current product lines. It also means gaining a competitive advantage before the new product is even launched, because we have learned how to learn about managing change. Stu Leonard, the Connecticut dairy store owner who achieves ten times more revenue per square foot of space than his competitors, invites his customers to a Sunday morning clinic in order to examine his practices on an ongoing basis. He uses this vehicle to assess continuously his relevance to his customers, and he has learned how to apply this information to improve his organization.

Building the renewal loop involves not so much a set of methods as it does a mindset whereby we constantly look back at the last accomplishment and ask two questions: What did we learn from that? What did we learn about how to learn from that event?

The DSD case cannot help us illutrate renewal, because it is too soon for that. We can, however, point to lessons learned. Jim Bern and his staff had, by the end of 1987, moved from deficits of $20 and $30 million to profits of $2 million. They had learned how to identify key success factors and build them into their goals, performance management systems, and reward programs. They had learned how to target change; make quality pervasive; and build, implement, and dismantle teams. Thay had also learned how to use training and development as intervention in their management styles and cultural values, and how to direct their efforts with vision. The question remains, have they learned how to do such things just once or have they learned to recycle and renew continuously as their environment changes?

APPENDIX 10–1
Key Questions to Explore in the Management of Change

Current State of the System

Which task, structure, systems, and processes are in need of repair? What standards must be applied to establish why they are not functioning as they should be?

How well are the current technical, political, and cultural dynamics aligned to support what is to be accomplished?

Is the vision clear? Is there commitment to it?

Are interfaces among functions and among the elements cited in the first question working smoothly?

What in the way we have configured our tasks, structure, systems, and processes makes it difficult to serve the customer fully?

Have we learned how to recognize the need for change? Do we know how to manage it?

Transition Management

Who are the key stakeholders in the changes being planned? What will be their positions with respect to the planned change?

Have we criticized our plans in terms of their ability to change key stakeholders while realigning the technical, political, and cultural systems?

Who will lead the transition? Who needs to be committed?

Have we built in ways of continuously assessing progress or the lack of it?

Desired Outcomes

Do we understand how we achieved the changes we obtained? Have we learned to reduce the cycle time required for total system change?

Have we ensured continuous renewal?

11

Flexible Arrangements

Bureaucracy, the rule of no one, has become the modern form of despotism.

Mary McCarthy, *The New Yorker*, October 18, 1958

It is an interesting paradox that the organizations that survived the 1980s because they successfully downsized, delayered, and made the necessary global arrangements to be competitive will have major adjustments to make in the 1990s in order to manage the "lean and agile" remains. In the 1970s, it was considered sound business practice to keep the ratio of reporting relationships at about one manager to eight employees. With the delayering of the 1980s, this ratio climbed to one to twenty in many organizations. Of course, the computer now makes much of the information storage and retrieval that was a major responsibility of these layers of management an electronic task. But so far the computer is not capable of mentoring, appraising performance, or planning career succession. (The computer can, of course, assist with the information bases needed for such activities.) Nearly every one of the 300 managers we interviewed in the late 1980s expressed the following frustrations:

1. They simply cannot do justice to twenty or more subordinates in terms of mentoring, career planning, and managing performance.
2. They find the organization has removed layers without removing the measurements, reporting requirements, and other bureaucratic rules.
3. Authorization levels (sign-off, personnel actions, etc.) have not been made commensurate with their broader responsibilities.
4. Downsizing has left the organization in shock, so that the old culture supports of trust and loyalty are gone precisely at a time when new global arrangements require

trust and cooperation between nations and merged organizations with very different cultures.

5. The hierarchy is still in place, with its old lines of authority and bureaucratic arrangements. Even more difficult, the mindset which went with it is still in place.

One manager characterized what remains in the organization as ''beeswax which has ossified without any of the supporting honey to provide the basic strength needed. Break a piece of the ossified structure and the whole thing shatters around you.'' The changes of the 1980s make it imperative to find new ways to empower and liberate the middle managers who must operate the lean and agile organization remains. From an organization point of view, this means that more flexible arrangements must be created. The rest of this chapter considers ways to create and manage such arrangements.

THE GREENFIELD

Many successful new plants were created in the 1980s (for example, Westinghouse's College Station, General Electric's Bromount, Digital's Enfield). This was one means organizations used in an attempt to build in flexibility. The idea was to isolate a manufacturing operation and through the development of a new vision create a self-contained operation that corrected the problems of older plants. The successful greenfield plant developed new definitions of the task, the power structure, personnel responsibilities, and so on. The success of such plants demonstrates that there are real alternatives to the old hierarchical labor–management structures. The problem had been that typically what is learned is not applied in other parts of the host organization. Indeed, most plant managers confess that they need a buffer between themselves and the rest of the organization in order to succeed.

At times, other plants within the organization try to transfer aspects of the greenfield without endorsing the total system designed for the greenfield. Thus, one often hears a greenfield manager say, ''Yes, they tried our skill-based pay plan, but abandoned it within a year.'' What needs to be transferred is the systematic way the greenfield operation goes about planning work. Consider the following example.

Enfield

Digital Equipment Corporation created an experimental plant in Enfield, Connecticut. The idea for the plant began when its first plant manager spelled out 31 characteristics of the plant he would most like to work in. When he communicated these, one person (a sponsor) at corporate headquarters was able to help him persuade others to build such a plant. A task force was established to transform the vision into operational plans. This task force helped to add the kinds of values needed. And although such values have continued to evolve over time, the current set agreed to by those who work in Enfield include: self-direction, respect of differences, growth and development, openness, initiative, flexibility, team spirit/collaboration, taking responsibility, informed participation, trust, careful risk-taking, big-picture focus, creativity, balance of work and family, and simplicity.

The plant's strategic vision has been articulated as follows:

> In Enfield we believe that all employees should understand our business, our competitive positions, our goals and our performance in order to:
>
> Ensure most effective utilization of technology.
> Participate fully in influencing product competitiveness and corporate performance.
> Have a reference point for decisions and actions that transcend personal and plant biases to do the right thing for Digital Equipment Corporation.
> Acknowledge and work to strengthen dependency on others (vendors, engineers, customers, and so on).
> Take appropriate risks after assessing the implications of actions in the broadest context possible, and encourage participation in community affairs.

This strategic vision and the values that accompany it might be discarded as just so many words if it were not for the following accomplishments:

- □ 40 percent time reduction in the standard module-building process
- □ one-day cycle time
- □ balanced line with continuous flow of daily shipments
- □ just-in-time inventory system, with no incoming inspection, stockrooms, or buffers in work in process

- □ 11–12 inventory turns
- □ output equivalent with that of other plants in the system, achieved with half the people and half the space
- □ scrap reduced by 50 percent
- □ 40 percent reduction in overhead, resulting in a lower breakeven
- □ MRP II Class A certification (an outside industry standard)
- □ MRP II Class A recertification (unannounced audit)

The core module teams drive the business. They develop basic operating systems for each new product improvement, test them, and transfer them to other manufacturing sites throughout the world.

Business planning is a regular responsibility of the module team. Each operating team has taken on responsibility for such processes as selecting and separating team members; administering salary and benefits; affirmative action; training and development; budgeting; planning, receiving, and distributing materials; shipping; performance contracts; engineering change orders; product quality; equipment maintenance; safety and first aid; problem-solving; and work schedules.

The earliest work of Enfield was guided by a basic philosophy that called for designing both the task process and the *social context* in which the task was to be accomplished. Periodically, the business teams conduct additional scans of the total work environment to assess how they are doing. The result is a continuous renewal of the plant and its people.

Lessons Learned

As indicated earlier, it is not the use of teams, different reporting structures, skill-based pay systems, tighter coupling of information systems to the worker, and so on, that can transfer to other parts of the organization. Such practices simply do not make sense at the corporate level or in the field sales organization. And yet, because they are concrete and visible, they have been the focus of attention. Indeed, Digital's experience suggests that the separate elements of Enfield do not even transfer to other manufacturing sites very well.

What Does Transfer?

Comparing Enfield with General Electric's Bromount or Westinghouse's College Station, one sees that what can transfer is the disciplined social and technical design of the work system. This means that what is transferred is the *systematic, social–technical planning and implementation process*. In order to transfer this process, there must be an assurance that the core elements are consciously attended to and *aligned*. In this chapter and in Chapter 12 on leadership, we propose the following as a minimal set of elements:

□ *Task*: The task is broken into its sequential parts and into challenging work systems for individuals and/or teams (see Chapter 12).
□ *Structure*: Charters and boundaries are constructed and reconstructed to permit responsiveness to customers (see Chapter 8).
□ *Systems*: The three core systems of information, measurement, and rewards are constructed to ensure goal accomplishment (see Chapter 12).
□ *Processes*: Key processes are continuously designed and reviewed to ensure that they add value (for example, meetings are planned and implemented so that they deliver the decisions needed).
□ *Individual development*: Processes are in place to ensure continuous development of individuals
□ *Alignment*: The five components listed above are aligned technically, politically, and culturally to ensure that there is internal system integrity (see Chapter 12).

Two points can be inferred from the review of greenfield and the literature on innovation. First, to transform an organization, major elements must be redesigned and then put into place as a total system. The new system must be seen holistically; it cannot be disassembled and transferred in separate parts. Second, creating new organizational arrangements requires the traditional skills for managing the task and a new set of skills for designing the social fabric of the new arrangement so that it can be aligned properly with the task requirements in a new system.

Several observers have identified requirements for organizations to survive in the future. In 1988, Peter Drucker envisioned a "shift from the command-and-control organization, the organization of departments and divisions, to the information-based organization."[1] Others have also recognized the need for new forms of organizations geared to delivering new products to market quickly without sacrificing quality. Researchers have found that organizations good at new product development use widely over-lapping development phases, self-organizing project teams, and cross-fertilization of project teams.

In the 1990s, we must take what we have learned about successful greenfields and innovations and apply it to flexible arrangements. Our bet is that the arrangements most likely to yield increased flexibility are personal contracts, coalitions, teams, and networks. Such arrangements have been around for decades, of course, but the social architecture—that is, the systematic con-struction of interdependencies among task structure, processes and so on—to support them has not been consciously designed and implemented. Nor has it been widely recognized before now that such arrangements need to be *temporary*; that is, they will be uniquely designed to accomplish a limited set of tasks, after which they will be dissolved and new ones developed. Each person in the organization will come to expect that a much larger percentage of his or her time will be spent within these temporary structures.

As companies continue to search for ways to become more flexible and more globally competitive, they must simultaneously find new ways to create unique approaches to tasks and integrate the results into the work of the organization. Flexible arrange-ments that build synergy must be created through the wise use of unique contributions from new work systems while at the same time overcoming constraints due to differences of time, geogra-phy, culture, and work styles.

Creating Flexibility: A Case Example

One high tech firm, which we will refer to as Image Maker, is the world leader in market share of its product line. It grew to its present position by buying its competitors, within two years of each other, in both Europe and Asia. After the acquisitions, Image Maker found itself with three completely different companies, each with its own organization and structure for marketing, engineering, manufacturing, service, and sales; each with overlapping affiliate operations; for example, all three country organizations had affiliates in Canada. It was obvious that competitive advantage could be gained by sharing technology across the three organizations, collapsing redundant structures, and restructuring its sales approach to include all products. The issue was, How does one do this? Obviously, one does not dismantle the acquisitions and require facilities in other countries to report to the parent company in the United States. There is an obvious need for country-by-country general managers, but that still does not solve the problem of duplicate departments—of engineering, marketing, and so on.

Image Maker decided to create temporary arrangements that would foster cross-discipline, cross-country communication and operations while at the same time restructuring on a permanent basis. Its approach was to form temporary networks of people to work on key strategic and operational problems with the idea that the network would be composed of any individuals who were needed to work on the chosen problem regardless of their country or departmental affiliation.

Over the next two years, the organization found that these temporary networks were an effective means of managing the enterprise. The various task forces, coalitions, workshops, and networks proved to be a way to get work done which cut across internal functional boundaries and ultimately even boundaries between the organization and its customers and suppliers.

Temporary Commitments: A Paradox for Flexibility

The modern organization places the individual in a stressful paradox. It demands of the individual that he or she work as though fully committed while at the same time be willing to shift product lines and move to a different plant, county, or country upon a moment's notice. The organization asks for commitment, concern, and loyalty and at the same time a willingness to shift, flex, and change.

Consider this paradox in terms of the notion of temporary commitments. Instead of making a long-term (blank-check) commitment to the organization, individuals need to be helped to make commitments to particular products, projects, and groups of people with the understanding that all of these commitments may be dissolved in the near future.

We believe three arrangements are especially well suited for the temporary commitment requirement. The first is the *coalition*, which may be defined as *an interacting group of individuals, deliberately constructed, independent of the formal structure, consisting of mutually perceived roles and membership, issue oriented, focused on a goal external to the coalition and requiring concerned member action.*

The coalition usually is small in numbers and operates in a face-to-face context. An informal group of engineers, manufacturers, and buyers might form a coalition to introduce laser cameras into their organization. They would work together to convince supervisors or other engineers of the utility of the new cameras. If successful, they might not meet again.

A related arrangement is the *network*, which may be described as *a set of connected coalitions, consisting of mutually perceived membership, issue oriented, and focused on external goals.*

The network may best be thought of as consisting of several coalitions and individuals who maintain influence with each other in order to pursue a common purpose. The network is usually not formally organized; that is, it operates outside of the structure of the organization. For example, networks have been developed in organizations to advocate that particular software systems (Word Perfect, Symphony, and so on) become the standard for the organization.

The third arrangement that can increase flexibility is the *temporary system*, which is *a time-bounded, human system constructed with purpose, structure, and procedures to manage a limited set of inputs.*

The temporary system, unlike coalitions and networks, is not a naturally occurring arrangement of people but must be consciously designed and implemented. As with other systems in an organization (a department, division, or other unit), the temporary system requires designation of purpose, a structure, processes, and membership. Its basic utility is that it begins with the knowledge that the arrangement is of limited duration. Time limits for temporary systems force those involved to reach clarity of task and role and to rely on commitment rather than hierarchical control. The lack of a long history of policies and other controls also contributes to its flexibility.

All three types of flexible arrangements—coalitions, networks, and temporary systems—can help organizations of the 1990s meet such emerging needs as:

- pursuing multiple, widely varied goals simultaneously
- developing short-term, intensive, effective, work relationships
- fostering innovation
- freeing individuals from the constraints of their country cultures by self-consciously developing unique, temporary cultures
- using human relationships to overcome bureaucracy

THE SOCIAL ARCHITECTURE OF THE TEMPORARY SYSTEM

A temporary system has all the properties of any human system. It operates on the basis of inputs, processes, and output. As stated above, however, it has the property of being time-bounded; that is, its participants know from the beginning that the system will be dissolved when it has served its purpose. Another unique feature of the temporary system is that, in contrast to permanent organizational systems, its structure consists of interlocking coalitions and networks rather than hierarchical authority arrangements.

Temporary systems have been used extensively as arrangements for inducing change. Some common examples include the company conference at which new directions are developed; investigative bodies, such as a special prosecutor's task force; and groups in psychotherapy.

Research has demonstrated conclusively that newly formed groups or temporary systems inevitably pass through several identifiable phases of development. Each phase is initiated not by an innate force for growth but by a requirement imposed upon it either from the larger environment of which it is a part or from the need to develop reliable ways of accomplishing its purposes. Initially (phase 1), a new temporary system is dependent on the permanent system for its assignment or charter. This dependency must be resolved in three ways. First, the new temporary system must quickly establish its area of technical direction. Second, it must learn to negotiate its relationships with the key stakeholders in the permanent system who have life or death authority over its charter (the political task). Third, it must develop a unique culture that can support the norms and values necessary for its own success.

When the temporary system is successful in resolving its dependency on the permanent system, it creates for itself enough autonomy to do its task in novel ways, thus capitalizing on the uniqueness of those in the temporary system while at the same time retaining enough linkage to ensure transfer of products and services back to the permanent system.

In phase 3, the temporary system needs to develop reliable, consistent ways of operating that are tailored to its specific task and configuration of people. Here there is a need to develop operating mechanisms that aid in technical design, conflict management, commitment, development, responsibility definition, and time use.

When temporary systems successfully work their way through phases 1 and 2, the individuals involved will typically experience a sense of confidence in one another's abilities. Phase 3 is usually referred to as the trust formation phase. Its benefits are that, in addition to providing a desirable working environment, phase 3 allows members to take risks with one another on task alternatives that invariably lead to innovativeness.

Uniquely, in temporary systems, even as the first three phases are being worked through, there is a sense that members are shortly to be separated and that the task must be completed. This is the final phase (phase 4). If this phase is not managed effectively, members may have a tendency not to make commitments because of the temporary quality of their work together. Explicit attention needs to be given at this point to dissolving face-to-face coalitions and designing separated networks.

Phases in temporary systems or other groups are not necessarily consecutive. A temporary system will sometimes move through all four phases in a few short hours and will typically recycle through the phases each time there is a new face-to-face meeting or new task inputs are received from the sponsoring organization. The temporary system may get "hung up" on a particular phase for an extended period of time.

Let us return to the case of Image Maker. The organization needed to solve several sets of problems never faced before. For example, how would it develop products systematically on a world-wide basis? Management decided, rightfully, that this was not a simple research and development question. Technology development that tries to keep cycle times to a minimum must interweave parallel activities in marketing, engineering, procurement, manufacturing, tooling, training, and so on; in this case, such activities must be orchestrated over the entire world.

Image Maker decided to create a temporary system composed of senior individuals from several different departments and several different countries to develop a generic model of technology development for the company. The group was given a charter, a budget, and a deadline and was told to take the time to become committed to one another, and to develop systems for measuring progress, rewarding performance, and providing each other with information. It was also given the help of consultants to tie the temporary system together technically, politically, and culturally.

The technology temporary system struggled through each of the four phases: gaining clarity, establishing membership and developing support for one another, finding procedures that worked effectively across the world, and planning for its own termination. Movement through the phases was facilitated by an outsider who helped the individuals understand that they were in the process of forming a temporary system. Even though members actually met face to face only three times during the year of the system's existence, by the second meeting they joked about moving in and out of phase two or four and were very proactive about managing themselves as a social system doing technical work.

Group members found it necessary to address more than the issue of how to build a technology development process worldwide. In order to achieve their purpose, they had to pursue more immediate questions relating to their own ability to function as a system: What really was their mission? What roles and procedures did they need? How could they distribute power effectively? How could they manage their own measurements, evaluations, and rewards? What unique values did they need to function as one team composed of individuals representing the cultures of several countries? And how could they attend to their own team development in such compressed time frames? In each phase, the members of the temporary system worked at aligning the technical, political, and cultural aspects of their work systems.

Temporary systems will naturally develop in phases, but can they be systematically designed and operated? Obviously, we believe they can. Required is that each manager operating in a temporary system divide his/her contribution between providing expertise on the task and being a "social architect" who designs and redesigns the temporary system in which the work is accomplished. Time spent on the "social" organization of a temporary system is quickly regained by the enhanced ability of such systems to solve new, complex problems.

A social architect, like a building architect, has two tasks. First, a blueprint must be developed in which the fine detail is laid out. Second, a rendering must be created that portrays the hopes and expectations of what the temporary system will be able to do when it is fully built. This second task creates the vision for rallying the members of the coalition, network, or project task force. It answers the question of why the hard work required in the blueprint is worthwhile. It leaps beyond what is known to what might be.

The members of several of the temporary systems that Image Maker created reported that designing and operating a temporary system created its own positive motivational conditions. It gave the members a feeling of increased control over their destiny. Establishing membership was experienced as a meaningful task in and of itself; it permitted work to be accomplished and built positive affiliation across cultures by reducing ambiguity and complexity.

Liaisons

Image Maker found that temporary systems need to maintain effective transactions with the individuals or units of the permanent organization that have a stake in the outcomes of the temporary system. To this end, key liaisons were designated who were not full members of the temporary systems, to prepare the permanent system to receive their products. One such role was the project sponsor—the person (or group) who wants the technical work of the project done and who will probably control budgetary support for the project, team, or network. The project sponsor defined the boundaries for the temporary system. Whoever plays this role needs to be explicit about the task to be accomplished, what decision-making power will rest with the members of the temporary system and what control the permanent system will have (the political requirement), and how free the temporary system will be to choose its own operating style (the cultural requirement).

Other liaisons may be needed to help with technical transactions, information about competitors, and so on. Each person in a temporary system will have technical, political, and cultural ties to individuals in the permanent system and require systematic support to manage these ties.

If sponsors, coaches, other stakeholders, and the members of the temporary system do not maintain effective relationships with the permanent system, the transfer of products and services from the temporary system will be blocked, and whatever competitive advantage the temporary system is supposed to give rise to will be lost to the NIH (not invested here) syndrome.

The sponsors and coaches who deal directly with members of the temporary system will need to develop explicit agreements about such inputs into the temporary system as information, finances, and support functions.

In the case of Image Maker, coaches and sponsors were designated who helped with such mundane matters as how to process a travel voucher because a determination had to be made as to whose budget paid for it to the other extreme of designing a world-wide conference in which the reports of the temporary systems could be reviewed, discussed, and assigned to the appropriate functions for implementation.

Internal Elements of a Temporary System Task

Task Definition

The first component to be designed is the task itself. What is to be accomplished? Sponsors may not be explicit about such matters. Differences in organization functions and cultures will surface immediately in the attempt to define the task. Differences in individual cognitive approaches to tasks will also surface. Frequent interactions with sponsors and other liaisons are needed in designing the task component. Elements requiring attention during task definition include at least the following:

- ☐ Project definition
- ☐ Standards of accountability
- ☐ Sources of competitive advantage
- ☐ Key success factors
- ☐ Work packages
- ☐ Technical work design (for example, Gantt charts, PERT, basic operations definitions)
- ☐ A map of stakeholders and their interests

Structure

The second component of the temporary system is structure. Structuring a temporary system really means developing the role specialization needed by the system. One such role is that of convener, a person who takes prime responsibility for seeing that times for meetings are clear, calling on members to contribute to meetings, and perhaps initiating agendas. Other roles may include paying particular attention to the process of face-to-face meetings (a process facilitator), watching for and supporting participation, acting as a third party when differences arise (an arbitrator), helping the group periodically check its progress, and ensuring that differences associated with language and country are managed well. Other roles may be developed that allocate substantive aspects of the task to the appropriate individual. For example, Jim will be responsible for information about competitors, testing of composite materials, and so on. As various forms of temporary systems develop, subgroups may have to be created for particular tasks. In such cases, conscious attention needs to be paid to what happens to the overall work when it is differentiated by subtasks. Members need to make sure that they have planned adequately for the reintegration of such subtask work into their project responsibilities.

Subgroup work is worthy of special attention because it may not be a familiar work pattern in all of the countries in which the organization has facilities. Since a temporary system is a system composed of human beings, it has special requirements that emanate from the people who have membership in it. To be a source of competitive advantage, the people component of temporary systems must be managed in as tough-minded a manner as the task itself. First, because of the diversity of the temporary system and because there should be equal participation in it, there is a need to develop commitment as the primary source of influence. Without commitment, temporary systems are likely to fail; control through obedience simply will not work. To sustain commitment, periodic events may need to be held in which members (either explicitly or symbolically) "sign up" for work directions, develop contracts with one another, and create other special agreements.

Ultimately, the temporary system products will be the result of a series of agreements or commitments between pairs of individuals and between individuals and the rest of the project team. When the members meet face to face, a danger is to overcommit without regard to the demands of the permanent system. Thus, a delicate balance needs to be achieved between zealous commitment and back-home requirements.

Given the hectic world of modern organizations, temporary systems lasting more than six months may need to add new members and release others. It is helpful, therefore, to develop explicit procedures for socializing new members into the system as well as for releasing members.

Similarly, once the purpose of the temporary system has been clarified, the need for additional or alternative expertise may become apparent, in which case the members of the temporary system need to establish selection criteria.

Identifying the core set of assumptions that members needed to make explicit and adopt was crucial to the success of Image Maker's temporary systems. Assumptions that varied world-wide included habits, ideas, and values: respect for the individual, fixing things before they "are broke," open confrontation, openness to customers. The temporary system needs to be explicit about the basic assumptions members adopt, to ensure that counterproductive implicit values that have been brought to the temporary system from different countries and cultures will not cause problems.

Values associated with experiencing meaning in work assignments must be defined for the temporary system. Research indicates that there is a wide variation in what constitutes a meaningful work effort. These variations need to be explicit, with acceptable parameters identified before the work is undertaken.

It can also be expected that conflict will arise in temporary systems, as it does in any human system. There are many different styles for managing conflict in permanent organizations, in networks, and in cross-cultural teams. Furthermore, individual preferences may exist for win–lose competition, confrontation, collaboration, compromise, or denial. The temporary system must find ways to be explicit about how it will handle conflict (see Chapter 9).

A powerful vehicle for developing cohesiveness in the temporary system is a reward and recognition system. Temporary systems need to be explicit about how rewards and recognition are distributed. A maxim that applies to all human arrangements is *a system will get what it rewards*. Since so many sources of work recognition are culturally mediated—that is, have value to only one particular culture—the temporary system must find ways of identifying what constitutes rewards and recognition for its members and then ensuring that the desired performance is followed by the identified reward. Team members within temporary systems need to develop processes for peer-performance review and communicate them to the permanent system. Reward and recognition systems need to be part of the fabric of the temporary system. The temporary process cannot work if all rewards, recognition, and career advances are controlled by the permanent system. In such a situation, conflicts of time allocation will always be resolved in favor of the demands of the permanent system, and temporary system work will become meaningless.

Temporary system coaches, sponsors, and other liaisons will need to work carefully with the managers of members of the temporary system. Joint assignments, career planning, and bonus allocations need to be negotiated as to who will have primary responsibility, the functional manager in the permanent organization or the temporary system members. At Image Maker, it was decided that temporary system members would have 20 percent of the responsibility for evaluations and bonuses. One study of matrix management showed that if X has two bosses, A and B, the key to the success of X is the quality of the AB relationship.

Finally, the temporary system has the opportunity to combine its own values, norms, rewards, and staffing processes into its own unique culture. If it does so successfully, ambiguity will be reduced and conflicting expectations created by multiple organizational assignments will be resolved. Defining unique cultures for global project teams should result in increased flexibility and therefore increased competitive advantage.

Processes and Procedures

The global temporary system needs two sets of procedures or operating guidelines—one set for face-to-face activities and another for dispersed or network activities. Procedures need to be established for five continuing management tasks:

- Creating and implementing agendas for each meeting or teleconference
- Identifying, establishing, and assigning responsibility for support functions
- Establishing concurrence processes
- Managing technical, political, and cultural conflicts
- Managing information technically, politically, and culturally
- Managing the temporary system interface with the permanent system.

Transforming Leadership

Management of the internal operations of the temporary system and the transactions between it and the permanent system is not enough. To obtain the hoped for competitive advantage that will justify the efforts associated with internal collaboration, resources must be transformed to generate product and service excellence. Temporary-system members must themselves become transforming leaders. To exercise such leadership, at least the following requirements must be met:

- A compelling vision must be developed of how things will be improved when the project team has completed its work.
- Consistent attention must be given to strengthening the temporary system.
- Member commitment must be built and maintained.
- The resources necessary for accomplishing the task must be acquired.
- The functioning of the temporary system must be periodically assessed to see what areas need renewal.
- The psychological and resource contracts with the permanent system must be periodically renewed.

A Temporary System for Change

In the last twenty years, managers have become accustomed to going off-site for special two- to five-day meetings. These off-sites qualify as temporary systems. When the group works off-site it has a task, structure, procedures, and may have temporary information systems. Usually there is not a temporary reward system. Some off-sites use a special measurement process to assess the impact of the sessions.

Increasingly, organizations are discovering that the off-site or temporary system can be used to initiate major change. Consider the following example.

The president of a computer company became impressed with the practice of many Japanese firms of developing partnerships with their suppliers. His own company was in the habit of putting nearly every tool, component, or part up for competitive bid on the assumption that this method would result in the lowest cost. He asked an outside firm to provide him with a competitive analysis of his company's sourcing activity. The study showed that, in fact, he might save his company $141 million if he purchased larger lot sizes and worked cooperatively with suppliers, which would include their involvement at a much earlier stage, such as at the time the project is being engineered and drafted. A consultant already on contract encouraged him to use an off-site to change his sourcing process.

The consultant arranged with the internal sourcing people to identify five key suppliers and invite them to the off-site meeting. The suppliers were interviewed, using the study that had already been conducted, to determine the major issues involved in working with the computer company. In addition, a large group from the computer company was selected to be interviewed and to participate in the off-site.

Their selection was achieved by developing a flow chart identifying who gets involved in sourcing from the idea stage through delivery to the customer. This resulted in selecting individuals from marketing, engineering, drafting, manufacturing, service, and sales.

The interviews of both suppliers and the company employees were summarized and reported at the off-site meeting. Five supplier teams were selected to participate.

Next, the actual temporary system (off-site) was designed and implemented. First, the task was defined as changing the relationship from supplier as provider to supplier as partner. The task was broken down into a set of specific changes, again based on the study. The suppliers were encouraged to be candid and the interview proved that they were. The meetings were structured around a leader, the vice president for manufacturing, and core teams composed of each supplier and the employees who interacted with that supplier. On the third day, division managers joined the teams, and on the fourth and last day the presidents of the companies were added.

The process was to do the initial diagnosis and problem solving in the core teams, share the ideas and conclusions with the division managers when they arrived, develop recommendations for change, and finally work out actual agreements when the presidents arrived on the last day. Agreements were turned into new contracts following the off-site meetings.

The information system was essentially the data collected ahead of time and the face-to-face interaction at the off site. Rewards were the consequence of the new agreements that resulted in savings in cost and time. For example, the company discovered that one supplier actually had better equipment for testing certain prototypes and was able to do away with its own internal testing functions.

The temporary system provided an intense, time-bounded arrangement for solving a major class of problems. One participant characterized it as the "swarm" method of solving problems; that is, all the key stakeholders swarmed all over the problem for four days. Several months later, an evaluation of the effort showed that the temporary system did indeed achieve its goals of changing the basic relationship with suppliers. Even though the temporary system concluded at the end of four days, its results transferred to the permanent organization because of the approval of the presidents at the end of the off site meeting.

TEMPORARY SYSTEMS AS A SOURCE OF COMPETITIVE ADVANTAGE

Organizations must operate effectively in the 1990s, often in many different countries simutaneously. They will, therefore, need to find ways of overcoming cultural differences that can retard global project work. The temporary system is ideally suited to achieve this objective because it creates a temporary culture specifically tailored to the needs of the assembled members. Furthermore, because of their cross-national membership, such systems can be powerful vehicles for the transfer of technologies across national borders. Too, there is a strong likelihood that the new products and knowledge developed in the temporary system will be transferred to the participating countries.

Another advantage of temporary systems is that they do not add to organizational bureaucracy because they are disbanded as soon as they have accomplished their defined purpose. The likelihood that members of such systems will achieve synergy is high: Participants must self-consciously create a system that will work or the temporary system will be dissolved. Also, by designing their own system, members increase their sense of controlling what would otherwise be an ambiguous situation.

Experience and research have led us to conclude that in today's lean and agile, global organization there is no longer the slack or the proximity that allowed small, unstructured groups of people to "slip off" and develop tomorrow's technology or strategy. Rather, the capable organization msut rely on the consciously designed social apparatus (such as the greenfields and temporary systems) to deliver tomorrow's technology and strategies. And, as such social systems become increasingly important, managers will need to learn the tools of social architecture as discussed in this chapter and Chapter 12.

Finally, as organizations learn to use temporary systems effectively, they are likely to adopt more flexible arrangements even in routine operations. As this happens, they will become more explicit about social architecture and thereby stand a better chance of being self-renewing.

12

Leadership

*The new leader . . . under an umbrella of visions and a set of values
. . . has got to be expert at allocating resources and sharing power.*
David Teger, Chairman, United Research

The need for leadership has been with us from the
dawn of history. Aristotle observed that the average
individual wants to be led. Children on a playground will accept
the dominance of the strongest individual because they know he
or she will protect them from bullies.

So strong is this need that before the emergence of the
written word, tales of mythical leaders were handed down from
generation to generation. Most of their feats were imaginary,
plausible only to those who believe in magic; nevertheless,
Achilles, Theseus, Roland, Siegfried, Saint George, all are part of
the heritage of Western civilization.

The Scottish philosopher David Hume proposed that Britons
should be led by a man who shared the values they held dear and
whose policies were regarded by a majority to be in their best
interest. The Encyclopedia of the Social Sciences defines leadership as "the relation between an individual and group built
around some common interest and behaving in a manner directed
or determined by him." Some current definitions of leadership
within organizations say essentially the same thing:

- Leadership is the activity of influencing people to strive
  willingly for group objectives.
- Leadership is the process of influencing the activities of an
  individual or a group in efforts toward goal achievement in
  a given situation.
- Today, our society is more than ever concerned with leadership. But whereas in the past we looked to statesmen to
  provide it, more emphasis is now placed on the role of
  business leaders in shaping the future. At the same time,

259

the role of business leaders is changing. At one time, a business leader could sit at the top of the organization and acquire, store, and edit information, dispersing it only on a need-to-know basis. Today, such information is still collected, but there is such an avalanche of it that it is shared unedited, and the key executive looks to the rest of the organization for help in understanding it.

As information proliferates, the need for the traditional controlling manager diminishes while the need for the true leader increases. A leader in the 1990s will integrate his or her control within the process of information flows, will be a team builder, and will redistribute power. Power will take the form of empowering others.

The ultimate challenge for the leader in the next decade will be to assume the role of social architect, mobilizing participation in whatever cultural change is appropriate for the organization's future survival and success. This new leadership style requires that managers' roles at all levels be transformed, with more time spent initiating problem-solving among team members, absorbing internal and external information to ensure the best possible decision-making, and for greater efficiency pushing decision-making down to the lowest possible level.

MANAGERS VERSUS LEADERS

One researcher, Zaleznik, reformulated the classic distinction between transactional and transformational leaders by calling the former managers, the latter leaders. He characterized leaders as personal, active, able to project ideas into images that excite people, developing options while depending on personal mastery of events for identity. Managers, on the other hand, he characterized as impersonal, reactive, passive; they coordinate, limit options, and prefer to work with people with whom they relate according to roles. Furthermore, leaders inspire, managers involve; leaders value end states, managers are instrumental.

Although there has been wide acceptance of this dichotomy in academic settings, in practice the variability within each category limits the usefulness of the distinctions. Some leaders are very impersonal; many managers are personal. Many managers and leaders alter their behavior depending on the situation. Organizations promote managers to executive positions, and many (not all) become leaders. Unfortunately, the bipolar distinction has often been used to distinguish heroes (leaders) from sluggards (managers). People frequently say, "He's too transactional" as a term of derision. And yet, to pick just one example, the plant manager who lets the day-to-day transactions drive his or her behavior is the backbone of the manufacturing sector.

More recent works on the subject distinguish leaders by the tasks they focus on and the way they execute those tasks. Leaders, according to these sources, distinguish themselves by their sensitivity to changes in environmental requirements (for example, globalization, quality), by their ability to capture disparate facts and understand the underlying trends, and by their ability to direct others toward important visions.[1]

THE LEADERSHIP CONTINUUM

We believe there is another way of making distinctions that integrates many of these views. Instead of a polarity, think of a leadership continuum. On the left the task is to constantly scan the external environment: What are our customers' needs? What are our competitors doing? Is our technology being replaced elsewhere? What will satisfy stockholders? At the extreme right side of the continuum the focus is on short-term planning, budgeting, organizing, and controlling. And in the middle the focus is on implementing strategy and converting current tasks, structures, systems, and processes so that they adapt to the new environmental demands. We will call this kind of leader the *social architect*. The left-hand aspect of leadership might be called transformational; the right-hand, transactional. In our formulation, the continuum is:

Transformational —— (Social Architect) —— Transactional

The differences are matters of the degree to which energy, efforts, attitudes, and behaviors are concentrated on certain tasks as contrasted with others. The transformational focus is visionary: It awakens the rest of the organization to environmental threats, mobilizes counterattacks, and so on. The internal focus is on social architecture: It shapes and reshapes the core aspects of the organization—tasks, systems, structures, processes—as needed for survival and growth. The transactional emphasis is implementation. Some rare leaders operate across the continuum; most operate on a much narrower spectrum.

To link our views of leadership to the competitive advantage model we have used throughout this book, consider the following. We have posed six critical questions in the right-hand column of the model.

1. To what extent do we understand and meet customer needs?
2. To what extent does my business have world-class performance in each source of uniqueness (technical, financial, marketing, organizational capability) and the ability to integrate the four sources?
3. To what extent do we have a shared mindset inside and outside the organization?
4. To what extent do we use all management practices to build shared mindset?
5. To what extent do we have the capacity for change?
6. To what extent do we have leadership throughout the organization?

In our formulation, the transformational leader will pay most attention to questions 1, 2, and 3. The social architect will focus attention on questions 3, 4, 5, and 6. Of course, wide variation does exist: Some transformational leaders may wish to address additional questions, and the same holds true for other types of leaders. As this book has illustrated, however, making sure that all six of these questions are answered and continue to be answered is a monumental challenge. Every leader runs the risk of diluting his or her influence by trying to maintain emphasis on all six.

As threatening as the forces of change may be, the leader must live with the motto, "Facts are friendly." He or she must constantly assess these threats and opportunities and transform data into information that can be used to develop competitive advantage. The transformational leader's task is to ensure that customers receive perceived value from their transactions with the firm and to generate sources of uniqueness that translate to customer value. In practice, this means being a frequent visitor at the customer's site and exposing one's own organization to the customer as broadly as possible.

The transformational leader derives competitive advantage from exploiting the organization's sources of uniqueness and its financial, strategic, and technological capability. Competitive advantage in the financial area is achieved by managing capital acquisition and resource allocations better than competitors; in the strategic area, it is achieved through the choice of product mix and features. Technology leads to competitive advantage when it enables unique products to be built with shorter cycle times.

For us, the transformational leader and the social architect meet and merge in the task of building organizational capability. To build such capability, we propose, one must begin with establishing the right mindset. In Chapter 3, we quoted John Sculley of Apple Computer: "To sell our product, we had to alter the culture, reshape the public consciousness. We had, in other words, to lay claim to *'share of mind.'* . . . Unlike share of market, share of mind is much more lasting."

PATH CHANGER, NOT PATHFINDER

John Muir, the noted conservationist, who wrote about his explorations of the mountains and canyons from Yosemite to what was to become Sequoia National Park, excited the imagination of many people. He founded the Sierra Club in 1892 and truly was a pathfinder. But it was Theodore S. Solomons, a charter member of the Sierra Club, who, a year after Muir's death, organized the necessary resources to preserve the paths Muir had explored for all those hearty enough to walk them.

The relationship between the two men perfectly illustrates our concept of the transformational leader and social architect. From our experience in organizations, we have become aware of the importance of the internal leadership role. We have met and worked with many individuals who are "the power behind the throne"—the people who "make it happen," who translate the CEO's vision into reality. But one must search diligently through the business literature to find much mention of internal leaders or social architects.

Business Week writes sketches of the Fortune 1000 CEOs. *Fortune's* October 1988 article on seven keys to leadership highlights only the top executives of organizations, except for two cases that highlight division heads (a female and a black). Only a few articles discuss the importance of what we are calling the internal leader or social architect in business, although in the political arena there is a wide and growing recognition of the importance of such figures as the White House chief of staff.

Thomas Watson, Jr., of IBM, has put the case quite clearly:

> Williams was my best friend. In the early 1950's we had gradually assumed the responsibility for running IBM. We made a good combination. He was totally policed as a man, orderly, and a little cautious; I was perhaps innovative, certainly highly motivated, and not cautious at all. Without him my success would certainly not have been possible and without me he, too, would perhaps not have had as much success as he did.

After studying 41 executives, Randall White, a research associate at the Center for Creative Leadership, recognized the need for the internal leader when he wrote: "All CEO's have flat sides, but the most successful ones play to their strengths—and build a staff that covers their weaknesses."

Accounts of geniuses who founded companies such as Polaroid's Edwin Land and Walt Disney, often describe the importance of the people who backed them up on the inside. Michael Eisner, CEO of Disney, describes himself and Frank G. Wells, COO of Disney, as having complementary foci. Eisner states: "Frank is a real full-time lawyer, and I am a gentleman lawyer. I'm a real full-time creative executive, and he's a gentleman creative executive." Wells comments: "Michael has enormous creative skills as well as being a terrific businessman. I'm more involved in a wide variety of business decisions and administrative chores."

One of the premiere external leaders featured in *Fortune* in early 1989 is now arguing that the organization of the 1990s, which has already done its homework on globalization, quality, and so on, will have need of individuals who can make the new organization, characterized by lean and agile structures work effectively.

Internal Focus

The primary focus of the transformational leader is on interpreting the external environment in terms of customer preferences, competitor advantages, global developments, and so on and developing a vision that will help the organization find new ways to outstrip the competition. The process, of course, never ends. Successful competitors keep finding ways to catch up to and outstrip the leader. The cycle itself shortens.

The social architect, or internal leader, on the other hand, focuses on constantly finding ways to transform task, structure, systems, process, and individual developments in order for the organization to support the vision and mission of the external leader. (Remember that the same person can be both the external and internal leader, although playing such a dual role effectively is extremely difficult.)

In Chapter 9 we examined the three subsets of the organization—the technical, political, and cultural. As the internal leader modifies and changes the organizational elements cited above, he or she must constantly reassess them to make sure that they are technically, politically, and culturally aligned with the rest of the organization. By attending to this matter of "fit" and by altering these elements as required whenever there is a shift in the environment or a new vision, the internal leader exercises leadership in building organizational capability.

The Development of Others

Another central focus for the internal leader must be the *empowerment* of others. This practice is at the root of organizational capability, especially during times of transition and transformation. How else can the vision be implemented except by individuals taking initiative?

Power stems from the belief that a person can take actions that will alter the external environment. To develop and sustain this belief is to empower. The psychologist Albert Bandura, noted for his work on beliefs and power, had identified four means of empowering others.

1. Through positive emotional support during experiences associated with stress and anxiety
2. Through words of encouragement and positive persuasion
3. By offering models of success with whom people can identify
4. By providing the opportunity for successful completion of a task[2]

With these four tactics the internal leader can empower others. No manager can afford to underestimate their importance. In fact, a compelling case has been made for the idea that, when the computer ultimately undermines the hierarchical organization as we know it today, the major responsibility of managers will become that of empowering others. The information systems expert[3] who formulated this theory then asked the rhetorical question, "What is required of managers in such a workplace?" Her answer stressed the "need for communication, for sharing meaning through inquiry and dialogue, and for engendering learning in others, in contrast to an earlier emphasis on contractual relationships or the authority derived from function and position."

Empowerment is increasingly being seen as the key component of effective leadership. In the findings of yet another expert, the sense of empowerment among employees yields the following results:

- People feel significant.
- Learning and competence matter.
- People are part of a community.
- Work is exciting.

A primary vehicle for development is not, as one might expect from theory, a training program but challenging assignments. For example, one organization recently combined the engineering and marketing divisions so that they are headed by one person and then changed the role of marketing product managers to that of business managers with profit and loss responsibilities. In still another company, engineering managers now manage prototype development in supplier organizations so that integration with manufacturing, which is outsourced, occurs at a much earlier point in time—reducing cycle time significantly and increasing the responsibilities of engineering managers. The ticklish task is to stretch the individual and yet be reasonably sure that the person can succeed—or, if failure occurs, to make sure the final outcome is learning, not punishment. As Fred Smith of Federal Express has written in his company's management handbook, "Fear of failure should never be a reason not to do something." As individuals develop, the level of supervision and instruction they will require for successful completion of a task declines.

Above all, the manager who seeks to empower others successfully must be willing to share power, take more delight in others' development than in having control, and realize that visions are realized only by teams, not by individual leaders alone.

Developing Capable Organizations: The Internal Task

Many managers believe that the essence of their job is to organize and implement the tasks they are assigned. Without well-designed task flows, flexible structures, coherent reward systems, and predictable processes (such as well-defined new product development cycles), the individual contributor's work is negated. Some experts see the whole difference between Japanese and American management as the U.S. practice of breaking down tasks to their simplest components and meting them out to individuals to be performed mindlessly versus the Japanese practice of opening up assignments to increase responsibility and give employees an understanding of the task as a whole. In 1988 in a speech to a group of American business leaders, Takeo Miura, Senior Executive Managing Director of Hitachi, said:

> We are going to win and the industrial West is going to lose out: there's nothing much you can do about it, because the reasons for your failure are within yourselves.
>
> Your firms are built on the Taylor model (the Father of USA's scientific management); even worse, so are your heads. With your bosses doing the thinking while the workers wield the screwdrivers, you're convinced deep down that this is the right way to run a business. For you, the essence of management is getting the ideas out of the heads of the bosses into the hands of labor.
>
> We are beyond the Taylor model: business, we know, is now so complex and difficult, the survival for firms so hazardous in an environment increasingly unpredictable, competitive and fraught with danger, that their continued existence depends on the day-to-day mobilization of every ounce of intelligence. Only by drawing on the combined brain power of all its employees can a firm face up to the turbulence and constraints of today's environment.

Task Analysis

Perhaps the movement in U.S. industry that most eloquently refutes the CEO's charges is the so-called High Performing Systems movement (see Chapter 9). High Performing plants are usually new facilities, although in a few instances old plants have been transformed along these lines. Usually such plants alter traditional U.S. management practices with semiautonomous business teams, inverted authority structures, skill-based pay, and highly participative management processes. They start down the high-performance route by dramatically redefining the core tasks to be performed.

Most such plants begin with a task-analysis process known as variance analysis. In this process, those who will perform the task work with production engineers to break it down into basic discrete, input-output steps, which are then configured into the most effective arrangements by those who will actually do the task. One Ford manager said this was one of the most dramatic differences and sources of learning for him in the organization's joint venture with Mazda. Once the model was designed, Ford production engineers expected to spend several months designing the production process. Mazda simply turned it over to the teams that would produce it and told them to design the process and the necessary tooling.

Key Requirement 1   The social architect must understand the fundamentals of task variance analysis and must create the conditions in which those who will produce the product or service can configure the most effective arrangements.

Process

An organization's processes will succeed insofar as they reflect well-thought-out management beliefs, values, and style. One Japanese expert has characterized this as *compressive management*. "The essential logic of compressive management is that top management creates a vision or dream, and middle management creates and implements concrete concepts to solve and transcend the contradictions arising from gaps between what exists at the moment and what management hopes to create"[4]

This writer also introduced the concept of inductive management, similar to what we have called empowerment. At the heart of inductive management is the idea that as middle managers resolve the vision into concrete concepts, they must create information, not just transact with it. Inductive management begins with the vision of the individual and then encompasses others who can commit to it. Resources must be allocated so that interaction is encouraged. Information creation expands from the individual to the group. 3M is the prime example of a project becoming a department and then—if successful—a division. Middle managers play a key role; they have the ability to combine strategic macro information and hands-on information. Middle management forges the organizational link between deductive and inductive management.

Key Requirement 2   The social architect must create the environment in which middle management can accomplish linkage between vision and practice.

Another process much needed and much misunderstood is conflict management. Most managers believe that one function of the organizational hierarchy is to resolve conflict, the idea being that whenever there is a "draw," the conflict is pushed up to a higher level of management for resolution. We would argue that conflict should not be the province of the structural hierarchy but of processes designed for its resolution, and that pushing a conflict up a level is actually a process failure. (This is not to say that certain conflicts, such as those pertaining to budget allocations, are not best handled by the hierarchy; our argument is that many conflicts could be handled more speedily and efficiently by the creation of adequate processes.)

The first step in managing conflict is to recognize that it has potential value as well as potentially debilitating consequences. Conflict may increase the motiviation and energy required to perform the tasks of the organization. It may increase the innovativeness of individuals and the system through greater diversity of viewpoints and a heightened sense of necessity. Each person engaged in conflict may develop increased understanding of his or her own position, because the conflict forces one to articulate one's views and to employ supporting arguments.

Two organizations that have recognized the utility of conflict are IBM and 3M. At IBM, the budget process must go through a series of concurrences and nonconcurrences specifically designed to generate conflict. Through this process it is believed that needed resources will be clearly identified. At 3M, innovative ideas are carefully nurtured to allow conflict-free gestation and are then forced through a series of confrontations before they are translated into a business product.

Andy Grove, the president of Intel, still teaches a course called Creative Confrontation, a course that sums up much of Grove's own philosophy. At Intel, Grove is famous for his "Andygrams," to which one key executive was introduced the hard way when his carefully written memo came back with a stamp that said: BULLSHIT! DO IT AGAIN! This kind of confrontation works, of course, only in a culture in which confrontation has been identified as a useful aspect of the management process (see Chapter 9).

Since before written history, humankind has been engaged in conflict, and much attention has been devoted to its examination. Many courses teach the basic principles of conflict management. Such approaches as breaking down the conflict situation into manageable subparts, building upon the successful resolution of the subparts, orchestrating escalation and reduction periods, and learning to shape potential solutions for maximum commitment are well known. Several organizations use third parties to resolve conflicts. Some organizations have gone so far as to appoint third parties at large; others third parties from departments not involved in the conflict. Still others build the third party role into the job descriptions of very senior executives. Yet very few organizations have adopted successful practices from other settings. One of the authors interviewed three key executives who had transferred from a company that had conscious conflict management processes to one that did not. While they reported that it was "very hard to know where you stand around here," they failed to perceive that the problem stemmed from the new organization's view of overt conflict as necessarily problematical and its resulting lack of accepted means of resolving it. We believe that effective conflict management can be a significant source of competitive advantage.

Many organizations fail to recognize that, when no processes for resolving conflict exist, the organization is thrown back on pushing everything up the hierarchy or removing those involved in the conflict. Constructive processes for managing conflict result in resolution; where they are absent, the recourse is control. When conflict is controlled rather than resolved, the antagonisms usually persist, so that continuing expenditure of energy and time may be required to keep the problem from erupting anew.

Key Requirement 3   The social architect must create conflict-resolution processes that provide real solutions and contribute to a sense that the manager can trust the organization to help him or her deal with such problems in a fair and expeditious manner.

To build a climate of trust is no small part of increasing organizational capability. Articles dealing with business management continually admonish top executives to "trust your subordinates." Certainly organizations proceed best when there is mutual respect and trust between layers of the hierarchy. Donald Peterson, the CEO of Ford, has been quoted time and again as saying that the company's turnaround required the establishment of new levels of trust among employees and managers. As he put it, "Anyone who will be affected by a decision ought to have the feeling that people want to know how he or she feels."

Any process installed in an organization can be subjected to the test of whether it will engender or reduce trust. A process will increase trust if it is consistent with the company's stated values, meets common standards of fairness, and if the why as well as the how is understood. In essence, the trust test helps ensure predictability, so that individuals know with certainty who is accountable and what the consequences of certain behavior will be.

Key Requirement 4   The social architect must create conditions in which trust prevails.

Systems

Another crucial component in building organizational capability is the information system. Like management systems, the company's information system is both a source of resistance and a potentially powerful tool. A computerized management information system may be resisted if it is used only for payroll and accounting functions. As it becomes more of a communications resource—as with IBM's internal PROFS system, which links virtually all 350,000 employees in 130 countries—it begins to increase organization capability by improving communication at all levels.

The challenge for the internal leader is to use the information system not only to communicate effectively but to enhance competitive advantage. This means, among other things, using the system to increase customer satisfaction. Both IBM and Digital Equipment Corporation give their customers direct electronic access to their order departments so that the customer does not have to maintain inventory. Both companies also use remote diagnostics so that the equipment placed in customers' settings signals problems before the customer is even aware of them.

A guiding principle for the social architect of information systems is to increase organizational permeability, or the ability of the information system to communicate directly with customers and suppliers. Customers should be able to make their requirements known by accessing supplier organizations' production information systems. Suppliers should be aware of their customers' requirements.

Increasing competitive advantage through the effective use of information systems will require the internal leader to stretch even further. Can the system be used for continuous or at least periodic assessment of customer satisfaction? Applications in manufacturing are already widely known, but can such systems be applied in areas of product testing to keep reducing the cycle between potential defect and corrective action? At Digital, as soon as a circuit board passes through its initial "melt" process, it is tested while still inside the machine, and the test results come out with the product.

More than any other technology, computer-driven information systems have the potential to reduce the power of managers who have operated as manipulators, dealers, and withholders of information. Many managers continue to prefer closed-loop control, because they do not trust their employees to respond properly to the computer. The challenge for the social architect is to use the computer to shift the entire organization from a control mentality to a commitment orientation, in which employees do the right thing because they believe in it and are rewarded for it.

As with other systems discussed earlier, the ultimate test of the effectiveness of an information system may be the degree to which it automatically helps the organization learn from its own actions. That is, to what degree is information positioned so that it helps to answer the questions, What are we learning about how to do our business? What are we learning about how to learn in this business?

Earlier chapters considered the importance of employee performance measurement and reward systems. John Trani, the president of General Electric's Medical Systems Business, argues, "If you measure something it will get better." During his tenure he has instituted practices for measuring the order cycle, defined as the time it takes between receipt of the customer's order and when the instrument is first used with a patient; inventory levels; headcount; productivity levels; per instrument costs compared to those of competitors. In each case, the measurement has resulted in time and cost reductions. We would add to Trani's principle, "After you have measured something, if you reward it, it will stay better." This is the principle of achieving congruence between measurement and reward. When these two systems are not in congruence, chaos results. For example, one company measured its service organization on the basis of keeping inventories low and reducing time to replace parts for customers. These two measures placed the service organization in deep internal conflict, resulting in neither low inventories nor improved responsiveness to customers. The two measures were imposed at different points in time without cognizance of the conflict they would create. Congruence of measurement and reward is evident at Nucor, a steelmaker that pays for increases in productivity over the standard, so that a worker at the foundry level may make as much as two to three times base salary, depending on productivity. The result of such a measurement and reward system is that both the company and the employee win.

Key Requirement 5   The social architect must ensure that the measurement, rewards, and information systems are congruent not only with each other but with the organization's goals.

Organizational Technical, Political, and Cultural Fit

The cornerstone of social architecture is to keep in alignment the *technical, political,* and *cultural* (TPC)[5] dimensions of the organization's tasks, structures, systems, processes and individual development. In practice, this means constantly evaluating whether changes are needed in these areas and by asking what such changes will do to the technical, political, and cultural dimensions of the organization. For example, organizing employees into semi-autonomous teams for particular work assignments will be much more difficult in an organization whose culture and reward systems are geared to promoting individual merit rather than egalitarianism. Ultimately, this means, for example, that introducing reduced cycle times may depend as much on creating the culture to support the reconfiguration of tasks as it does on doing a new variance analysis. Businesses often founder in the acquisition process because they are not able to achieve a TPC fit within their acquisitions when they begin introducing aspects of the parent organization.

The importance of achieving TPC alignment has been well demonstrated in the electronic components industry. Most manufacturers abandoned the long-line assembly process during the last two decades. Usually the change came about as a pure survival tactic to defend themselves against their Japanese competitors. Going from piecemeal to complete component manufacturing obviously required technical adjustments in the form of task redefinitions. More dramatic, however, has been the shift in the political and cultural dimensions. Teams, which are responsible for total components, now do the work that middle-level managers used to do, with many teams responsible for their own compensation arrangements and for hiring and dismissal practices. All of these activities used to belong to management and were the cornerstone of management power. Organizational cultures have shifted from reliance on the individual performer to new norms that support team functioning. Redesigning the assembly process from a technical viewpoint turned out to be fairly simple compared to shifting the bases of power and to developing norms for team governance.

Key Requirement 6   The social architect takes primary responsibility for assuring that the technical, political, and cultural dynamics of the organization are properly aligned with tasks, structures, systems, processes, and individual development.

CONCLUSION

Except in small or medium-sized companies, the requirements for leadership are greater than one individual can manage. In all organizations the ideal is to spread leadership through all levels. This chapter has argued for a continuum of leadership ranging from primary emphasis on interaction with the environment to translating strategies into congruent internal tasks, structures, systems, and processes to exercising leadership in the daily activities of planning, controlling, staffing, and so on.

A common requirement throughout the leadership function is to develop individuals so as to maximize their leadership potential. We saw earlier that Takeo Miura of Hitachi has claimed that Western culture will have to take second place in tomorrow's world because it has not recognized the core requirement to tap into the intelligence of all who work in organizations. And while his conclusion is justified, there are some significant counter-trends, such as those represented by High Performing Systems.

Finally, we proposed six key requirements for individuals seeking to be the social architects of more capable organizations:

- To reconfigure the nature of work tasks so that they challenge both the minds and skills of employees
- To create organizations in which the natural role of middle managers is to constantly renew the linkage between vision and practice
- To create and maintain effective conflict-management processes
- To build an organization in which employees trust and respect one another, their managers, and the organization's rationale
- To ensure that the basic systems of measurement, rewards, and information are congruent with each other and with the goals of the organization
- To ensure that the organization's technical, political, and cultural dynamics are in alignment with the tasks, structures, systems, and processes of the organization

13

The Capable Organization: Key Questions and Principles

In the past, competitive advantage was derived primarily through financial, strategic, and technological means. Throughout this book we have stressed *organizational capability* as a fourth major source of competitive advantage. With organizational capability a company is able to adapt more quickly than its competitors to the full range of external threats (new competitors, products, new technology, competitor marketing campaigns, lower competitor costs, increased competitor service) and internal threats (labor and demographic changes, loss of key personnel, reduced quality of product, loss of vision, work-force stagnation).

Organizational capability represents the proficiency with which managers understand principles and apply processes consistent with those principles to manage people for competitive advantage. It may be viewed as competing from the inside out: Customer value comes from putting into place management practices that meet customer needs and instill a shared mindset among employees and customers. For the capable organization, the focus is not just on building internal efficiencies such as reduced product-cycle times but on translating internal efficiencies into value-added goods or services to customers. Emphasis is not on creating a vision that will help make strategic allocations but on creating a vision that results in strategic unity for both employees and customers. The focus is not on leaders who give direction to employees but on internal leaders with external vision who engage employees to meet customer requirements.

We believe that organizational capability is based on a set of *principles*, not practices, that will be stable over time. Management practices focus on what managers do and where they spend their time. Concentrating on principles helps to identify the key questions and concepts that underlie and influence management practice. Managers who understand the principles of organizational capability and who are able continually to adapt their practices to those principles will be able to sustain their competitive advantage. Those who understand and implement the principles of organizational capability avoid the ''quick-fix'' trap of copying a competitor's practice only to find that the practice copied does not fit the organization.

LOGIC FOR COMPLETE COMPETITIVE ADVANTAGE

The logic of building competitive advantage through organizational capability is reviewed in the left-hand column of Figure 13–1. The premise of this logic is that what individual employees do as leaders (bottom of the framework) can be connected to business conditions (top of the framework). When managers are able to translate business conditions into individual employee actions, they have learned how to build competitive advantage from the inside out. In the right-hand column of Figure 13–1, we identify seven critical management questions. By examining these questions, all employees can better understand how competitive organizations are built.

Building competitive advantage from the inside out begins by understanding the business milieu and niche in which they work—the economic and social changes that affect a business. Chapter 2 reviewed some of the major economic, political, and social changes that influence all organizations. Understanding how these conditions increase the pace of change illuminates why organizations must become more flexible, open, and responsive to milieu conditions. An increased pace of change increases the amount and intensity of competition as new competitors enter markets. The Epilogue to this book projects that a major management concern of the 1990s will be understanding and managing the environment. We see an increasing need for managers to understand business, social, and environmental conditions.

To respond to increased competition, managers must learn how to build a sustained competitive advantage. In Chapter 2, we defined two essential elements of competitive advantage: (1) perceived customer value and (2) uniqueness. Perceived customer value is present when employees understand and meet customer needs. Uniqueness is present when the organization develops capabilities that are idiosyncratic and nonimitable. By developing

Figure 13–1
COMPETITIVE ADVANTAGE MODEL

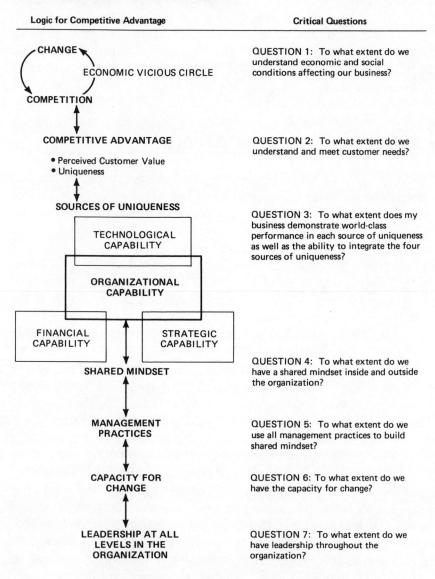

Logic for Competitive Advantage	Critical Questions

CHANGE
ECONOMIC VICIOUS CIRCLE
COMPETITION

QUESTION 1: To what extent do we understand economic and social conditions affecting our business?

COMPETITIVE ADVANTAGE

• Perceived Customer Value
• Uniqueness

QUESTION 2: To what extent do we understand and meet customer needs?

SOURCES OF UNIQUENESS

TECHNOLOGICAL CAPABILITY

ORGANIZATIONAL CAPABILITY

FINANCIAL CAPABILITY   STRATEGIC CAPABILITY

QUESTION 3: To what extent does my business demonstrate world-class performance in each source of uniqueness as well as the ability to integrate the four sources of uniqueness?

SHARED MINDSET

QUESTION 4: To what extent do we have a shared mindset inside and outside the organization?

MANAGEMENT PRACTICES

QUESTION 5: To what extent do we use all management practices to build shared mindset?

CAPACITY FOR CHANGE

QUESTION 6: To what extent do we have the capacity for change?

LEADERSHIP AT ALL LEVELS IN THE ORGANIZATION

QUESTION 7: To what extent do we have leadership throughout the organization?

unique capabilities that add value to customers, organizations attain and sustain competitive advantage in the marketplace.

As we have seen, there are three traditional sources of uniqueness—financial, strategic, and technological capabilities. As managers master and develop unique competencies in each of these three domains, they can more fully meet customer needs. Chapter 3 proposed that a fourth source of uniqueness is organizational capability and that it complements the other three, adds value to customers, and, in many cases, is the most difficult area to copy. Managers who are able to understand and integrate all four sources of uniqueness are more likely to build competitive organizations.

To better understand organizational capability, we have identified four critical elements of capable organizations. First, capable organizations have a shared mindset both inside and outside the organization (Chapter 4). Second, they use management practices to build a shared mindset (Chapters 5–8). Third, they create a capacity for change through understanding influence (Chapter 9) and managing organizational systems (Chapters 10–11). Finally, they empower all employees to think and act as leaders (Chapter 12).

As both managers and employees build bridges between business context and individual employee actions, they are more able to build a competitive advantage that is not easily duplicated by competitors.

QUESTIONS AND PRINCIPLES FOR COMPETITIVE ADVANTAGE

The framework of Figure 13–1 may be understood through seven key questions (right-hand column). Managers seeking to build sustained competitive advantage should continually ask these questions to ensure that actions correspond to business conditions. To respond to the questions, we have identified key management principles (Figure 13–2) that lead to more effective management practices. As executives ponder these questions and respond to them by applying appropriate principles, they more ably lead their organizations to sustained competitive advantage.

Leadership

To review, and in some cases extend our previous arguments, let us start with the final question and work backward to understand the key principles on which organizational capability is founded.

Figure 13-2
QUESTIONS AND PRINCIPLES FOR ORGANIZATIONAL CAPABILITY

Questions	Principles
• To what extent do we have leadership throughout the organization?	1. *External leadership* the ability to translate external needs to internal vision 2. *Internal leadership* the ability to translate vision to employee action
• To what extent do we have the capacity for change?	1. *Symbiosis* the ability to remove boundaries between external threat and internal action 2. *Reflexiveness* the ability to learn from previous actions 3. *Alignment* the ability to integrate tasks, structures, processes, and systems at the technical, political, and cultural levels 4. *Self-renewal* the ability to change over time
• To what extent do we use all management practices to build shared mindset	1. *Integration* — the ability to integrate all the management practices 2. *Unity* the ability of management practices to build internal and external unity

Key questions	Key principles
• To what extent do we have a shared mindset inside and outside the organization	1. *Internalize customer values* the ability to make customer values employee values 2. *Mindset dispersion* the ability to build a shared mindset inside and outside the organization
• To what extent does my business demonstrate world-class performance in each source of uniqueness as well as the ability to integrate the four sources of uniqueness?	1. *Paradox* the ability to deal with competing demands
• To what extent do we understand and meet customer needs?	1. *Customer intelligence* the ability to scan continuously and learn from customers 2. *Competitor intelligence* the ability to examine continuously and learn from competitors
• To what extent do we understand economic and social conditions affecting our business?	1. *Continuous learning* the ability to learn continuously about business conditions that affect the firm

To what extent do we have leadership throughout the organization?

In capable organizations management is able to *translate external understanding into internal vision*. Based on this principle, leaders look squarely at the external environment as it really exists (not as we might like it to be) and compare their company's performance with that of competitors. This leadership principle requires the creation of a vision the leader articulates, owns passionately, and promotes at every opportunity both inside and outside the organization. Based on our view of competitive advantage the criteria for developing this vision are as follows:

- Will the vision lead to products and services that the customer perceives as unique and valuable?
- Will the vision maximize shareholder value?
- Will the vision prepare us to deal with the increasing pace of change?
- Does the vision include technical, strategic, and financial capabilities that exceed those of our competitors?

In Figure 13–1, principle 1 looks outside the organization; principle 2 builds leadership by looking inside: *translating vision into action*. Consistent with this leadership principle, we have proposed a process for moving from a vision to action:

Step 1: Translate vision into a shared mindset both inside and outside the organization.

Step 2: Apply the shared mindset to a set of improvement activities that build the capacity for change (which we have identified as the ability to reduce the time between an environmental change and organizational implementation or response).

Step 3: Adapt human resource practices to help implement the capacity for changes, and shape employee thinking and behavior.

Principle 2 enables leaders to translate concepts into reality, to transform vision into action, and to build competitive advantage with customers by shaping employee behavior.

In one company we recently visited, this principle was not applied. The senior managers had taken two years to draft statements of their vision, mission, strategy, objectives, operating principles, and values. After two years, these six documents were finally prepared and agreed to by the top managers. However, as we delved deeper into the organization, we found that the written documents had little if any impact. One cynical employee told us that the greatest value of the document was that the managers had spent much of the previous two years in off-site meetings writing the statements and thus had not been around to get in the employees' way. Principle 2 states that the leadership vision must influence employee action; that leaders focus vision on employees, not platitudes, and that leaders lead by empowering others.

External leadership aligns the organization with environmental changes and customer needs; internal leadership—which we have called social architecture—translates the external requirements into organizational tasks, structures, processes, and systems, which are continuously aligned technically, politically, and culturally.

Leadership is not just the realm of top managers. Every employee must feel empowered to think and behave as a leader within his or her domain. The capable organization reflects a breadth and depth of leadership in all departments and at all levels. Leadership capability is the integration and sum of individual leaders.

Early chapters cited leaders who implemented the two principles of leadership and built organizational capability. Chapter 1 discussed Marriott Corporation, which, having developed competitive advantage in the areas of both financial management and customer service, turned its attention to becoming the employer of choice. Borg-Warner also illustrated the shifting requirements for leaders when top management was forced to buy the company to stave off an external buyer. These managers recognized that managing the finances associated with the leveraged buyout was only part of the leadership requirement. The long-term key to success was a shift in mindset, with managers coming to see themselves as owners rather than agents. Changes in the reward, training, and communication systems enabled employees to shift mindset and helped the firm reach its new financial objectives. Baxter Healthcare used the occasion of a merger to increase organizational capability. It developed a set of principles (for example, select the best manager regardless of company, freeze external hiring) that allowed it to improve the organizational capability of the newly formed organization. All of these examples illustrate the core leadership requirements of constantly adjusting the business environment as changes occur among customers and competitors and then redesigning and implementing internal systems to align the tasks, structures, processes, and systems to the new external requirement.

While the need has always existed to exercise external and internal leadership simultaneously, the increasing rate of external changes requires that the amount of time between identification of an external change and adaptation to it inside the organization must constantly be reduced. Such accommodation occurs as a function of the deployment of organizational processes to manage people for competitive advantage.

Throughout the book, specific examples have demonstrated the importance of these two leadership principles: translating external understanding into internal vision and translating vision into action. When management practices are consistent with these principles, organizations experience a reduced cycle time between external change and internal accommodation. Leadership that is based on these two principles is destined to build organizational capability and competitive advantage.

Capacity for Change

Having established the principles of leadership to build a capable organization, the question becomes:

To what extent do we have the capacity for change?

The key indicator of capacity for change is the ability of organizations to reduce the cycle time of *all* their activities—product development, customer feedback, management-system design and implementation, and so on. To reduce these cycles, we offer four principles.

The first principle is *symbiosis*, or building a bridge between the requirements of the external environment and internal capability. Chapters 2 and 3 demonstrated that the pace of changes in the external environment was increasing exponentially at the same time that competition was growing in intensity. We saw how Borg-Warner diverted a takeover, and we examined how Baxter Healthcare used a merger to transform both organizations. Chapter 10 traced how a division of a large organization learned to go from loss to profit. In Chapter 11, we saw how global organization links all countries. In all cases, the organizations increased their capacity for change by designing internal processes that could cope with external changes. They insisted on symbiosis between the rate of external change and the design of organizational systems. The symbiosis principle invokes different criteria for success. For example, we do not just require rapid adjustments in selection, development, and evaluation; we require that such adjustments can be justified in light of their contribution to competitive advantage, that is, customer value and uniqueness.

The second principle of capacity for change is *reflexiveness*, or the ability to learn from past experiences. We have seen that managers who have a capacity for change have the ability for self-assessment and are able to experience continuous learning. These managers are able to be self-critical and to understand the need to redesign tasks, structures, processes, and systems in response to external changes. Organizations demonstrating the reflexive principle learn from successes and failures and are able to avoid persistent problems.

The third principle of capacity for change is *alignment*, or the ability to integrate tasks, structures, processes, and systems at the technical, political, and cultural levels. An organization that introduces quality circles at the shop-floor level may have successfully adapted to increased demand for quality. But quality circles have not increased the company's capacity to (1) understand changing customer needs or (2) ensure that the company is competitive in terms of product costs and production schedules. The organization seeking to build capacity for change based on the alignment principle, when faced with a quality issue, needs to ask the larger question: "What is it about our management of tasks, structures, processes, and systems that allowed us to get out of touch with the customer's need for quality?" Each of these areas is a building block for change, but it is the systematic alignment of the underlying technical, political, and cultural dimensions (Chapters 10 and 12) that ensures the capacity to change.

We have illustrated the alignment principle in several chapters. Marriott's decision to become the employer of choice (Chapter 1) defined the task as a capacity to become the employer of choice. In contrast, management might have defined the task as a new recruiting program, in which case it would have missed identifying environmental factors as well as major competitors. In Chapter 10, which examined capacity for change, the case study illustrated how one division manager transformed a large financial loss into profit by realigning the technical, political, and cultural dimensions of the organization's tasks, structure, and systems.

The fourth principle of capacity for change is *self-renewal*, or the ability to change over time. The capacity for change is not embedded in the single instance of change but in the pattern of successfully changing in the face of a need to change over time. General Electric managers consider the ability of their fourteen core businesses to generate a pool of cash part of their capacity for change because the cash can be poured back into particular businesses as needed or to buy related businesses that will increase market share. The other part of GE's capacity for change lies in the values it has integrated into all its businesses. For example, GE promotes organizational learning by reducing the layers of bureaucracy between tasks and the people required to do them. By removing bureaucratic procedures, employees are required to renew themselves to meet the business challenges that fall on them. Notice that the capacity for leanness is justified both as an internal operating process and in terms of its world-wide competitive advantage. The self-renewal capacity for change comes from the ability for the change to endure over time.

Management Practices

As a function of *management practices*, the behavior of individuals transforms organizational requirements into customer satisfaction and competitive advantage. Management practices comprise the formal processes for governing how employees think and behave and are embedded in an organization through policies, operating procedures, and traditions. They determine the kind of information employees receive, and how and when. They also affect how individuals behave—where they spend their time, with whom, and doing what. Managers employ these practices as tools throughout an organization to shape and direct employee attention, time, behavior, and energy. Thus, we turn to the third question that creates organizational capability.

To what extent do we use all management practices to build shared mindset?

The two principles that affect management practices are (1) integration of practices and (2) creation of unity.

The first principle for using management practices to build shared mindset is *integration*, or the ability to ensure that all practices complement each other and intertwine. Chapters 6 through 8 reviewed the ways management practices may be integrated to build organizational capability. We described the case of Whirlpool, in which the chairman recognized the need to customize the three-year executive-development program to help the company respond to external change. The decision was made to focus the first year on managing change, the second on developing global markets, and the third on increasing competitive advantage. Integration occurred throughout the program as the company linked external changes and internal action. This practice changed the way the executive program was evaluated, because it was no longer appropriate simply to get "reactions" to the teaching. The real evaluation came in assessing the later behavior of the executives: Did they manage change better, become more globally oriented, and meet the requirements of their external constituents? Integration of management practices offers a consistent and focused approach to organizational capability.

The second principle for applying management practices is *creation of unity*, or the ability to ensure a unity inside and outside the organization. Business strategies have a dual purpose. One is to improve resource allocation, involving decisions such as whether to buy or sell businesses, increase investment in research and development, or fund capital projects.

A second purpose of business strategy is to create a common focus within and without an organization. The creation of unity is a critical success factor in building organizational capability. Internal unity exists when employees have shared understandings of what is expected and how to behave. External unity exists when customers agree to a company's values. The creation of the unity principle applied to management practices ensures that each practice is used to share information and create consistent behavior. Chapter 6 discussed how staffing and development can be used to generate employee competencies and bring employees and customers together into a common focus. Chapter 7 reviewed the means by which employee performance appraisal and rewards can be used to reinforce employee behavior and increase customer commitment. Reward systems that enhance organizational capability routinely encourage employees to adopt behaviors that coincide with customer values, implement strategies, manage change, and establish a shared mindset. Chapter 7 provided several examples of companies—AT&T, Avon, Rubbermaid, Walmart—that have turned to the creation-of-unity principle of giving pay increases based on improved performance. This system ties reward distribution directly to customer response to the company's products and services.

By applying the principles of integration and creation of unity, a company's management practices improve the "line of sight," or the connection between internal practices and external customer expectations. While the importance of making this connection may seem obvious, we could not find more than 50 companies that tie some of their management practices to external criteria, nor more than a dozen that evaluate all of their management practices against external criteria. Management practices are more likely to be designed with the customer in mind if this is a part of the organization's mindset; thus we turn to our fourth critical management question.

Mindset Inside and Outside an Organization

We have argued that a foundation for a capable organization is a shared mindset both inside and outside the organization. Mindset represents the patterns people inside and outside an organization use to process, store, and retrieve information about the organization. Shared mindset represents the harmony, or unity of mind, that helps organizations gain a competitive position by developing congruence with customer expectations. The shared mindset may be formed around goals and means (processes, work systems, management activities). When both employees and customers understand and agree on the ends and means of an organization, a shared mindset is formed. The fourth critical question is, then:

To what extent do we have a shared mindset inside and outside the organization?

Two principles may be used to respond to this question. First, we have proposed the principle of *internalizing customer values*, which requires the ability to translate the needs of customers into the core values of employees. Second, the principle of *mindset dispersion*, which requires the ability to have the mindset widely dispersed both inside and outside the organization, helps managers focus on instilling a shared mindset.

We have illustrated the application of these principles throughout the book. Chapter 4 considered two organizations with very different mindsets. In the first, employees were accustomed to dialogue, debate, and open exchange of ideas. Employees experienced mindset dispersion by crossing organizational boundaries, forming committees from different functions, and moving quickly up and down the hierarchy to lobby for a position. In the second company, employees also experienced mindset dispersion as they had to accommodate themselves to formal procedures, standardized systems and processes, and deferring to those in authority.

We pointed out that Disney has done a world-class job in applying both principles. It has implemented the internalization of customer values and mindset dispersion by generating a commitment to guest service that permeates a host of employee activities: Disney employees receive extensive orientation to learn not only their own jobs but the objectives of the company. They come to believe in and share the processes Disney uses to meet guest goals; Disney sets standards and offers incentives based on the extent to which employees meet accepted work standards; employees are encouraged to share the vision and goals of Disney—to be a location where guests can escape from their daily routines and have a good time.

Apple, Disney, and Nordstrom have defined their strategy in terms of mindset dispersion—of capturing *mind share*, not just market share. When someone in New York, Toronto, Des Moines, or Tokyo says it's time to take a vacation, Disney wants that thought to be, "I need a weekend in Disneyworld." Apple wants its customers to think, "I need my MAC to solve this problem." Nordstrom's customers come to experience a shared mindset of outstanding customer service—being called by their names, finding the store will replace items unconditionally, to cite just two examples. As mindset dispersion occurs among customers and employees, Nordstrom, Disney, and Apple managers have built organizational capability and secured competitive advantage.

To build capable organizations, we have indicated four key questions that can be posed centering around shared mindset management practices, capacity for change, and leadership. We have suggested a series of principles to translate into management action (Figure 13–2). To ensure that organizational actions are aligned with business conditions, three additional questions can be identified.

Sources of Uniqueness

Organizations compete by offering customers value in ways that cannot be easily copied by competitors. Customers who primarily value lower-priced products or services buy from firms that have financial capability, or the ability to produce goods or services at reduced costs. Those who primarily value product variety and features seek firms with strategic capability, or the ability to deliver differentiated products. Those who primarily value product innovation seek out firms that have technological capability, or the ability to design, engineer, and manufacture the products desired. Customers who primarily value a high quality of service and long-term relationships rely on firms with organizational capability, or the ability to manage people and processes to meet customer needs. In reality, customer values are complex and require that organizations gain capability in all four areas. Thus the question:

To what extent does my business demonstrate world-class performance in each source of uniqueness, as well as the ability to integrate the four sources of uniqueness?

When managers are able to deliver customers added value through developing competencies in each capability, they build sustained competitive advantage.

The fundamental management principle to ensure sources of uniqueness is *paradox*, requiring the ability to deal with competing demands. The four sources of uniqueness pose a number of paradoxes for managers. They must learn to make trade-offs between:

□ *Financial and technological capability*

Do managers invest limited resources in returns to investors (for example, dividends) or in plant and equipment?

Do managers encourage short-term performance or invest in long-term research and development?

□ *Technological and strategic capability*

Do managers put resources into facilities and process technologies or product features?

Do managers foster basic research or research dedicated to specific customers?

☐ *Strategic and organizational capability*

Do managers spend time with customers or employees?

Do managers fund new products or increase employee salaries?

☐ *Financial and organizational capability*

Do managers allocate profits to dividends, reduced prices for customers, or employee compensation?

For each of these trade-offs managers face a paradox: to succeed, they must simultaneously accomplish multiple agendas.

Through developing organizational capability, as we have defined it, managers may follow two paths to resolve the paradoxes. First, financial, strategic, and technological capabilities may be accomplished only as managers develop competencies in their respective areas. Financial capability is built by employees who understand financial management, including capital allocation, cost allocation, and valuation principles. To secure technological capability, employees must develop competence in design, engineering, information systems, and manufacturing. Strategic capability requires employees who can grasp customer expectations and understand market research and distribution channels. Developing employee capability in each area assures that the organization will meet customer values better than its competitors. Developing the competencies to achieve these capabilities requires that management focus on organizational capability—shared mindset, management practices, capacity for change, and leadership.

Second, the ability to integrate across financial, technological, and strategic capabilities derives from organizational capability. While this capability helps to develop personal competencies, it also encourages organizational competencies, or the ability to work across boundaries in an organization. Shared mindset blends the unique requirements of each capability into a common commitment to customer values. Management practices can be devised to ensure that competencies in each of the capabilities are merged. For example, when training programs use cross-functional teams— with members who have competencies in finance, engineering, manufacturing, marketing, and human resources, individuals can become aware of their unique contributions as well as forge personal competencies into organizational competencies. Building capacity for change through understanding the technical, political, and cultural processes encourages looking across the organization and building integrative competencies. Leadership, as we described in Chapter 12, encourages individuals to integrate personal competencies into organizational competencies by translating vision into action and viewing customer requirements in terms of personal goals.

The ability to resolve paradoxes may develop as managers apply the principles of organizational capability. Competing demands may be reshaped to become complementary demands. Departments and functions that operate independently may become interdependent, and personal competencies may be melded into organizational capability. Through organizational capability, synergy is likely to result as the whole organization becomes more competitive than any of its individual parts.

Competitive Advantage

We have broken down competitive advantage into two elements (Chapter 2): perceived customer value and uniqueness. All the uniqueness in the world does not build competitiveness unless it meets customer values. Being constantly aware of and driven by customers allows managers to organize their activities to their maximum value, as summarized in the question:

To what extent do we understand and meet customer needs?

Without constantly posing this question, managers' actions may be efficient but not effective.

Two principles are central to this question. *Customer intelligence*, or the ability to learn continuously from customers, focuses attention outside rather than inside the organization. Much of our discussion of organizational capability has centered on examples of organizations that have outstanding customer intelligence. In a development program at Baroid's, employees interviewed customers as part of their training. Customer intelligence derived, in part, from requiring that all management practices be directed to outside the organization as well as to inside. External leadership, as reviewed in Chapter 13, focuses on how employees build bridges between their organization and customers.

Competitor intelligence, or the ability to continuously examine and learn from competitors, benchmarks an organization against its competitors. Benchmarks have been applied in many areas—product design, manufacturing processes, product costs, marketing approaches. We have argued that benchmarking, or competitor intelligence, should also include organizational processes. Measuring an organization against competitors on each of the four components of organizational capability should provide insight into competitive advantage.

- □ *Shared mindset* To what extent does our shared mindset internalize customer values and have broad dispersion compared with competitors?
- □ *Management practices* To what extent are my management practices integrated and focused on unity compared with competitors?
- □ *Capacity for change* To what extent does my organization experience symbiosis, reflexiveness, alignment, and self-renewal compared with competitors?
- □ *Leadership* To what extent does my organization experience internal and external leadership compared with competitors?

By focusing organizational capability questions on competitors, managers identify the uniqueness of their processes. Unique organization processes enhance competitiveness.

Business Conditions

Any examination of competitive advantage must begin and end with business conditions. Business conditions represent the social, political, and economic factors that affect an organization. Being able to meet customer needs today does not guarantee that we will be able to do so tomorrow. Understanding the forces that will create tomorrow's customer values will ensure that today's management meets tomorrow's needs; thus the question:

To what extent do we understand economic and social conditions affecting our business?

Managers who understand economic and social issues will increase the organization's competitive position.

The primary management principle that establishes awareness of business conditions is *continuous learning*, or the ability to constantly learn about conditions affecting the business. Continuous learning may be the most critical principle. It requires an acceptance of and commitment to today's actions while simultaneously challenging them. It requires dedication to current competencies while building future competencies. It requires the ability to focus on winning today and at the same time conceptualize the keys to winning tomorrow. Through continuous learning today's successes become tomorrow's legacies, and tomorrow's challenges become today's opportunities. Continuous learning ensures that managers understand and are able to translate management principles to action. The epilogue to this book reviews the importance of understanding the environment and how it may affect all organizations throughout the 1990s.

CONCLUSION

Seven management questions and fourteen management principles underlie this book. By continuously asking these questions and understanding the principles on which responses are founded, managers build more capable organizations.

The primary message of our book is straightforward. Organizational capability is a critical fourth source of competitive advantage. It requires that everything managed inside the organization be coupled to what is happening outside the organization—business conditions, customers, competitors. It requires the kind of leadership that understands external demand and is able to translate that demand into a set of organizational processes that result in a shared mindset among suppliers, employees, and customers; a set of management practices that are justified in light of their contribution to competitive advantage; and a capacity for change within each employee as well as within organization as a whole.

In brief, we believe that developing organizational capability and building competitive advantage from the inside out has become and will continue to be a primary management agenda. The concepts we have presented may serve as a foundation on which to build this agenda.

Epilogue

Reducing Future
Threat Potential

> We cannot know the future. The best we can do is to make decisions
> today that hold up in the future.
>
> Peter Drucker

In the 1950s the issue was: How to capture the postwar raw
    resources

In the 1960s it was: How to cope with unparalleled growth

In the 1970s it was: How to cope with Japanese quality
    standards

In the 1980s it was: How to cope with the new Asian and
    European competitors

In the 1990s it will be: _____

What you fill in the blank with could determine your company's future. You might be tempted to say, "How to become global." If you say this you have certainly picked a major issue, and one that you must solve to be a significant player in the twenty-first century. In our opinion, however, you have not picked the issue most likely to permeate every other source of competitive advantage—namely, the increasing toxification of the environment.

There are at least two reasons why you might not have picked this issue. First, you may not think of environmental toxification as a business issue. For you, this may appear to be the problem of governments, environmental groups, perhaps even of radicals. Second, you might argue that this issue has been with us for several decades and point to emission controls, toxic waste laws, and so on. If either of these arguments is yours, or if you did not choose the environmental issue for some other reason, please read further to see if we can convince you to change your priorities. Your business may depend on it.

You might also be wondering why the subject is included in a book on building organizational capability. Quite simply, it is because the issue of environmental toxification will become a critical element in every source of competitive advantage—economic, technical, marketing, and organizational.

The challenge to business is to recognize indicators of environmental pollution at their earliest appearance, before they become major problems, and then to try to act on them in a way that produces a competitive advantage. For example, as long ago as the Truman Administration of the 1940s, a few people began to point out that the consumption of nonrenewable energy sources was increasing exponentially. But no one became very excited about the matter until in the early 1970s the oil-producing nations imposed artificial controls on production and distribution, which in effect simulated what would happen when the supply really dwindled.

One company that did take the warnings seriously invested in its own small refinery and access to oil. During the period of large oil price increases it was able to continue manufacturing its plastics at a cost six times less than that of some of its major competitors. Temporary corrections in the forms of conservation and increased drilling throughout the world now mask the underlying problem—but the oil depletion continues and will remain a major problem while other aspects of the total system producing environmental toxification become abundantly clear.

From a business perspective, a second set of indicators appeared in the last decade, having to do with the environmental pollution produced by manufacturing plants. Companies that use or emit fluorocarbons, asbestos, fiberglass, iron filings, and other toxic materials in the manufacturing process have increasingly been controlled, which in turn has increased production costs.

Related signs of the same problem take the form of class action suits against manufacturers of asbestos, fiberglass insulation, and tampons and of depressed sales of foods supplemented with red dye or sobesterol or that naturally contain high cholesterol.

More recently, the problem has manifested itself in the presence of waste products. Plastic bags containing contaminated hospital waste have washed up on the New Jersey shore or been

found in the stomachs of sea animals. Garbage scows around the
world have been prevented from dumping wastes into traditional
ocean dumping grounds. A law against ocean dumping, which
New York City has ignored since the late 1930s, has suddenly
been brought to the attention of the courts. City after city has run
out of land-fill space. The Great Lakes, Chesapeake Bay, and the
Mediterranean all move inexorably toward becoming giant cess-
pools. The shoreline of the Aral Sea in Russia, once the world's
fourth largest inland body of fresh water, has receded by 30 miles
in the last two decades. The sea now contains no fish, so that in
order to maintain jobs, frozen fish from the ocean must be flown
into the cannery, which now stands on an alkaline flat.

Finally, the indicators become interdependent. The polluted
air produced in the U.S. Midwest shows up in the form of acid
rain in Canada, the rip in the ozone layer creates a world-wide
greenhouse effect; the fishing industries, which rely on clean
ocean waters, find concentrates of poison appearing in their catch.

At the end of 1988, *Time* devoted the issue typically reserved
for the person of the year to the planet Earth, which it portrayed in
dire ecological straits. *National Geographic* published a similar volume, with a holographic cover that communicates both the technical progress and the environmental problems of this fragile
planet.

The problem that the preceding indicators point up and the
media have now discovered with a vengeance is the exponential
growth of the toxification of the earth. In the decade of the 1990s,
every man, woman, and child will be affected by environmental
toxification. Every business and every government agency will
feel the problem. All business leaders and all politicians will have
to accommodate their agendas to the issue. For business managers, toxification will be to the 1990s what globalization was to
the 1980s, what quality was to the 1970s, and what growth and
change were to the 1960s.

Time identified four types of dangers. First, extinction: The
destruction of forests (eight million hectares burned in 1987 in the
Amazon alone) and other habitats is driving 100 species of plants
and animals to extinction every day. It pointed out that the genetic
material being lost forever may contain secrets for fighting dis-
eases or improving crops. Second is the global warming caused by
emissions from cars, factories, and power plants. Third is waste:
As nations produce millions of tons of household garbage and

industrial toxic waste, there is no place to dispose of it. Finally, there is population growth itself. The world's population, now at 5 billion, is increasing by 80 million every year. The swelling population is wreaking havoc on the environment as forests are chopped down, grasslands are overgrazed, and croplands are overplowed in a desperate effort to produce more food. The importance of all this is perhaps best summarized by Smithsonian Institution biologist Thomas Lovejoy: ''I am utterly convinced that most of the great environmental struggles will be either won or lost in the 1990s. By the next century it will be too late.''

Are business leaders and politicians ready to deal with the problem of toxification? Have businesses taken the necessary steps to determine what the impact of toxification will be on their products and services? Have some visionary leaders already piloted new businesses that will capitalize on detoxification? If you believe that environmental pollution will be a major issue for business in the next decade, then consider the following steps:

1. Assume that even with reduced product cycles, product responsibility will be stretched in many directions—companies will need to take responsibility for any toxification that occurs in the process of obtaining raw resources; packaging and distributing their products; and for toxic wastes which are or are caused by their products.
2. Determine the impact on competitive advantage of dealing with the toxification issues involved in:
   obtaining resources needed to build products
   manufacturing processes
   customer concern about effects on them and their environment
   discarding products that contain potentially toxic wastes.
3. Determine the impact on competitive advantage if your company is perceived by customers as:
   a polluter
   uncaring about this small planet
   unconcerned about conserving energy and resources

Notice the words—''if you believe.'' These are at the crux of getting your company ready for the future. To take constructive action, that is, to use what will happen in the future for competitive advantage, you must believe that toxification will be a key issue and potential opportunity in the next decade. We believe that future events brought about by our past and current practices will have major impact on the very survival of whole industries, and that companies in every industry will need to contend with the issue of toxification in some form in order to remain successful.

There are two avenues to competitive advantage with respect to environmental toxification. The first, and most obvious, is to figure out ways to beat competitors by reducing the impact of toxification in acquiring resources and in production and distribution. The second is to find ways to turn toxic waste into financial gain. Convincing the country in which you wish to build a plant that you can do it with less environmental damage than your competitor may gain you access. Designing and producing process controls which reduce the release of toxic materials during manufacturing or processing and then marketing those controls may become a new source of business. For example, several oil companies claim that the toxic-free refinery is now technically possible. If these are built in the 1990s, who will profit from their construction? Finding ways to recycle and renew resources will shift from "nice-to-do" in the 1980s to profitable and required activities in the 1990s. According to David Van Seters, a Canadian management consultant, examples of new business opportunities are:

Recycling technology, including developing new separation technologies

Waste-to-energy incinerator construction

Ground water contaminant monitoring

Toxic real estate assessment

Compact sewage treatment systems for single subdivisions or office buildings

Advanced hazardous-waste management techniques

Water and sewer system repair and expansion

Air emission monitoring and control

Environmentally clean and safe consumer products

Research and development for less harmful technologies[1]

Once again, organizational capability will become key because what will be needed is a new mindset that regards the problems of toxification as important and that seeks new opportunities for business in solving such problems.

To put it simply, every business will be impacted by what is happening in the environment. Some organizations are more prepared because they have developed a capability to understand how external changes will affect them.

In the rest of this Epilogue, illustrations are provided describing how a few organizations have been building the capacity to anticipate the impact of world changes.

PREDICTING THE FUTURE

If there is one lesson to be learned from the statements of prognosticators, it is that trying to predict the future is a futile task. For example, in 1835, Thomas Tredgold, a British railroad designer, declared that "Any general system of conveying passengers at a velocity exceeding 10 miles an hour is extremely improbable." A week before the Wright brothers' successful flight at Kitty Hawk, *The New York Times* ridiculed the notion that man might fly. In 1945, Vannevan Bush, then president of the Carnegie Institution of Washington, offered his advice to President Harry Truman on the atomic bomb. "The bomb will never go off," Bush declared, "and I speak as an expert on explosives."

In our own time, a leading futurist offered "convincing evidence" that industry was on an irreversible move from north to south. He initiated the so-called Sun Belt–Frost Belt debates, his argument being that economic vitality was moving from the Northeast and Midwest to the Southeast and West. Today, many parts of the Frost Belt are returning to prosperity, while the Sun Belt has collapsed into only a few "sunspots." Since 1980, for example, eight Sun Belt states have experienced net emigration, while five Frost Belt states have shown net immigration. One Sun Belt state, Texas, has crippled the FSLIC with the largest failure rates of savings and loans ever recorded in a single year. Housing starts are up in Boston and down in Dallas (and this was true before the oil glut took affect).

Two leading futurists would have us believe that predicting the future is now technologically reliable and that most trends are readily discernible. As they put it, "Part of the process is knowing what to look for. Still another part of the process is knowing what it is when we find it." They would also have us believe that predictions proceed quite directly from the collection, analysis, and synthesis of data and the extensive use of computers. Now, from the perspective of 1990, it might be useful to examine some of their predictions. In 1980, they predicted that by 1990 all automobiles would be 92 percent plastic. General Motors has one that almost meets this figure. Most other cars contain about 100 pounds (1.5–2 percent) of plastic. They also predicted in 1980 that there would be fewer people living in poverty once welfare practices were reformed by the late 1980s! While some of their other predictions have turned out to be correct, we can see that their accuracy rate is far from 100 percent.

If the experts can't predict the future with any certainty, is there any reason for managers to try understanding it well enough to build it into their tool kits? How much time and other resources should be devoted to making assumptions about the future? Are there experts who can be relied on to help us understand potential future impacts on particular businesses? What core set of indicators gives managers the best chance of reducing the likelihood of major negative impacts on their businesses? Despite the riskiness of making projections, we believe that anticipating future threats and opportunities that will impact the success of the business is very much part of a manager's job—and has in many instances been done successfully.

The task is twofold. First, it is necessary to determine what "data" must be gathered. That is, what sources have to be reviewed, what general areas are most sensitive to environmental changes and are, thus, likely to impact one's organization. Second—and more difficult—the data must be intepreted in such a way that it takes on meaning. The ultimate goal of study of the future is to discover what the data mean for the business and how the information gathered can be used as a source of competitive advantage.

The task is not likely to be a popular one. U.S. industry is ridiculed the world over for its focus on the short term (usually the next quarter's financial statements). In such an environment, focusing on the future is difficult, although not impossible. What follows is a perspective on the core tasks associated with the maintenance of a futures perspective, the benefits and costs associated with such tasks, and several examples from major corporations that have taken certain predictions and assessed their likely impact on the company's long-term strategy. Several examples are also cited of organizations that do commit regular resources to scanning the future. Finally, practical suggestions are given as to ways future perspectives can be used to influence management planning.

METHODS OF VIEWING THE FUTURE

As we examine the extensive literature on such issues as future population growth, world economic growth, and economic restructuring from the perspective of its relevance to the manager, it becomes increasingly clear that we must understand the methods used to arrive at predictions if we are to have confidence in their substance.

Examination of the literature suggests that four basic methods are used. First is *extrapolation*, or trend analysis or forecasting, which is based on the assumption that the future will continue the patterns of the past. If the population is known to be growing at a rate of 2 percent a year, forecasters assume it will do so in the future. In forecasting, short-term fluctuations are disregarded in order to arrive at a trend.

Obviously, the weakness of any trend portrayal is that few things continue to grow or develop at a fixed rate. (If we encountered a child at the age of 4 who had grown 5 inches in the last year, using extrapolation would lead us to predict that the individual would be 13 feet tall at the age of 34.) There is a need to improve trend predictions by accounting for growth curves. The Delphi technique, a methodology that was used more in the 1960s than it is today, is a useful tool. In this method, a group of experts is convened and their opinion solicited about such things as (1) the likelihood of an event occurring, (2) the cross-impact of its occurrence on other events, and (3) how soon the event is likely to occur. The results are summarized and then resubmitted to the same or another group through several more iterations until the desired consistency of predictions is obtained.

One corporation, Security Pacific, has come to believe that its managers need to be informed about trends that are likely to impact its business and has established a small group that is responsible for identifying such trends. The group's charter is "to understand contemporary challenges to business and to search for new corporate structures and styles of leadership." In its first few years of existence, the group published fifteen short trend papers that typically cover a particular topic in depth and then outline the group's recommendations. Topics have included cor-

porate social responsibility: paradox and challenge; work: changing motivations and values; the era of the communications link;
the tin collar worker: an introduction to robotics; food: sustenance
and political weapon; the last baby boomers; Pacific Rim 2010: a
scenario for the Pacific Basin.

The papers in the series are well thought out and point to
choices that loan officers and other commercial officers need to
make on a daily basis. To the degree that the trend papers are read
by managers (and the human resource staff reports that they are),
they represent an ideal form of prediction about the future, because the discrete, isolated events identified are then viewed in
the light of potential trends. With them managers are helped in
making choices as the future evolves.

A special form of trend analysis is the technological forecast.
Depending on the business, such forecasts can be of central importance. The technological forecast is a prediction of the future
characteristics of machines, procedures, or techniques, usually in
terms of such characteristics as levels of technical performance—
for example, speed, power, temperature, accuracy. When done
well, this kind of forecast takes the current state of technology and
identifies likely future developments, taking into account limiting
factors as well as potential advances.

An excellent example of the technological forecast is represented by the following quote by Ian Ross, the president of Bell
Labs, discussing the technological possibilities of miniaturization
in 1986:

> The first challenge, of course, is to continue to reduce the size of
> elemental components. This depends largely upon our ability to
> improve lithography with visible light. We've gone from minimum
> line widths of 25 microns—1/1000 inch—down to the present indus-
> try averge of 2.5 microns—1/10,000 inch—approaching the wave
> length of light. But we're shortly going to run into the limit of wave
> length of visible light, and that will be a problem. Using visible
> light and all the tricks we can conceive of, we might ideally get
> down to line widths of a half micron. Under practical conditions,
> however, this is more likely to be 1 micron. . . . In the lab today,
> transistors with critical dimensions of 0.1 micron have been made,
> have been shown to operate, and have been shown to perform
> according to theory. So possibly we may be able to achieve struc-
> tures of about a tenth of a micron minimum dimension, with about
> a hundred atoms within that minimum dimension. This could lead
> to a billion components on a square centimeter of silicon. That is
> not very restrictive.[2]

The risk with all such technological forecasts is that a replacement technology may alter the nature of the limitations involved. Think about what Ross might have said in the late 1950s if he were using the vacuum tube as the limiting factor in forecasting the future capacity of computers.

Another approach futurists take is to try to *"experience" the future* through the use of *models, games,* and *simulations*.This encourages the integration of several trends and allows for predictions concerning the cross-impact of several technologies. Such models are currently used to predict the impact of a warming trend on the earth. These simulations must integrate trends relating to industrial waste, weather patterns, sunspots, and so on. The U.S. Navy tests model ships and submarines at the Naval Ship Research and Development Center at Carderock, Maryland, in a model basin that looks like a large indoor swimming pool. Medical schools are increasingly using robot patients, actually computer-controlled mannequins with skin-textured plastic coatings. One physician said he could demonstrate the sounds and responses of several different types of heart attacks, some of which might never actually be encountered in the teaching hospital. War games have, of course, been used for many years, and their level of sophisticiation and realism has increased considerably.

A third method of anticipating the future is *scenario development*. A scenario is essentially an elaborate exploration of a "what if" question. Its purpose is to make us aware of potential problems that might occur if we were to take a proposed action. We can then either abandon the action considered or prepare to take precautions that will minimize the problems that might result. Shell Oil has developed a futures group that provides company planners with three 25-page scenarios each year. The data used in these scenarios come primarily from studies done throughout the year covering issues and alternatives in the social, economic, political, and technological environments. In addition, outside consultants are used for certain specialized inputs. The group that prepares the scenarios is small, but contains a mix of skills and personalities. Disciplines include economics, engineering, law, and sociology.

The preparation of these multiple scenarios is part of the formal planning process. As part of the scenario development approach, company planners review and comment on the drafts prior to their presentation to senior management. Each scenario requires a different corporate strategy.

In 1984, the Florida legislature commissioned a Washington consulting group to create three scenarios for the state. The first focused on Florida's future should a cataclysmic event take place. The scenario examined what might happen if a major hurricane, such as those that have occurred about every 25 years on the East Coast, were to happen again. The legislature reported that this scenario was highly useful, because it pointed out that about 90 percent of the current population had never experienced such a hurricane, thereby leading the legislature to institute new procedures for both educating and evacuating people. The second scenario examined what would happen if current growth levels of population, industry, and tourism were to continue at the same rate over the next 25 years. This scenario left little doubt as to the impact of such growth on the water table, the Everglades, inland waterways, and so on. Again, the legislature acted on the scenario, in this case by initiating efforts to control growth.

Scenario development, at its best, does what forecasting cannot do; namely, it recognizes the cross-impacts of interdependent events, as modeling does, while going even further to present the holistic picture. It is the difference between the architect's blueprint and the rendering. Early forecasters, for example, began to see what it would mean to be able to mass produce automobiles and to sell them at a price affordable to most people. They forecasted the number of automobiles (although most forecasts turned out to be quite conservative), the need for interconnected roads, and even the problem of traffic jams. However, few, if any, forecasts anticipated the automobile's impact on textile, rubber, and precious metal industries; the shift of population from urban areas to suburbs; the consequence to the family; the impact of one-person, one-car commuting.

In the 1990s, business leaders are likely to find that the most significant predictions are contained in an unpretentious book by Stanley Davis called *Future Perfect*.[3] To come up with his scenarios, Davis asked himself, "What if we shifted the management paradigm from one which believes that the essential management task has to do with people, capital, and technology and treats time, space, and mass as obstacles to overcome to a paradigm in which time, space, and mass are the resources to be managed?"

One example Davis uses to answer his own question deals with the product-repair process. Traditionally, products are serviced as follows: a product in the customer's setting breaks down, and the customer calls the manufacturer, who must find the appropriate service agent. The service agent then goes to the customer setting, identifies the problem (and may or may not have the needed replacement part), fixes the problem, and proceeds to another customer waiting for service.

Davis offers the following scenario (already followed in several industries): a customer learns that a repair was made on a product several days ago, and this notification is the first he hears of the need for repair. The point Davis makes is that, for the customer, no time has elapsed between identification of a problem and its solution. This scenario is, of course, a reality for certain computers, elevators, and so on. For example, many new elevators now have self-diagnostics, which can broadcast information on an impending malfunction to the manufacturer, who then delivers the module needing repair before the service engineer arrives. The service repair person replaces the module in which the impending defect is to occur, and it is repaired back at the manufacturer's site. Then the customer is notified. Davis's point is that the task is to manage time so that no expensive downtime occurs for the customer.

Another of Davis's scenarios involves the Federal Express Company, which has found ways to reduce pick-up, transfer, and delivery time better than any of its competitors. Federal Express is also, from Davis's point of view, in the business of managing space because, in effect, the company shrinks the space between a package's point of origination and its point of delivery. Davis does more than simply spin out scenarios of what will happen if managers shift their focus to time, space, and mass. He integrates these scenarios by making inferences about what must happen to organizations in this new context. The Davis scenarios provide the manager with the keys for unlocking the future, but the big job is still to translate the knowledge gained into competitive advantage for the manager's unique business.

Whether the basic starting point is a trend, a simulation, or a scenario, an essential task of leadership is to integrate information about the future into a concrete focus for energy—a vision. We commented earlier on the role a vision plays in successful leadership. Since a vision necessarily implies the future, its effectiveness over time will depend in large part on how well it integrates predictions of external events into its view of where the company is headed.

FUTURE TRENDS AND STRATEGIC PLANNING

One member of the World Future Society surveyed corporations to determine how they were using internal staff to connect predicting the future and strategic planning. Here are some noteworthy findings:

The First National Bank of Minneapolis conducts an annual social–environmental audit of the Twin Cities metropolitan area. The audit attempts to measure the existing quality of life, using ten indicators. The results of the audit are used in setting bank priorities and specifying actions the bank ought to pursue.

Bethlehem Steel uses a panel of top managers selected from each department to receive reports from departmental task forces on issues that are likely to affect the steel industry in the next 10 to 20 years.

Mobil Oil's Long-Range Analysis Group develops regional and global scenarios concerning the supply of and demand for energy in general and with respect to hydrocarbons in particular. The scenarios are used in the company's strategic decision-making, and they provide a long-range conceptual framework for divisional and corporate planners.

Uniroyal has a technological and social audit staff, which develops scenarios regarding future use of its products; recently a set of scenarios was developed that outlined how Uniroyal's businesses and staff functions might be operating in 15 or 20 years.

Business International, a New York City-based research firm, holds forecasting round tables in virtually every country in the world.

The Prudential Insurance Company employs a full-time forecaster to identify relevant trends, challenges, and opportunities likely to appear over the next 30 years. He also conducts regular training programs on his findings for managers.

Volvo assigns the task of exploring the future to its divisions, except when there is an issue of general interest to the company, in which case the central staff handles it. The divisions develop 25-year projections of business, political, social, economic and technological environments.

Western Electric's Corporate Environmental Scanning Program takes a broad look at future trends and presents its analyses and predictions at an annual planning conference.

Weyerhaeuser has new business planners specifically assigned to identify potential for new business. They construct scenarios demonstrating ways in which the company might take advantage of that potential.

Coca-Cola uses an analysis of current/future resources, both physical and human, and the total business environment as a preliminary step in the planning process. Strategies and goals are worked out principally on the division level, due to the decentralized nature of the firm.

APPLYING FUTURE TRENDS TO STRATEGIC PLANS

A human resource group in a Fortune 100 company has developed a process for integrating future trend analysis into the strategic planning process. As strategic plans are being developed, the company tries to determine the trends that are most likely to have impact on what is being planned. About 40 percent of the company's sales are to major communications industries and federal agencies. Sixty percent are directly to households. The company operates in most countries throughout the world.

Two years ago a group of strategic planning managers found useful the following trends identified by the human resource staff:

The explosive growth of technology- and information-based industries will lead to a shortage of such skilled employees as electronic engineers and software professionals. This means that we will have to be more aggressive and innovative in our recruiting, retention, and compensation programs; place greater emphasis on such "quality-of-life" considerations as flex-time, flexible benefits, and child-care support programs; and pay considerably more attention to strategic human resource planning and development.

Increasing world-wide competition will require further focus on productivity, quality, and employee participation. The company must expand its quality circle and employee involvement programs and focus on developing more and better employee communications. The international nature of our competition also means that we will be doing more off-shore product sourcing, which in turn can be expected to place a greater strain on our labor relations as numbers of U.S. jobs continue to shrink.

Although the rate of medical cost increases will decline, because of the aging of the population and other factors, these costs will continue to escalate in excess of the CPI rate. The company needs to introduce employee wellness programs and other preventive-care techniques; change the design of its health care plan to shift and/or reduce costs, including offering employees various plan options; and so on.

The age profile of the U.S. population is changing as the postwar baby-boom group matures and the baby-bust group of the 1960s moves into adulthood. The company will have to become more innovative in the areas of job design, early retirement, career pathing, rewards, and recognition in order to deal effectively with employee frustrations resulting from blocked promotion opportunities.

The aging of the population will place an increasing strain on both Social Security and the private pension system, one result of which will be the elimination of mandatory retirement laws. The company will need to place greater emphasis on its savings plans and other fixed contribution plans to supplement retirement benefits; and it should continue to pursue a variety of phased retirement approaches.

The percentage of U.S. workers represented by labor unions will continue to decline, resulting in increased union efforts to organize white-collar workers. Pattern bargaining is rapidly disappearing in the United States as foreign competition forces U.S. labor to compete in the world market.

Employment in the company's headquarters area will continue to decline as existing businesses mature and productivity improvements drive staffing levels down. If the small town in which the company's headquarters is located is to remain a viable corporate location, decisions will have to be made to locate new or expanded businesses in the area.

Minorities now represent 22 percent of the total U.S. population, with further increases projected in the Hispanic and Asian populations; the participation rate of married women under age 50 in the labor force is now the same as that of men. The company's work force does not reflect these trends. Continuing significant attention to affirmative action issues will be needed.

At the federal and state levels, there is an evolutionary trend to restrict the right of companies to fire employees without "just cause," or to terminate operations without the payment of heavy penalties. It is likely that these trends will require the company to expand its protection to include employees' "property rights" in their employment contracts.

This is the kind of thinking, summarizing, and recommending that a company should expect from its human resource department. It identifies the trends likely to have a strategic impact, and it makes recommendations to strategic planners. In addition, it forms the basis of the human resource group's own functional strategic plan.

FUTURE TRENDS AND THE MANAGER

We have proposed that the manager can increase his or her ability to be a full strategic partner by understanding how to bring future perspective to the planning table. The accuracy and focus of trends and scenarios will contribute significantly to a company's competitive advantage. The manager can draw upon the work of futurists by reviewing the literature, using the services of the World Future Society in Washington, developing an in-house capability, or joining an association of related industries. A future study, almost by definition, is rarely timely for a particular decision. Its main contribution to decision-making is to build an appreciation in the manager's mind that allows him or her to take more future-oriented considerations into account when making a decision.

The World Future Society points out that the process of thinking about the future should always be tailored to the specific needs of the organization in question. For example, a company whose environment is simple and stable obviously does not need complex studies. The society's recommendations to managers involved in considering the future are:

☐ Seek the seekers.
☐ Find allies within the company.
☐ Plan to learn first and then plug the techniques into a planning system.
☐ Decrease the resistance to change by minimizing the introduction of such considerations and techniques as a "big new deal." Trumpeting the exotic, complexity, newness, and originality of future studies is not the best way to influence managers.

Being knowledgeable about future possibilities and finding ways to get such knowledge into the strategic plans of the company are obviously not easy. Giving your company the opportunity to plan and create its future is, however, essential to its competitive vitality.

Return for a moment to consideration of the opening scenario of this Epiloque. Environmental pollution will be a major issue that every company will have to cope with in the final decade of this century. As horrifying as are many of its implications, use the issue to embrace the turbulence of the future. Ask the best minds in your company what the impact on your product lines will be in terms of the following four questions:

- □ What is there about the way we obtain resources for our products or services that contributes to toxification?
- □ What is there about what we do to transform these resources that contribues to toxification?
- □ What is there about our customers' use of our products or services that increases toxification?
- □ Which of our products or services contributes to toxification after being discarded by customers?

In the 1990s, you can be assured that foreign governments, our federal government, states, and municipalities, as well as consumers, will be asking these questions about your products.

Notes

Chapter 1 Changing Vistas for Management Thought

1. This metaphor comes from remarks by Richard Scott.

2. The term "organizational capability" was originally used by Igor Ansoff. We appreciate his letting us use and expand on the concept. We hope that our discussion extends his thinking and helps further explore this concept. In addition, the concept has been used by Prahalad and Doz (1987), Ulrich (1987, 1989), and Ulrich and Wiersema (1989).

3. The numbers we use in this example are not exact, but are close representations of what happened in Borg-Warner. The intent of this case is not to sell LBOs as a business decision, but to demonstrate the importance of using people management tools (rewards, development, and communication) to accomplish a financially driven business strategy.

4. For a more complete description of the Baxter Healthcare merger, see Rucci, LaFasto, and Ulrich (1990); and Ulrich, LaFasto, and Rucci (1989).

5. We are indebted to discussions with Wayne Brockbank for his insights on this concept. Further examination of this topic can be found in Brockbank and Ulrich (1989).

6. Some outstanding work focuses on the identification of paradoxes within organizations. See Quinn (1988) and Cameron, Quinn, and Sutton (1989).

Chapter 2 Forces for Change

1. See work on the overall rates of change and their implications by Thurow (1981, 1985), Ulrich and Wiersema (1989), and Peters (1987).

2. For an examination of the impact of the global organization, see Prahalad and Doz (1987).

3. See Keen (1988) and Bower and Hout (1988) for reviews of the importance of time as a source of competitiveness.

4. See Porter (1981, 1985).

5. For examples of public agencies that have focused on competitiveness, see Ulrich, Quinn, and Cameron (1989).

6. Hayes, Wheelwright, and Clark (1988) offer an extensive review of the manufacturing side of competitiveness. This book attempts to complement their view with a greater focus on the organizational issues related to competitive advantage.

Chapter 3   Competitive Advantage from the Inside Out through Organizational Capability

1. For a discussion of the quick-fix trap, see Kilman (1984).

2. A more complete discussion of how the FAA managed its people skills is given in Ulrich (1985).

3. See Cascio (1987) for a discussion of the percentage of operating budgets dedicated to people.

4. A discussion of SPOTS can be found in Brockbank and Ulrich (1990).

5. See Pucik (1984).

6. The importance of customer service has been well documented in a number of recent books, including Albrecht and Zemke (1985), Normann (1984), and Lund and Handsen (1986).

7. A series of research articles and conceptual papers on the importance of customers have been prepared by Bowen (1986), Bowen and Greiner (1986), and Schneider and Bowen (1985).

8. See Stalk (1988) and Bower and Hout (1988).

9. See Bowen (1986) and Schneider and Bowen (1985).

10. In the process of writing this book, one of the authors was building a house. He quickly learned that the relationship between the builder and contractor was the most critical factor in getting the house built. The positive relationship established a trust between the two parties so that disagreements could be worked out openly and honestly.

11. See Albrecht and Zemke (1985), p. 18.

12. This argument has been well articulated by Barney (1986), Davis (1984), Sims, Giola, and associates (1986), and Brockbank and Ulrich (1988).

13. We recognize that other authors have examined each of these elements using different terminology. Our objective here is to amplify these discussions by (1) extending previous thinking about each independent element, (2) integrating the elements into a unit to form *organizational capability*, and (3) linking organizational capability to competitive advantage.

Chapter 4   Creating Shared Mindset

1. We are indebted to Wayne Brockbank for his insights in this chapter. Much of the material in this chapter has been discussed in Brockbank and Ulrich (1988).

2. For an excellent discussion of culture, see Wilkins and Ouchi (1983), Davis (1984), Schwartz and Davis (1981), Deal and Kennedy (1982), and Schein (1984, 1985).

3. For a thorough review of the cognitive literature, see Bandura (1969), Mahoney (1981), Mahoney and Arnkoff (1978), Beck et al. (1979), and Mahoney and Freeman (1985). Efforts to apply cognitive theory to organizations can be identified in Weick (1976, 1979a, 1979b, 1988), Schwenk (1986), and Sims et al. (1986). Research on information saliency as a determining factor in organizational cognition has been done by Salancik and Pfeffer (1978) and Simon (1979).

4. The centrality of information as a means of creating cognitive patterns among individuals in organizations has been well studied by Berger and Luckmann (1966), Salancik and Pfeffer (1977, 1978), Pfeffer (1981), O'Reilly (1982, 1983), Schwenk (1986), Weick, Gilfillan, and Keith (1973), and Schwenk (1986).

5. This debate can be reviewed in articles by O'Connor and Barrett (1980), Staw (1977, 1980), Staw and Ross (1987), and Mahoney (1981).

6. This topic can be reviewed in articles by O'Connor and Barrett (1980), Staw (1977, 1980), Staw and Ross (1987), and Mahoney (1981).

7. See Weick (1976, 1979a, 1979b, 1988) and Sims et al. (1986).

8. Schein's work on culture (1985, 1986) is an outstanding illustration of shared mindset.

9. See Schein (1985, 1986).

10. Richard Stevenson, "Watch Out Macy's, Here Comes Nordstrom's," *New York Times Magazine*, August 27, 1989.

11. Stevenson, op. cit.

12. This research supports many of the issues raised in this chapter. See Ulrich, Brockbank, and Yeung (1990).

13. Deming's work (1988) has received wide international acclaim. His dedication to statistical tools to evaluate, assess, and stabilize processes has been credited, in part, with the Japanese quality and productivity gains.

14. See work on corporate cultures by Deal and Kennedy (1982), Schein (1985), and Schwartz and Davis (1981), which highlights the *internal*

314   NOTES

cultures that may exist within a business. Less work has focused on the *external* cultures that may exist through the eyes of a business's stakeholders. See Brockbank and Ulrich (1988) and Ulrich (1989).

15. Throughout Peters' work (1982, 1984, 1987, 1988), the concept of complete customer satisfaction plays a critical role. From this perspective, the customer perception of service becomes a driving criterion for business performance.

16. See Peters (1987).

17. The argument that customers may be heavily involved in management processes has been argued in Ulrich (1989). He proposes that human resource practices become more open to customers as a way of building complete customer commitment.

18. We agree with Schein (1985) that there is no one way to diagnose a shared mindset. We also believe that the list of questions used to diagnose existing mindsets proposed by Tichy (1983) and Schein (1985) are outstanding. We will not replicate those questions here, but refer the reader to them.

Chapter 5   Management Practices

1. We are indebted to discussions with Ram Charan on this concept. He discusses levers for managers that can be used to help accomplish business strategy. Our use of the term "management practices" parallels his concept.

2. In other works, we have defined the strategic business partner role of human resource professionals. See Ulrich (1987), Ulrich and Yeung (1989), and Ulrich, Brockbank and Yeung (1990). We believe the strategic business partner role is important not only for human resource professionals but for other staff positions as well. The partnership role offers staff the opportunity to become leaders.

3. See Ulrich (1986, 1987).

4. See the excellent works on the combination of many human resource practices into categories by Tsui and Milkovich (1985) and Fombrun, Tichy, and Devanna (1984).

5. See Drucker (1988).

6. This research comes from a study called OASIS, sponsored by Hay Associates, University of Michigan, Ann Arbor; and Strategic Planning Associates. It is available from the authors.

7. We are indebted to Steve Kerr for his observations on this topic. We appreciate his insights on the history of both the selection and development processes.

8. Again, we are indebted to Steve Kerr for this concept. He has helped us gain broader understanding of the reward concept.

9. For a more extensive look at organization design, see Galbraith (1973, 1977).

10. See Ulrich (1989) for the complete argument for how human resource practices build customer commitment.

11. This research has received extensive support. See Salancik (1977), Staw (1976, 1977, 1980, 1981) and Weick (1988).

12. It should be noted that other institutional practices may be used to create shared mindsets besides human resource practices. In work by Brockbank and Ulrich (1988), strategic-planning processes, the role of top management, and physical facilities are also described as institutional processes that create shared cognitions.

13. See Ulrich (1986).

14. We are again indebted to and recognize Wayne Brockbank for using the word "criteria" to define the rationale for how human resource practices are employed. We hope we have not misrepresented his logic.

Chapter 6   Creating Competencies

1. See Drucker (1988) for a discussion of the importance of hiring decisions.

2. See Gerstein and Reisman (1983) to identify the strategic implications of staffing.

3. This data comes from the OASIS research program; more information on it is available from the authors.

4. A number of statistical tools have been used for planning the size and composition of the work force and projecting the future needs of the business. For a good overview of these tools, see Burack (1985) and Dyer (1985).

5. A number of authors have examined succession planning. This work covers many of the choices we discuss in this chapter. A good summary can be found in Friedman (1985).

6. For a good review of the succession-planning systems in these companies see Mahler (1984).

7. In a study of the Fortune 1000, Wiersema (1986) found that internal and external promotions affected degree of strategic redirection within a company.

8. More information about dual career ladders can be found in the excellent book by Dalton and Thompson (1986). The authors track

the career stages of technical experts and demonstrate how these stages may be linked to reward systems.

9. For a review of these transitions, see articles by Bolt (1987), Beckhard (1985), and Schein (1988).

10. This report is available from the Center for Executive Development, Cambridge, Massachusetts.

11. See Tichy (1989), which describes the goals and processes used at the Crotonville, New York, facility.

12. For a more complete discussion of the use of development and other human resource practices with customers, see Ulrich (1989).

13. We are indebted to Bob Eichinger for sharing this information with us. We believe the research from the Center for Creative Leadership is outstanding in its ability to capture processes for developing employees.

Chapter 7 Reinforcing Competencies

1. See Ouchi (1977, 1979) and Ouchi and Johnson (1978) for discussions of how organizations generate controls over individuals.

2. A number of researchers have identified the characteristics of goals that influence individual behavior. For a review of this literature, see Locke and Latham (1984) and Locke et al. (1981).

3. See Chapter 9 of Deming (1988) for a more complete discussion of the nature of operational definitions.

4. See Friedman and Levino (1984) on the General Electric appraisal process.

5. This research has been reported by Whetten and Cameron (1984).

6. We are indebted to Steve Kerr for his insightful comments and discussions on how rewards affect individual behavior. See his outstanding article that discusses how to use rewards to shape behavior (Kerr, 1989).

7. See Kerr (1989) for a more complete discussion.

8. The 7 percent figure comes from Lance A. Berger, an executive vice president at the Hay Group, who reports on the Hay data base of 2,500 companies and finds that only about 5–7 percent use one-time payments as incentives.

9. Job content has received extensive attention. See Herzberg's (1965) classic distinction between motivation and hygiene factors and satisfiers and dissatisfiers. This work has been extended by Hackman and Oldham (1975) and Lawler (1986).

Chapter 8 Sustaining Competencies

1. Others have done outstanding jobs classifying types of organization structures and defining their strengths and weaknesses. See Hall (1977), Mackenzie (1986), and Jaques (1989). Much of this material is drawn from work by Donald Kane, a former General Electric employee responsible for organization planning.

2. A number of organizational analysts have described the functional organization, including Fayol (1959), Urwick (1943), Gulick and Urwick (1937), Taylor (1911), and Weber (1947).

3. This research has received extensive attention. The original research is found in Rumelt (1974).

4. For a more complete discussion of the matrix organization, see Davis and Lawrence (1977) and Galbraith (1973, 1977).

5. See Prahalad and Doz (1987) for an examination of the product organization as a global structure.

6. See Peters (1988). He describes the organization of the future as a circle that customers enter through loosely defined boundaries. See also Mills (1985). He describes the organization of the future as a network of relationships, often drawn as a complex spider web. This image of a spider web, with transactions and teams formed around project demands, is an appropriate image for our discussion.

7. See Harrigan (1985a, 1985b).

8. See Ouchi (1980) and foundation work by Williamson (1975, 1979, 1981, 1983, 1986).

9. Williamson (1975) argues that market-control mechanisms fail because of individual opportunism, bounded rationality, organizational change, and small-numbers bargaining over time. Williamson suggests that hierarchies may replace market-control systems. We use Ouchi's term ''bureaucracy'' in lieu of ''hierarchy.''

10. The amount of time spent on communication comes from many research efforts. Mintzberg (1973) found that managers spend extensive amounts of time in short-term, face-to-face communications. In other research, managers suggest that communication is their most critical activity and the one they spend the most time on.

11. Contact authors for details of this study.

12. See *Fortune*, November 10, 1986.

13. See Lengel and Daft (1988).

Chapter 9 Influence Management for the 1990s

1. See MacMillan and Jones, 1987.

2. See MacMillan and Jones, 1987.

3. See French and Raven, 1962, pp. 607–623.

4. R. Waterman, *The Renewal Factor*. New York: Bantam Books, 1987.

Chapter 10   The Capacity for Change

1. These competencies are derived from a University of Michigan study of more than ten thousand managers. Ulrich, Brockbank, Lake, and Yeung did the original research, and it is reported in Ulrich, Brockbank, and Yeung (1989, 1990).

2. See Tichy, 1983. This contribution to our understanding of change cannot be overestimated. It has its roots in the early works of Bob Chin and Ken Benne and extends their thinking to most formulations of change. Not only are the concepts useful, they are inherently practical for the managers of change.

3. Gardner, 1961.

Chapter 11   Flexible Arrangements

1. Drucker, 1988.

Chapter 12   Leadership

1. See Tichy and Devanna, 1986. This is a useful contemporary treatment of leadership, both practical and data based. See also the excellent historical treatment of leadership by Burns (1978).

2. Bandura, 1977, pp. 4–24.

3. Zuboff, 1988.

4. Nonaka, 1988.

5. See Tichy, 1983.

Epilogue   Reducing Future Threat Potential

1. David Van Selers, *Ann Arbor, Michigan, News*, March 18, 1990.

2. Ian Ross, "Research and Development: Key Issues for Management," *The Conference Board*, #842, Bell Labs, 1986.

3. Davis, 1987.

Bibliography

Albrecht, K., and R. Zemke. 1985. *Service America: Doing Business in the New Economy*. Homewood, IL: Dow Jones-Irwin.

Andrews, K. 1980. *The Concept of Corporate Strategy*, 4th ed. Homewood, IL: Dow Jones-Irwin.

Ansoff, H. I. 1988. *The New Corporate Strategy*. New York: John Wiley & Sons.

Baars, B. J. 1986. *The Cognitive Revolution in Psychology*. New York: Guilford Press.

Bandura, A. 1969. *Principles of Behavior Modification*. New York: Holt, Rinehart, and Winston.

Bandura, A. 1977. Self-efficiency: Toward a unifying theory of behavioral change. *Psychological Review* 84(2):4–24.

Barney, J. 1986. Organizational culture: Can it be a source of sustained competitive advantage? *Academy of Management Review* 11(3):656–665.

Beck, A. T., A. J. Rush, B. F. Shaw, and G. Emery. 1979. *Cognitive Therapy of Depression*. New York: Guilford Press.

Beckhard, R. 1985. Whither management development? *Journal of Management Development* 4(2):10–16.

Bennis, W. and B. Nanus. 1985. *Leaders: The Strategies for Taking Charge*. New York: Harper & Row.

Berger, P. L., and T. Luckmann. 1966. *The Social Construction of Reality: A Treatise in the Sociology of Knowledge*. New York: Doubleday.

Bolt. J. F. 1987. Trends in management training and executive education: The revolution continues, *Journal of Management Development* 6(5): 5–15.

Bowen, D. E. 1986. Managing customers as human resources in service organizations, *Human Resource Management* 25:371–384.

Bowen, D. E., and L. E. Greiner. 1986. Moving from production to service in human resource management. *Organizational Dynamics*, Summer, pp. 34–45.

Bower, J. 1970. *Managing the Resource Allocation Process*. Homewood, IL: Richard C. Irwin.

Bower, J. L., and T. M. Hout, 1988. Fast-cycle capability for competitive power, *Harvard Business Review,* November–December, pp. 110–118.

Bowes, L. 1987. *No One Need Apply: Getting and Keeping the Best Workers.* Boston: Harvard Business School Press.

Brockbank, J. W., and D. Ulrich. 1988. Institutional antecedents of shared organizational cognitions. Working paper, University of Michigan, Ann Arbor.

Brockbank, J. W., and D. Ulrich. 1990. Avoiding SPOTS: Creating strategic unity. In H. Glass (ed.), *Handbook of Business Strategy 1990.* New York: Gorham, Lambert, in press.

Brockbank, J. W., D. Ulrich, and A. Yeung. 1989. The strategic context of human resource management. Working paper, University of Michigan, Ann Arbor.

Burack, E. H. 1985. Linking corporate business and human resource planning: Strategic issues and concerns, *Human Resource Planning* 8(3):133–145.

Burns, J. M. 1978. *Leadership.* New York: Harper & Row.

Cameron, K., R. I. Sutton, and D. A. Whetten (eds.). 1988. *Readings on Organizational Decline: Frameworks, Research, and Prescriptions.* Cambridge, MA: Ballinger Publishing Co.

Cascio, W. F. 1987. *Costing Human Resources: The Financial Impact of Behavior in Organizations.* New York: Van Nostrand Reinhold.

Cummings, L. L. 1984. Compensation, culture, and motivation: A systems perspective. *Organizational Dynamics* 12(3):33–44.

Dalton, G., and P. Thompson. 1986. *Novations: Strategies for Career Management.* Glenview, IL: Scott, Foresman & Co.

Davis, S. 1984. *Managing Corporate Culture.* Cambridge, MA: Ballinger Publishing Co.

Davis, S. 1987. *Future Perfect.* Reading, MA: Addison-Wesley Publishing Co.

Davis, S., and P. Lawrence. 1977. *Matrix.* Reading, MA: Addison-Wesley Publishing Co.

Deal, T. E., and A. A. Kennedy. 1982. *Corporate Cultures: The Rites and Rituals of Corporate Life.* Reading, MA: Addison-Wesley Publishing Co.

Dember, W. 1974. Motivation and the cognitive revolution, *American Psychologist* 29:161–168.

Deming, W. E. 1988. *Out of the Crisis.* Cambridge, MA: MIT Press.

Devanna, M. A., C. J. Fombrun, and N. M. Tichy. 1984. A framework for strategic human resource management. In Fombrun, C. J., N. M.

Tichy, and M. A. Devanna (eds.), *Strategic Human Resource Management*. New York: John Wiley & Sons, pp. 33–51.

Drucker, Peter. 1988. Management and the world's work. *Harvard Business Review*, September–October, pp. 65–76.

Dyer, L. 1985. Strategic human resources management and planning. In Rowland, K., and G. R. Ferris, *Research in Personnel and Human Resources Management*. Greenwich, CT: JAI Press.

Evan, W. M. 1966. The organization set. In Thompson, J. D. (ed.), *Approaches to Organizational Design*. Pittsburgh: University of Pittsburgh Press, pp. 173–191.

Fayol, H. 1959. *General and Industrial Management*. London: Pitman.

Fombrun, C. J., N. M. Tichy, and M. A. Devanna. 1984. *Strategic Human Resource Management*. New York: John Wiley & Sons.

Freedman, E. 1985. *Strategic Management: A Stakeholder Approach*. Boston: Pitman.

French, J. R., and B. Raven. 1972. The bases of social power. In Cartwright, D., and A. Zander (eds.), *Group Dynamics*. Evanston, IL: Row, Peterson.

Freud, S. 1925. *Collected Papers* (4 vols.). London: Institute for Psychoanalysis and Hogarth Press.

Friedman, S. D. 1985. *Leadership Succession Systems and Corporate Performance*. Career Center Research Report, Columbia University Graduate School of Business, New York.

Friedman, S. D., and T. P. Levino. 1984. Strategic appraisal and development at General Electric. In Fombrun, C. J., N. M. Tichy, and M. A. Devanna (eds.), *Strategic Human Resource Management*. New York: John Wiley & Sons.

Friedman, S. D., N. M. Tichy, and D. Ulrich. 1984. Strategic human resource management at Honeywell Inc. In Fombrun, C. J., N. M. Tichy, and M. A. Devanna (eds.), *Strategic Human Resource Management*. New York: John Wiley & Sons.

Galbraith, J. 1973. *Designing Complex Organizations*. Reading, MA: Addison-Wesley Publishing Co.

Galbraith, J. 1977. *Organization Design*. Reading, MA: Addison-Wesley Publishing Co.

Gardner, J. 1961. *Self Renewal: The Individual and the Innovative Society*. New York: W. W. Norton & Co.

Gerstein, M., and H. Reisman. 1983. Strategic selection: Matching executives to business conditions, *Sloan Management Review*, Winter, pp. 33–49.

Giola, D. A., and C. C. Manz. 1985. Linking cognition and behavior: A script processing interpretation of vicarious learning, *Academy of Management Review* 10(3):527–539.

Gulick, L., and L. Urwick (eds.). 1937. *Papers on the Science of Administration.* New York: Institute of Public Administration, Columbia University.

Hackman, R., and G. Oldham. 1975. Development of the job diagnostic survey, *Journal of Applied Psychology* 60:159–170.

Hall, D. T. 1984. Human resource development and organizational effectiveness. In Fombrun, C. J., N. M. Tichy, and M. A. Devanna (eds.), *Strategic Human Resource Management.* New York: John Wiley & Sons, pp. 33–51.

Hall, R. 1977. *Organizations: Structure and Processes,* 3d ed. Englewood Cliffs, NJ: Prentice Hall.

Harrigan, K. R. 1985a. *Strategic Flexibility.* New York: Lexington Books.

Harrigan, K. R. 1985b. Vertical integration and corporate strategy, *Academy of Management Journal* 28:397–425.

Hart, C. 1988. The power of unconditional service guarantees. *Harvard Business Review,* July–August, pp. 54–63.

Hayes, R. H., S. C. Wheelwright, and K. B. Clark. *Dynamic Manufacturing: Creating the Learning Organization.* New York: Free Press, 1988.

Herzberg, F. 1965. *Work and the Nature of Man.* Cleveland: World.

Heskett, J. 1986. *Managing in the Service Economy.* Cambridge, MA: Harvard Business Review.

Holtax, L. (with J. Heisler). 1989. *The Championship Spirit: A Championship Season at Notre Dame.* New York: Pocket Books.

Jaques, E. 1989. *Requisite Organization.* New York: Cason Hall and Company.

Jung, C. G. 1933. *Psychological Types.* New York: Harcourt, Brace, and World, 1933.

Keen, P. 1988. *Competing in Time: Using Telecommunications for Competitive Advantage.* Cambridge, MA: Ballinger Publishing Co.

Kerr, J., and J. W. Slocum, Jr. 1987. Managing corporate culture through reward systems. *Academy of Management Executive* 1:99–108.

Kerr, S. 1989. Some characteristics and consequences of organizational rewards. Working paper, University of Southern California.

Kilman, R. 1984. *Beyond the Quick Fix: Managing Five Tracks to Organizational Success.* San Francisco: Jossey-Bass.

Kotter, J. 1988. *The Leadership Factor.* New York: Free Press.

Kurke, L., and D. Ulrich. When do theories of environmental selection and adaptation best apply? Working paper, University of Michigan, Ann Arbor.

Lawler, E. E., III. 1971. *Pay and Organizational Effectiveness*. New York: McGraw-Hill Book Co.

Lawler, E. E., III. 1981. *Pay and Organizational Development*. Reading, MA: Addison-Wesley Publishing Co.

Lawler, E. E., III. 1984. The strategic design of reward systems. In Schuler, R. S., and S. A. Youngblood (eds.), *Readings in Personnel and Human Resource Management*, 2d ed. St. Paul, MN: West Publishing Co.

Lawler, E. E., III. 1986. *High Involvement Management*. San Francisco: Jossey-Bass.

Lengel, R., and D. Daft. 1988. The selection of communication media as an executive skill, *Academy of Management Executive* 2(3):224–232.

Levinson, H., and S. Rosenthal. 1984. *CEO: Corporate Leadership in Action*. New York: Basic Books.

Locke, E. A., and G. P. Latham. 1984. *Goal Setting: A Motivational Technique That Works*. Englewood Cliffs, NJ: Prentice Hall.

Locke, E. A., K. Shaw, L. M. Saari, and G. Latham. 1981. Goal setting and task performance: 1969–1980, *Psychological Bulletin* 90:125–152.

Lund, R., and J. Hansen 1986. *Keeping America at Work*. New York: John Wiley & Sons.

Mackenzie, K. D. 1986. *Organization Design*. Norwood, NJ: Ablex Publishing Company.

MacMillan, I., and P. Jones. 1987. *Strategy Formulation: Power and Politics*. St. Paul, MN: West Publishing Co.

Maddi, S. R. 1976. *Personality Theories: A Comparative Analysis*. New York: Dorsey Press.

Mahler, W. 1984. *Succession Plannning in Successful Companies*. Midland Park, NJ: Mahler Publishing Company.

Mahoney, M. J. 1981. Psychotherapy and human change process. In *Psychotherapy Research and Behavior Change*. Washington, DC: American Psychological Association.

Mahoney, M. J., and D. Arnkoff. 1978. Cognitive and self-control therapies. In Garfield, S. L., and A. E. Bergin (eds.), *Handbook of Psychotherapy and Behavior Change*, 2d ed. New York: John Wiley & Sons.

Mahoney, M. J., and A. Freeman. 1985. *Cognition and Psychotherapy*. New York: Plenum Press.

Maslow, A. 1965. *Eupsician Management*. Homewood, IL: Richard C. Irwin.

McClelland, D. 1971. *Assessing Human Motivation*. New York: General Learning Press.

McGregor, D. *The Human Side of Enterprise*. New York: McGraw-Hill Book Co., 1967.

Mills, D. Q. 1985a. *The New Competitors*. New York: Free Press.

Mills, D. Q. 1985b. Planning with people in mind, *Harvard Business Review* 63(4):97–105.

Mintzberg, H. 1973. *The Nature of Managerial Work*. New York: Harper & Row.

Mirvis, P., and D. Berg (eds.). 1977. *Failure in Organization Development and Change: Cases and Essays for Learnings*. New York: John Wiley & Sons.

Nonaka, I. 1988. Toward middle-up-down management: Accelerating information creation, *Sloan Management Review*, Spring.

Normann, R. 1984. *Service Management: Strategy and Leadership in Service Businesses*. New York: John Wiley & Sons.

O'Connor, E. J., and G. V. Barrett. 1980. Informational cues and individual differences as determinants of subjective perceptions of task enrichment. *Academy of Management Journal* 23(4):697–716.

O'Reilly, C. 1982. Variations in decision makers' use of information sources: The impact of quality and accessibility of information, *Academy of Management Journal* 25:756–771.

O'Reilly, C. 1983. The use of information in organizational decision making: A model and some propositions. In Cummings, L. L., and B. M. Staw (eds.), *Research in Organizational Behavior*, Vol. 5. Greenwich, CT: JAI Press, pp. 103–139.

Ouchi, W. G. 1977. The relationship between organizational structure and organizational control, *Administrative Science Quarterly* 22:95–113.

Ouchi, W. G. 1979. A conceptual framework for the design of organizational control mechanisms, *Management Science* 25:833–848.

Ouchi, W. G. 1980. Markets, bureaucracies, and clans, *Administrative Science Quarterly* 25:129–141.

Ouchi, W. G. 1981. *Theory Z: How American Business Can Meet the Japanese Challenge*. Reading, MA: Addison-Wesley Publishing Co.

Ouchi, W. G., and J. Johnson. 1978. Types of organizational control and their relationship to emotional well being, *Administrative Science Quarterly* 23:293–317.

Ouchi, W. G., and M. A. McGuire. 1975. Organizational control: Two functions, *Administrative Science Quarterly*, pp. 559–569.

Peck, M. S. 1985. *The Road Less Traveled*. New York: Touchstone Book/ Simon & Schuster.

Peck, M. S. 1987. *The Different Drum*. New York: Touchstone Book/Simon & Schuster.

Peters, T. J. 1984. Strategy follows structure: Developing distinctive skills, *California Management Review*. Spring, pp. 111–125.

Peters, T. J. 1987. *Thriving on Chaos*. New York: Harper & Row.

Peters, T. J. 1988. Restoring American competitiveness: Looking for new models of organizations, *Academy of Management Executive* 2:103–109.

Peters, T. J., and R. H. Waterman, Jr. 1982. *In Search of Excellence: Lessons from America's Best-Run Companies*. New York: Harper & Row.

Pfeffer, J. 1981. Management as symbolic action: The creation and maintenance of organizational paradigms. In Cummings, L. L., and B. M. Staw (eds.), *Research in Organizations*, Vol. 3. Greenwich, CT: JAI Press, pp. 103–139.

Porter, M. 1981. *Competitive Strategy*. New York: Free Press.

Porter, M. 1985. *Competitive Advantage*. New York: Free Press.

Prahalad, C. K., and Y. Doz. 1987. *The Multinational Corporation*. New York: Free Press.

Pucik, V. 1984. White collar human resource management: A comparison of U.S. and Japanese automobile industries. *Columbia Journal of World Business* 19:3–20.

Quinn, R. E. 1988. *Beyond Rational Management*. San Francisco: Jossey-Bass.

Rausch, E. 1985. *Win–Win: Performance Management/Appraisal*. New York: John Wiley & Sons.

Rucci, A., F. LaFasto, and D. Ulrich. 1990. Managing organizational change: A merger case study. In London, M., E. Bassman, and J. Fernandez (eds.), *Human Resource Forecasting and Planning for the 21st Century*. Westport, CT: Greenwood Press Inc.

Rumelt, R. P. 1974. *Strategy, Structure, and Economic Performance*. Boston: Harvard Business School.

Salancik, G. R. 1977. Commitment and the control of organizational behavior and belief. In Staw, B. M., and G. R. Salancik (eds.), *New Directions in Organizational Behavior*. Malabar, FL: Robert E. Drieger, pp. 1–54.

Salancik, G. R., and J. Pfeffer. 1977. An examination of need-satisfaction models of job attitudes, *Administration Science Quarterly* 22:427–456.

Salancik, G. R., and J. Pfeffer. 1978. A social information processing approach to job attitudes and task design, *Administrative Science Quarterly* 23:224–253.

Schein, E. H. 1984. Coming to a new awareness of organizational culture. *Sloan Management Review* 25:3–16.

Schein, E. H. 1985. *Organizational Culture and Leadership*. San Francisco: Jossey-Bass.

Schein, E. H. 1986. Current issues in human resource management, *Conference Board Research Bulletin*, pp. 190–207.

Schein, E. H. 1988. Management education: Some troublesome realities and possible remedies, *Management Education* 7(2):5–15.

Schneider, B., and D. E. Bowen. 1985. Employee and customer perceptions of service in banks: Replication and extension, *Journal of Applied Psychology* 70:423–433.

Schwartz, H., and S. Davis. 1981. Matching corporate culture and business strategy, *Organizational Dynamics*, Summer, pp. 30–48.

Schwenk, C. R. 1986. Information, cognitive biases, and commitment to a course of action, *Academy of Management Review* 2:298–310.

Sculley, J. 1988. *Odyssey: From Pepsi to Apple*. New York: Harper & Row.

Shook, R. L. 1988. *Honda: An American Success Story*. Englewood Cliffs, NJ: Prentice Hall.

Simon, H. A. 1979. *Models of Thought*. New Haven, CT: Yale University Press.

Sims, H. P., D. A. Giola, and associates (eds.). 1986. *The Thinking Organization*. San Francisco: Jossey-Bass.

Skinner, B. F. 1971. *Beyond Freedom and Dignity*. New York: Alfred A. Knopf.

Stalk, G., Jr. 1988. Time—the next source of competitive advantage, *Harvard Business Review*, July–August, pp. 41–53.

Staw, B. M. 1976. Knee-deep in the big muddy: A study of escalating commitment to a chosen course of action, *Organizational Behavior and Human Performance* 16:27–44.

Staw, B. M. 1977. The experimenting organization, *Organizational Dynamics* 6:2–18.

Staw, B. M. 1980. Rationality and justification in organizational life. In Staw, B. M., and L. L. Cummings (eds.), *Research in Organizations*, Vol. 2. Greenwich, CT: JAI Press, pp. 45–80.

Staw, B. M. 1981. The escalation of commitment to a course of action, *Academy of Managment Review* 6:577–587.

Staw, B. M., and J. Ross. 1987. Understanding escalation situations: Antecedents, prototypes, and solutions. In Staw, B. M., and L. L.

Cummings (eds.), *Research in Organizational Behavior*, Vol. 9. Greenwich, CT: JAI Press.

Taylor, F. W. 1911. *Principles of Scientific Management*. New York: Harper & Row.

Thurow, L. 1981. Revitalizing the U.S. economy, *California Management Review* 13:101–127.

Thurow, L. 1985. *The Zero Sum Solution*. New York: Simon & Schuster, 1985.

Tichy, N. M. 1983. *Managing Strategic Change: Technical, Political, and Cultural Dynamics*. New York: John Wiley & Sons.

Tichy, N. M. 1989. GE's Crotonville: A staging ground for corporate revolutions—Lessons for the CEO. Working paper, University of Michigan, Ann Arbor.

Tichy, N. M., and M. A. Devanna. 1986. *The Transformational Leader*. New York: John Wiley & Sons.

Tichy, N. M., C. J. Fombrun, and M. A. Devanna. 1982. Strategic human resource management, *Sloan Management Review* 23(2):47–60.

Tichy, N. M., and D. Ulrich. 1984. Revitalizing organizations: The leadership role. In Kimberly, J., and B. Quinn (eds.), *Transforming Organizations*. New York: John Wiley & Sons.

Tsui, A., and G. Milkovich. 1985. Dimensions of personnel department activities. Paper presented at the Academy of Management, August.

Ulrich, D. 1983. Governing transactions: A framework for cooperative strategy, *Human Resource Management* 22(1–2):23–39.

Ulrich, D. 1984. Specifying external relations: Definitions of and actors in an organization's environment, *Human Relations* 37(3):245–262.

Ulrich, D. 1985. Federal Aviation Administration management: Myth versus reality, *MTS Digest* 4:7–11.

Ulrich, D. 1986. Human resource planning as a competitive advantage, *Human Resource Planning* 9(2):41–50.

Ulrich, D. 1987a. Organizational capability as a competitive advantage: Human resource professionals as strategic partners, *Human Resource Planning* 10(4).

Ulrich, D. 1987b. Strategic human resource planning: Why and how? *Human Resource Planning* 10(1):25–37.

Ulrich D. 1989a. Assessing human resource effectiveness: Stakeholder, index, and relationship approaches. *Human Resource Planning* 12(4):301–315.

Ulrich, D. 1989b. Executive development as a competitive weapon. *Management Development* 8:11–22.

Ulrich, D. 1989c. Executive development as competitiveness. In Vicere, A. (ed.), *Executive Education: Process, Practice, and Evaluation.* Princeton, NJ: Peterson's, pp. 109–120.

Ulrich, D. 1989d. Human resource as a competitive advantage. In Kilman, R., and I. Martin (eds.), *Making Organizations More Competitive.* San Francisco: Jossey-Bass.

Ulrich, D. 1989e. Tie the corporate knot: Gaining complete customer commitment. *Sloan Management Review,* Summer, pp. 19–28.

Ulrich, D. 1990. Competitive advantage through organizational capability: The central role of human resource management. In Glass, H. (ed.), *Handbook of Business Strategy 1989/1990 Yearbook.* New York: Gorham, Lambert, pp. 15.1–15.15.

Ulrich, D., W. Brockbank, and A. Yeung. 1989. Human resource competencies in the 1990's: An empirical assessment of what the future holds. *Personnel Administrator,* November, pp. 91–93.

Ulrich, D., W. Brockbank, and A. Yeung. 1990. Beyond belief: A benchmark for human resources. *Human Resource Management,* in press.

Ulrich, D., F. LaFasto, and A. Rucci. 1989. Why Baxter moved quickly to absorb American Hospital. *Mergers and Acquisitions* 24(1):54–59.

Ulrich, D., R. Quinn, and K. S. Cameron. 1989. Designing effective organization systems. In Perry, J. L. (ed.), *Handbook of Public Administration.* San Francisco: Jossey-Bass.

Ulrich, D., and M. Wiersema. 1989. Gaining strategic and organizational capability in a decade of turbulence. *American Management Executive* 3(2):1–5, 122.

Ulrich, D., and A. Yeung. 1989. Human resources in the 1990's: Trends and required competencies. *Personnel Administrator,* March, pp. 38–45.

Ulrich, D., A. Yeung, and J. W. Brockbank. 1990 Human resources in the 1990's: Forging personal competencies into functional capability. In *Personnel Management Services.* New York: Simon & Schuster, in press.

Urwick, L. F. *The Elements of Administration.* New York: Harper, 1943.

Watson, J. B. 1924. *Behaviorism.* New York: W. W. Norton & Co.

Weber, M. 1947. *The Theory of Social and Economic Organization,* trans. A. M. Henderson and T. Parsons. New York: Free Press.

Weick, K. E. 1976. Educational organizations as loosely coupled systems, *Administrative Science Quarterly* 21:1–19.

Weick, K. E. 1979a. Cognitive processes in organizations. In Staw, B. M., (ed.), *Research in Organizations,* Vol. 1. Greenwich, CT: JAI Press, pp. 41–73.

Weick, K. E. 1979b. *The Social Psychology of Organizing*. Reading, MA: Addison-Wesley Publishing Co.

Weick K. E. 1988. The enactment of organization through commitment. Working paper, University of Michigan School of Business, Ann Arbor.

Weick, K. E., D. P. Gilfillan, and T. Keith. 1973. The effect of composer credibility on orchestra performance, *Sociometry* 36:435–462.

Whetten, D. A., and K. S. Cameron. 1984. *Developing Management Skills*. Glenville, IL: Scott, Foresman & Co.

Wiersema, M. 1986. Executive succession, top management team consolidation, and corporate strategic redirection. Ph.D. dissertation, University of Michigan, Ann Arbor.

Wiersema, M., and D. Ulrich. 1990. Strategic redirection and the role of top management. In Glass, H. (ed.), *Handbook of Business Strategy 1989/1990 Yearbook*. New York: Gorham, Lambert, pp. 14.1–14.15.

Wilkins, A., and W. G. Ouchi. 1983. Efficient cultures: Exploring the relationship between culture and organizational performance, *Administrative Science Quarterly* 28:468–481.

Williamson, O. E. 1975. *Markets and Hierarchies: Analysis and Antitrust Implications*. New York: Free Press.

Williamson, O. E., 1979. Transaction cost economics: The governance of contractual relations, *Journal of Law and Economics* 22:233–261.

Williamson, O. E. 1981. The modern corporation: Origins, evolution, attributes, *Journal of Economic Literature*, 19:1537–1568.

Williamson O. E. 1983. Organizational innovation: The transaction cost approach. In Ronen, J. (ed.), *Entrepreneurship*. Lexington, MA: Lexington Books, pp. 101–134.

Williamson, O. E. 1986. The multidivisional structure. In Barney, J. B., and W. G. Ouchi (eds.), *Organizational Economics*. San Francisco: Jossey-Bass, pp. 163–187.

Yeung, A., W. Brockbank, and D. Ulrich. 1989. Understanding culture and human resource practices: An avenue to strategic business partners. Working paper, University of Michigan, Ann Arbor.

Zuboff, S. 1988. *In the Age of the Smart Machine*. New York: Basic Books.

Index